One Young Man and Total War

(from Normandy to Concentration Camp,

a Doctor's letters home)

One Young Man and Total War

(from Normandy to Concentration Camp,
a Doctor's letters home)

The Pentland Press Limited
Edinburgh • Cambridge • Durham • USA

© Robert Barer 1998

First published in 1998 by
The Pentland Press Ltd.
1 Hutton Close
South Church
Bishop Auckland
Durham

British Library Cataloguing in Publication Data.
A catalogue record for this book is available
from the British Library.

ISBN 1 85821 569 2

Typeset by CBS, Felixstowe, Suffolk
Printed and bound by Bookcraft Ltd., Bath

To the family

CONTENTS

ILLUSTRATIONS

Front Cover Illustrations (Top to Bottom)
Nijmegen Bridge 1944
Captain Robert Barer, MC, RAMC
Brussels 1944
Sandbostel POW Camp

FOREWORD

by
Lord Carrington

To those of us who lived through and fought in the Second World War, Captain Barer's letters and experiences are evocative of those momentous years. The long period of waiting in England before D-Day. The difficulties of a young man recently married but separated from his wife and only meeting her at irregular intervals. The routine and yet the uncertainty of what the future held, mixed with the humdrum affairs and concerns of everyday life. All this is vividly recalled in Captain Barer's letters.

Although the letters from Normandy and Germany were obviously censored, they depict very accurately the experiences of the British Liberation Army during those momentous months. For Captain Barer, the culmination was the liberation of Sandbostel Prisoner-of-War Camp and, more particularly, that side which housed the political prisoners. He it was who was first there and having to deal with the appalling conditions and horrors which were beyond belief to all of us who saw them. It was an experience which remained with him for the rest of his life and, as a doctor dedicated to healing, it was perhaps even worse for him than for others.

He was a brave and good soldier and obviously a devoted husband as these interesting and moving letters demonstrate.

September 1997

PREFACE

Our Generation

On a lovely May day in 1939 five friends, four boys and a girl, set out in a borrowed car from London to Cambridge. Nearing the end of their BSc year, they went ostensibly to a meeting of the Physiological Society. In the event, much time was spent picnicking, which was just as well, since it was perhaps the last really carefree day for six years. In a few months there would be war. Eric, the science student, was called up at once and survived six years in the Army. Of the four medical students, all qualified in 1942. Dai became ill while sitting his final exam; he passed but died six months later of TB meningitis. He was a fine fellow and had this disaster been delayed only a few years, he could have been cured by the new antibiotics. Dennis and Robert served as MOs in the final campaign in North-West Europe. They met once in Holland when Dennis had just survived being run over in a slit trench by a German Tiger tank. Robert and Gwenda, already firm friends, were to marry on Robert's 'last' leave before D-Day, though unforeseen circumstances gave them a little more time together. By the time he was released in 1946, they had a son, Robin Geoffrey. Robert's letters to Gwen form the rest of this tale. All, of course, were censored and little could be told of the events which unfolded as he journeyed with the Guards Armoured Division from Normandy to the mouth of the Elbe. Thus much of the content is personal but battles were foretold when he warned that mail would be delayed and some things could be reported after they were over. Some notes are interleaved to show what was going on when the letters were written.

ACKNOWLEDGEMENTS

These letters lay untouched for more than forty years until after my husband's death in 1989. I was reading through them when I received a letter from the Imperial War Museum. It enclosed a report on Sandbostel POW/ Concentration Camp which Robert had written in 1945 and had recently been handed in at the British Embassy in The Hague by a Dutchman, Herr Ing. Boonenburg. Now, nearly eighty years old, he had gone to receive a campaign medal. He had served in the Dutch Resistance and, on the liberation of southern Holland by the British Army had been attached as an interpreter to the 94th LAA Regiment, in which Robert was MO. He is still in touch with old comrades and knew Robert well. Philip Read and Stephen Walton of the Imperial War Museum, Department of Documents, asked to keep this report and other memorabilia of my husband. The original letters, many documents and photographs are now in their Archives and are available for research.

Stephen Walton has encouraged me to publish the letters and been most kind and helpful. Ulrike Jordan, of the German Historical Institute London, requested permission to reproduce extracts from the letters for her book *Conditions of Surrender* (1997, Tauris, London), which includes contemporary and later articles from both sides about the conditions in the early months after VE Day. She had found, in the Stuttgart Bibliothek fur Zeitgeschichte, a diary written by Elfie Walther, who, as a young girl, had been drafted with others to 'clean up' in Sandbostel and had recorded her dreadful experiences. Ms Jordan, found Ms Walther and I was able to get in touch with her. She has given me permission to publish her diary extracts and in a most rewarding correspondence, we are discovering our shared views on the Nazis and more recent terrible régimes. I also have permission from the Stuttgart Bibliothek and the publishers, Tauris. The photographs of the Nijmegen Bridge and Brussels on the cover are from the Imperial War Museum (crown copyright, with permission) and that of Sandbostel comes from the Grenadier Gazette No. 16, 1993 in which Colonel H.S. Hanning published an abbreviated version of the Sandbostel report which, sadly, coincided with an obituary of L/Sgt, later Major, Fred Hutton who had won the Military Medal for his bravery during the assault on Sandbostel.

The explanatory notes in italics are mine. Our son Robin has written linking passages to show the events which were taking place when the letters were written. An important source was *The Guards Armoured Division*, Major General G. L. Verney, Hutchinson, 1955.

I wish to thank our good friend Professor Jack Reeves of Denver (with whom we were dining in Munich in 1971, see final chapter) for urging me to publish, as perhaps the most important thing I might ever do! Finally, without the loving help and support of our three sons, it would not have happened.

GRB1998

ABBREVIATIONS

ADS	Advanced Dressing Station
APO	Army Post Office
ASU	Advanced Surgical Unit
ATS, WAAF	Women's Army and Air Force
BMJ	British Medical Journal
CCP	Casualty Clearing Post
CCS	Casualty Clearing Station
DDMS, ADMS	Deputy and Assistant Director of Medical Services
DPH	Diploma of Public Health
EM	Electron Microscope
EMS	Emergency (war) Medical Service
FA	Field Ambulance
FDS	Field Dressing Station
FRS	Fellow of the Royal Society
MOH	Medical Officer of Health
NAAFI, ENSA	Feeding and Entertainment Organisations for Troops
POW	Prisoner of War
RAMC	Royal Army Medical Corps
RAP	Regimental Aid Post
RMO	Regimental Medical Officer
SEAC	South East Asia Command
UC, UCH	University College and University College Hospital, London

May 1939
Dennis, Eric, Dai, Robert and Gwenda

CHAPTER I

Last student days

Robert Barer was the third and youngest son of Nathan and Rachel Barer. They were Russian Jews, married in Odessa in 1903 where Max was born. They moved westward because of the pogroms. Jo was born in Warsaw but they moved again to Belgium. After the outbreak of war they arrived in England in 1914. Robert was born in 1916, lucky to be a British citizen by birth and always proud of it. In the twenties the family did not parade their Russian origin for there was much antagonism to the Soviets; the Zinoviev letters had had their effect and revolution was widely feared. The family was naturalized in 1929. Robert became a medical student at University College, London in 1935 and simultaneously studied Physics at evening classes. He was a brilliant student who was inspired by the Biophysicist and Nobel Laureate A.V. Hill. He wanted to become a biophysicist himself and apply quantitative physical methods to biological and medical research. War was looming and terrible events were taking place in Germany. He belonged to an organization which assisted Jews to escape. He used to climb into the London docks at night to help men who had stowed away on North Sea ships and transfer them to other ships going to the Far East. He did not rate their chances highly. One night he fell from a high wall and broke some ribs but he dared not get treatment for fear of exposing the group . . .

In 1939 when war broke out he was ready to enter University College Hospital (UCH) as a clinical student. All medical students who had reached that stage were obliged to finish their studies because the need for doctors would certainly be great. Our group was sent to Cardiff for a year to escape the anticipated air raids on London. Instead there came the 'cold war' and we had a delightful time staying in a holiday home on the seashore in Barry and wandering up and down the beautiful coast, swimming and walking on the Welsh hills. We joined classes with Cardiff students and became aware of the conditions of south Wales miners. The first shock was when a 14-year-old boy was brought in after a roof fall and died. The Sunday after the Dunkirk evacuation, we went into Cardiff and saw exhausted men lying all over the city, sleeping on the pavements. Trains had distributed the defeated troops all over the country. We listened aghast in the students' union to the radio bulletin telling us that France had surrendered . . . In the next few weeks an invasion was expected – roads were blocked with lumps of concrete – male students were enlisted in the Home Guard and trained with rudimentary weapons; I drove an ambulance in the blackout, terrifying! There were dogfights of fighter planes over the Bristol Channel and the sea was polluted with oil from a sunken tanker. In the middle of August 1940 we returned to London just as the Blitz began. Every day there were battles of fighter planes over south-east England – the London docks were set on fire. In September it was clear that the RAF – the Few – had defeated the German attempt to win air superiority and the invasion threat retreated. Now night bombing started as we returned to University College Hospital for the new academic year. Both of us were bombed in the first weeks. My digs were hit and I spent a night on a bookshelf in St Pancras town hall, arriving at the hospital the next day in pyjamas. Robert was in an Anderson shelter in the garden of his north London home when it was severely damaged by a bomb blast. Everyone carried on regardless. As students, we alternated two weeks helping in Casualty and fire-watching on the hospital roof, and two weeks in the country at our 'base hospital' attending lectures and ward rounds. In Casualty the patients smelled terribly – many had spent their nights in the Underground where there were no washing facilities . . . In the theatre we assisted with air-raid casualties, many of them had crush injuries from falling masonry. One night all lights went out and we continued operating with hurricane lamps . . . After one terrible night we wandered all over the west end of London. John Lewis's department store was burning, Oxford Street, Tottenham Court Road and Charing Cross Road were all blocked by bomb craters – it was silent with no traffic. We really wondered if the capital could continue to function, but it did . . .

Robert qualified in November 1942 with the highest results in the whole of London University. Young doctors were called up after only six months' hospital experience. He took a busy surgical job in east London to prepare himself for active service. In August 1943 he reported for duty at the RAMC training centre at Aldershot. His letters begin there.

CHAPTER II

Call-up, RAMC training, training with Guards Armoured

Division in Yorkshire, head injury, marriage

1)

Officers' Mess
No. 1 Depot, RAMC
Church Crookham
Aldershot

Early August 1943

Dear Gwenda,

After living the life of a hunted animal for 24 hours, I am now beginning to feel myself again, apart from the shot of TAB in my left arm and tetanus in my right. I arrived yesterday in mufti, complete with two heavy bags and a few auxiliary parcels, only to discover that the mess was about a mile away from the place at which I had to report. There was no means of transport and I couldn't get a taxi. Furthermore I had to be at the mess within an hour and in uniform. I begged to be allowed to change into uniform in the local lavatory and packed my immediate requirements into a couple of smaller bags. On emerging from the lavatory I was greeted by a succession of salutes and heel clicking from everyone in the neighbourhood, which I pretended not to see. I went into the guard room to leave my heavier bags and someone sprang to attention and roared out something at the top of his voice whereupon several other people jumped up and started waving rifles about. I thought I should be arrested for coming into the wrong place but it seems they were only being polite, so I left my bags and departed. About a hundred yards down the road I saw an officer approaching, so remembering E [*a fellow student who was a recluse and avoided human contact*], I crossed the road and pretended not to see him (I later found I was reported to the colonel). The worst experience was yet to come. After 20 minutes walking in the terrific heat I came upon a platoon of troops marching down the road. I hastily distributed my load between my arms, deciding that I could not possibly salute with both arms full. As we approached the Sergeant saluted and yelled 'Squad! Eyes right' and a dozen pairs of eyes stared at me. I smirked sweetly at them but I don't think this can have been right as the old Sergeant looked very upset and I thought he was going to burst into tears.

Fortunately things improved in the afternoon when I went around with one of my room mates, a GP named B, aged 45, who fought as an ordinary soldier in the last war and won the Military Cross. Incidentally I got a terrible scare as the Colonel told me that I was Grade B and only fit for home service. This turned out to be a mistake and it was actually B who was gassed in 1917 who was Grade B.

2)

Officers' Mess
No.1 Depot, RAMC
Church Crookham
Aldershot

7.8.1943

Dear Gwenda,

I've been here a week now and have enjoyed it very much. It seems strange doing lectures again without you and I find myself saving you a seat or trying to copy something I've missed from your notebook. It's quite a temptation to write to you every night but if I did that my letters would be very dull so I content myself with pretending you are here and telling you all about the day's events every evening when I go to bed. We certainly lead a busy life here. We are called about 6.30 a.m., breakfast at 7.30 and march off to the depot at 8. There we have drill for an hour. The drill sergeants are very good. I have been most impressed by their high standard of education and excellent command of English. They tend to be rather sarcastic and some of their remarks are not exactly drawing room. One of them said we marched 'like a lot of burglars in a virgin's bedroom'. After drill we have various lectures and demonstrations. This morning, for example, we had a demonstration of Military Law, at which various offenders were charged with petty crimes such as going out of bounds or being absent without leave. The military code is firm but fair and a man has to be pretty bad before he is sent to the detention barracks. There are numerous safeguards and the right of appeal. We have had a certain amount of gas training but most of this comes next week. We have all had to have a two minute exposure to DM (dimethyl-something arsene). We were marched into a chamber and made to jump up and down in the gas. It caused some coughing and a burning sensation in the nose. We then put on our gas masks

4

and ran up and down for ten minutes. Some people were sick in their respirators. We were all coughing and sneezing by now. We took off our respirators and began to feel the delayed effects of the gas. I suffered most discomfort in the nose and sinuses, slight nausea and, worst of all, a dull ache in the gums and teeth. The effects gradually wore off in an hour or two. This gas is not particularly lethal but is used to cause great depression and demoralisation. I shudder to think what the effects of ten minutes exposure would be like. I gather that next week we are liable to have some of the stuff shot at us without warning.

Lectures go on till 6 p.m. with breaks for lunch and tea. Then we have PT for one hour. This is apt to be rather murderous and most of the older men have to drop out for some of the exercises. It is extremely well run by a staff of instructors who were well known sportsmen in civil life. It ends up with an all-in game of handball. I got my shirt literally torn to shreds in one game. One of the men in a previous batch was concussed and unconscious for 5 days! For the first few days one's muscles feel like taut violin strings and every movement is agony, but this is beginning to wear off now. One of the veins in my upper arm has ruptured in 3 places! All this leads up to our physical efficiency test in the 3rd week, in which we have to climb 10ft walls and swing across ponds on a trapeze. It doesn't seem to have affected my girth yet though, as one of my room mates, helping me on with my battledress remarked, 'Gosh, you look like twice round the gasworks!' After supper our time is our own, but as you can imagine we don't feel like doing anything very strenuous. Most of the chaps settle down to a steady evening's drinking. We had a terrific drinking party the other day as one of the instructors, a little Irishman named Capt. Gilbert is getting married. He is a great chap and has the DSO and OBE. The Colonel, Gilbert and another instructor were in Tobruk together. The Colonel was in charge of the hospital and could not leave, but Gilbert and the other chap slipped out one night, tagged on to the end of a German column, yelled 'Heil Hitler' when anyone approached and escaped into Egypt. Gilbert had the extraordinary experience of running a Syrian brothel for some months. His prophylactic measures were so good that there were only 4 cases of VD among many hundred men using the brothels. He is very bitter about the nonsense people talk in Parliament and elsewhere about 'official brothels'. It's quite clear that if energetic measures were enforced on the spot, inside the brothels, VD could be prevented. He had to do all this work unofficially as questions would have been asked if it had leaked out. As he said 'if you examine an ATS girl with an auroscope it will be a case of rape by the time it gets to Parliament.' I had hoped to be able to get some leave this week-end, but as luck would have it I'm orderly officer today and MO tomorrow. I'm afraid

I'm on again next Saturday, but I hope to have a couple of hours off next Sunday to get up to town and collect some clean sheets. I'm afraid time will be so short that it won't be worth meeting, but I think I shall be able to manage the weekend after that (Sunday). Being orderly officer is quite instructive. I had to go round at mealtimes and ask the men if they had any complaints. The men's food is really excellent. At tea they each get an enormous hunk of cheese (at least 4 ounces [*civilian ration was about 2 oz/ week at this time*], a big helping of lettuce and tomatoes, bread and butter, cake and tea. This will be followed by a hefty supper. They get 4 really good meals a day and the variety is excellent. In fact their food would suit me much better than our own, which is very good but more 'dainty'. One of the sergeants told me that years ago when he was a recruit the food was appalling. The potatoes were never properly peeled and often had lumps of clay stuck to them.

Love
RB

3)   Crookham

                                                                  15.8.1943

Dear Gwenda,
Thanks for your letter. Am sorry about your Mother [*cancer of the breast had just been diagnosed*].

Things have gone on in much the same way during the last week. I have just had more TAB on one arm and vaccination on the other. In addition someone contrived to break my left big toe during the 'handball' so I'm feeling rather black and blue. Fortunately two pairs of socks, army boots and strapping combine to make a good splint for the toe and my activities have scarcely been hampered. I still manage to do the PT which has lost most of its terrors by now, in fact it was almost amusing to have the new batch complaining that we were too rough in the handball – they will get used to it in time. Incidentally with regard to your kind offer to repair my shirt, I'm afraid that it would be beyond even your remarkable capabilities in 'alteration' . . . as it was literally torn to shreds off my back, leaving my hairy chest exposed. We have a pretty awful physical efficiency test on Tuesday . . . The Colonel says he has invited a lot of big noises from London specially to see me fall into the water! This event is apt to be rather amusing (for the onlookers) as if you don't quite make the other side on your first swing on the trapeze, you are just left swinging in an ever decreasing arc of a pendulum until you have to let go and fall into the water. Although these tests are pretty hard they are not so hard as the new tests now being introduced which all officers and men are expected to pass eventually. They include swimming a certain distance in full battle dress, carrying boots and a rifle. You may wonder how the average recruit is able to pass such a severe test. The fact is that the Army PT and general training has improved people's condition enormously. Moreover there are now a number of Physical Development Centres to which new recruits who are of obviously poor physique can be sent before doing their primary training. There they are given extra food and are put through a graded course of exercises, with definite rest periods throughout the day. The average weight gain at one of these centres is 6 lb, which is pretty good remembering that the fat ones will have lost weight. The commandos have now become obsolete, as the whole army is being trained on commando lines.

We have had several field exercises this week to teach us a little about military tactics and enable us to site aid posts and units of a field ambulance. Incidentally, don't be misled into thinking that a field ambulance is a single ambulance car. It is actually a big unit consisting of 18 ambulances, a lot of trucks and motor bikes, 13 officers and about 200 men. In action it is split up into a number of casualty collecting posts (CCP) and an advanced dressing station (ADS). Away in front of the CCPs is the regimental aid post (RAP) run by the RMO and the most forward unit. The ADS may be operating many miles behind the forward area and the casualty clearing station (CCS) is many miles more behind that. The first hospital proper is generally a matter of hundreds of miles from the fighting and this is the first place at which nurses appear, though in exceptional cases and if conditions are safe they may be employed at a CCS. Very little beyond first aid and treatment of shock is done before the CCS stage, though there are a number of advanced surgical centres for very urgent cases. All this requires an immense amount of organisation. Even the correct siting of an RAP, which we had to do, entails a thorough exploration of the ground over a distance of several miles, working out the best routes for stretcher-bearers and most economical use of transport. The stretcher-bearers' job must be one of the most difficult in the army. It is exceedingly dangerous and nerve-racking and they don't have the advantage of being able to hit back. The physical strain is very great, as we soon found out when we carried a man a hundred yards on a stretcher. Having got some idea of the large amount of organisation required for the apparently simple task of running an RAP, I am afraid I shall always look back with burning shame on my signature on the famous '2nd front' telegram to Churchill. It is so easy to talk about 'throwing in a couple of divisions', but one does not realise that each division consists of 1 tank brigade and 2 infantry brigades (with 1 doctor to each) plus field, anti-tank and anti-aircraft artillery, engineers, workshops, signallers, transport, cooks and a host of other people. It is quite amazing that anything ever gets done at all.

At long last I have seen a proper demonstration of Thomas' splint drill. It is quite complicated and requires at least two people, but the end result is extremely efficient. The army has also invented a very neat method of applying extension and splintage in cases of fractured femur using only the man's rifle, handkerchief and bootlace.

I am going on my hygiene course in a week's time and expect to get leave next Sunday. Can you meet me at the Dominion [*cinema, Tottenham Court Road*] about 12 noon? It may be our last chance for some time. I shall let you know if anything prevents my coming. I probably won't have to go back till about 9 p.m. Let me know if this is OK.

Love RB

4)

Officers' Mess
Army School of Hygiene
Mytchett
Aldershot

15.8.43

Dear Gwenda,

The hygiene course has been absolutely fascinating so far. I am sure you would enjoy it immensely. It is a great pity that our student hygiene course could not have been run on similar lines. All the army teaching is refreshingly practical, and every method used has to be capable of working under adverse conditions. The methods of water purification are remarkably good and simple. They consist of rapid active sedimentation with aluminium gel, followed by rapid filtration through special metal filter candles, then chlorination by means of a special stable bleaching powder. Thiosulphate tablets are added to remove the taste of chlorine. The whole thing can be done in a couple of hours and the final result is excellent. Before pumping the water the MO has to test it for poisons. This again is very simply done, as is also the determination of the amount of chlorination needed. Remember that all the tests have to be carried out in the field. Another thing we have to do is to construct and run various destructors, disinfectors and incinerators. This is great fun, as great emphasis is placed on improvisation. The army has discovered that crude waste oil mixed with water, when ignited on a hot metal plate is capable of generating great heat at negligible cost. These 'oil-flash' burners are very simple to make and can be used for all sorts of purposes. We have had several lectures and films on the fly. I never realised how interesting the life cycle and habits of the fly could be till now. This sort of thing is simply not touched on by the ordinary books. Did you know that the fly will not pass through a fairly large hole provided that the surroundings are bright? A fairly large mesh curtain therefore serves very well to exclude flies from a cookhouse. Also once a fly gets into a wire mesh cage through a large hole, it cannot find its way out until dark. This is used in making fly traps. We have to make fly traps varying from wires coated with 'tanglefoot', a mixture of castor oil and resin, to large mesh cages baited with meat. The importance of fly control was brought home to us when we heard about what happened at El Alamein, when we nearly lost Egypt due to a plague of flies. The men were literally covered from head to foot by flies. Eating and drinking became impossible as the food was covered by a solid mass of flies before it reached the mouth. Sleep was out of the question. The RAMC had to organise a special corps of 500 men to deal with this horror.

Our TAB seems to have been very effective in Libya, as we had very few cases of Typhoid. The Germans on the other hand seem to have slipped up badly and were riddled with it. The hygienists claim that it lost them the battle of Egypt when they were within 20 miles of Alexandria.

Regarding TAB, there was a large batch of our prisoners in Benghazi, kept under incredibly filthy conditions (those who saw them swore they would never forgive the Germans for what they did); whereas the German guards and local population were very prone to Typhoid, no cases occurred among the prisoners, though they all had dysentery and every other imaginable disease.

Apparently there was some Typhus among the population of Derna. The Germans solved the problem of delousing very simply by burning all their clothes and not giving any in return! Most of the population died of exposure. We have now got a very effective secret antilouse powder but the vaccine problem is still unsolved.

Prof. Gilding is a very interesting man. He escaped 3 times from a German prison camp in the last war. On the last occasion he and a friend got out and made their way in British uniform to within 50 yards of the British trenches before they were recognised.

Love, RB

5)   Scarborough

                                                                Early September 1943

Dearest Gwenda,

Sorry about the official envelope. I expect you thought I'd been killed already – but it was the only one to fit your photos.

I've been moving about for a bit for the last few days and have not been able to give an address. When I arrived near York I found I had to report to the Director of Hygiene and my heart sank, but fortunately he was only on duty while the DDMS was away on an exercise [*DDMS, Deputy Director of Medical Services – chief MO in a corps*]. I stayed 2 days until he came back. I then had a colossal stroke of luck, for he posted me to the crack division of a crack corps – namely the Guards Armoured Division! Many people say it's the best in the army so I've stopped worrying as to whether I shall see any action. The whole corps is a field force, that is to say everyone from the Generals down live under camp conditions and get extra 'hardship' allowance – there are no static hospitals, nurses or ATS in the corps. By the way I am not sure how much of this I'm allowed to tell, so don't talk too much.

I had quite an amusing time near York. The place was teeming with brass-hats and there was scarcely no one below the rank of Major. Nevertheless they were all very friendly and decent. They had the most mischievous little kitten I have ever seen and it was very funny to see some of the Colonels playing and talking to it in baby language. All the Colonels I have met so far have been surprisingly progressive in their outlook and the only Blimpish views I've heard have come from young Lieutenants who probably say things hoping to curry favour with the Colonels. I even heard the senior Colonel praise Russia for having set up a successful socialist state! I was shown around the headquarters area by one of the MOs. He was a King's man and knew Mary Pringle [*fellow student*]. Some of the MOs have to work under difficult conditions and as you can imagine it's not easy to keep things clean and sterile in tents.

When the DDMS came back he sent me to the ADMS [*Assistant Director of Medical Services*] of the Guards Armoured Division near Scarborough. I spent the night at a Field Dressing Station. This was the first one in the country and most of the officers are away making a training film. The next day the ADMS came down and he was absolutely charming. He promised to get me the right sort of job as soon as he could, after I have learnt a bit about army procedures. He then sent me off to Scarborough to do a locum for the RMO to the 94th Light AA Regiment. This is quite a different thing

10

from the ordinary static AA (anti-aircraft) battery. It comprises 900 men and a large number of Bofors guns – special light highly mobile AA and anti-tank guns. As soon as I arrived they forced a hearty tea into me, pushed me into my private jeep and drove me 10 miles out on the cliffs to stand by at a gunnery practice. When I arrived I marched up to the Colonel and gave him my best Crookham salute. He flung me the hell of a salute in return, but then I saw the Brigade Major convulsed with laughter and on turning round I saw the Colonel shaking hands with two brass-hats who had chosen to turn up at the same time as I had. They turned out to be no less than the Commander of the Royal Artillery and his adviser.

The gunnery practice was most interesting. The target consisted of a long flag towed from a wire by a plane. The Bofors are most beautiful guns and it is most fascinating to watch shells going up round the target. Just occasionally one of the shells bursts prematurely and someone gets injured.

The Colonel and officers are an extremely jolly lot and the mess is quite informal – the Colonel does not even sit at the head of the table.

One of the officers is an author but publishes under a pseudonym which he refuses to tell, so no one knows what he has written. We have also got people with degrees in French, Classics and Architecture, so they are pretty accomplished. I do PT on the sands with my men. They have just come back from a battle course and are pretty tough. Sick parades are usually quite interesting and contrary to what people say, I've seen a lot of 'real' medicine. People are always getting hurt and there is quite a lot to do. Soldiers always seem to shoot unaccountable temperatures, with no other physical signs. Catarrhal jaundice is common too and special army instructions have been issued regarding it. VD however is extraordinarily rare, and owing to good prophylactic measures they have only had one case in the last 18 months.

I have a very nice sick bay in a commandeered private hotel, with hot and cold in every room.

Scarborough itself is a very nice place. The town is built on a number of hills and the surrounding country is very beautiful. The hills make walking in army boots rather difficult and I go in constant dread of slipping down on my backside in the middle of the main street. If I'm still here at Christmas you might be able to come down.

I'm afraid I don't know where I shall be going after next week, but I rather fancy I shall be attached for a while to a field dressing station. These have been described as 'travelling morgues', as all the worst cases are sent to them for resuscitation.

In the meantime write to me

Lieut. R Barer RAMC

94th Light AA Regt RA
Scarborough
Yorks.

Love, RB

6)   Scarborough

                                                       9.9.43

Darling Gwenda

Thank you for your letter and the magazine. It would be very nice to get it regularly as otherwise one feels very out of touch . . .

I'm still here with the gunners but my stay is drawing to a close so it's not much use writing to me here. I don't know where I'm going yet but will let you know as soon as possible. I'm having a simply grand time at present. All the officers in this division have to ride motor bikes so I have been dashing around the country at high speed wearing a crash helmet. It's amazingly easy to learn and it seems almost impossible to fall off – much easier than an ordinary bike. The only snag is that our particular bikes are extremely heavy and once a bike falls down it is almost impossible for one man to lift it. The main danger seems to be that the bike may fall on your leg in a spill and I have been practising throwing myself clear. One of these days I'll give you a ride on my pillion!

The gunners are really a grand lot. I've been going around to various messes – the other day I had to go out to a magnificent country mansion now used as the artillery HQ, in order to condemn a number of tins of milk which had gone bad. The surrounding country was simply breathtaking and we must certainly come here together some time.

The Colonel is a very charming man. He has been a soldier for 25 years but has a degree in Law. He has a lot of interesting stories to tell. One night while we were talking about books and authors he said that he had once written a book which had been reproduced in 3 languages. We were very impressed but when he produced the book it turned out to be the instructions for carrying out the death penalty written in English, Arabic and Hebrew! He told us some very funny stories of a very enthusiastic but rather unfortunate young officer whom he had under him in N. Ireland at the beginning of the war. During the height of the IRA troubles this man had left a large truck full of machine guns, quite unguarded in the middle of the main square in Belfast, while he went off to lunch! Another time this chap found a Colorado beetle [*a potato pest against the importation of which exceptionally strict measures were taken*]. He put it in a match box in his pocket and together with the Colonel took it to the chief representative of the Ministry of Agriculture in Belfast. When they got there after a lot of trouble with wire-pulling, he began to produce a wonderful schoolboy collection of articles from his pockets – money, india rubber, penknife, string, chewing gum etc. but no beetle! The Colonel went hot and cold with embarrassment and stammered his excuses, but the officials were none too pleased. They left the building in grim silence and were walking along the road when suddenly they saw the beetle crawling along the pavement! If it had got free it might have caused thousands of pounds worth of damage. My sick parades continue to be interesting, it's remarkable how commonly various types of synovitis occur. One has to be pretty well up in skins too. I lecture to my medical orderlies daily. Some of them are quite good but one or two find the terminology a little difficult. Incidentally I had a man with 'herbaceous cyst' the other day. I've just concluded a rather exhausting 3 day inspection of all the billets and cook houses. Quarters for 900 men are no small matter! It's remarkable how many little points crop up – things which would seem trivial normally but which might cause trouble when dealing with large numbers. For example in one place I found that when the blackout boards were taken down they were put in front of the fireplace, blocking the ventilation – quite a factor when there are 6 men in a room normally big enough for one. In another place mosquitos were breeding in the fire buckets – easily avoided by changing the water weekly. In another the cookhouse was unbearably hot. They could not keep the window open as the draught blew the fire out. This was soon remedied by providing a board to deflect the draught.

These and many other little points soon made me realise how very important the MO can be in securing the most comfortable conditions for the men. The other officers do their best but they don't realise the importance of these things. I think I shall probably become a sanitary inspector after the war!

Another problem I have had to deal with is that of the swimming bath. The open-air baths are beginning to get too cold for teaching beginners and we have been offered the use of a closed bath on Saturday mornings. Unfortunately this is of an archaic type, which is only emptied once a week on Saturday afternoons, so that the water is at its dirtiest on Saturday mornings. I had to give an opinion on its suitability. I am hoping to get some help by means of the Horrock's test (i.e. determination of the amount of chlorination needed to sterilise the water). I did one at the beginning of the week and shall do another on Saturday morning to see if there is much change.

All this seems rather a far cry from electron microscopes, but it's nonetheless interesting and at the moment important. The incompetent or lazy MO would be an absolute menace. It's a pity that some of our more vociferous young preventive medicine enthusiasts are not trying this but then I expect they're too busy learning physics – incidentally if the MRC wants physicists why doesn't it try physics departments instead of medical schools? [*A reference to friends in our year who had been recruited to an army research establishment.*]

It's too early to start talking of leave just yet. In any case this division has been in every county in England and we might quite easily get shifted to Watford next week, so don't despair. I'm longing to see you and will do my best.

Love

RB

PS. I do hope everything turns out all right for your mother. [*Her operation for surgical removal of a breast was imminent.*]

7)   Scarborough General Hospital

                                            15.9.43

Dear Gwenda

I hope your mother is well on the way to recovery by now. I am afraid I've got a bit of a shock for you, but as you will see from this letter there's nothing at all to worry about. The fact is I've been concussed! It's been quite an interesting experience and I'm better now. Any peculiarity in the handwriting is entirely due to the fact that I've got nothing to rest the paper on and one eye is bandaged up. I'm afraid, so far as I know, that it was all due to the motor bike. I had been making good progress in riding all last week and having conquered the intricacies of rough riding over bumpy fields they sent me out on Sunday on a long 2 hrs country ride. The roads were wet but I enjoyed the ride and felt full of confidence. I got back rather early and went out again for another 20 minutes. I remember turning back home again and feeling elated at going at 55 and then opening the throttle still more. That is my last memory. I don't know what happened even yet. It's an absolutely textbook case of concussion. I have vague memories of an army Doctor bending over me in some sort of vehicle, and burbling your name but the whole thing seemed at the time like a rather pleasant dream. I then remember vaguely being sent up to a ward and put in a bed with the foot raised. I seemed to have caused quite a stir as they phoned through to the hospital that I was moribund and bleeding from the nose and ear. I had been unconscious for about an hour. At the hospital I shook the House Surgeon by being pulseless and pallid. They left me alone and in a couple of hours I had recovered completely! Of course the bleeding from the ear was just blood which had collected from the cuts on my face and the bleeding from the nose was due to superficial abrasions. I had a few cuts over the right eyebrow and cheek and one on the lower eyelid. By an odd coincidence the House Surgeon was away for the week and the House Physician was in charge. She turned out to be one of the Cardiff girls, a Miss Reece [*I think her other name was Gwyllian or something – we had spent a year at the Cardiff Royal Infirmary. Our year was sent there to escape expected bombing. It did not happen and we arrived back in time for the London Blitz!*]

She sutured my main cuts under not too good local anaesthesia, but found my skin too tough for her wrists. Fortunately my Chief, Major McArthur from the field dressing station had just arrived and he finished the job. They were afraid to touch my eyelid and waited for the Surgeon, Guy Thomson, a London man. He put 3 horsehair sutures without anaesthetic at all, as it was so near the eye. It wasn't pleasant but I managed all right. They say there won't be much of a scar and in any case I hope to get more honourable wounds on the other side to match, so I don't think it will spoil my facial beauty though you'll have to wait a while before I get a photo done. They say my face looks pretty funny at the moment as the R side of my nose and lips are about 5 times as big as the left! The biggest nuisance is having my right eye bandaged up. You've no idea how difficult monocular vision is – I have almost no sense of depth at all. They x-rayed me yesterday and found nothing. I think that about covers my injuries apart from a few bruises and abrasions. You see, dear, I've been quite frank with you and told you everything as I know you'd worry otherwise. Please believe me when I say that I am perfectly all right and have developed no sequelae and what's more I don't intend to develop any. I'm afraid that as a matter of army routine they're going to send me to a head injuries centre at Newcastle in a couple of days but it's merely a matter of . . . and they have to make a fuss of RAMC officers. I've no doubt I shall see a neurologist and a psychiatrist and an electroencephalographist and a lumbarpuncturist and God knows what. I'm having great fun practising extensor plantars and other weird and wonderful reflexes for the neurologist and as for the psychiatrist what we told DM will be nothing compared to the history I'm concocting [*obviously some joke we perpetrated on a fellow student!*] I think it would make even Freud blush! Don't be surprised if you see my case written up in the BMJ! Miss Reece told me that they're getting a new HP in a couple of days – none other than F of Cardiff. I'm afraid I've not had time to write much about other things. I enjoyed my stay at the AA regiment enormously and the Colonel has just been to see me – also believe it or not the Padre who is a nice young chap and not at all bigoted.

Please, darling, don't get all excited and come flying down here – in any case I shall probably be moved soon and will let you know where I go.

Concussion seems to be a most wonderful natural protective reaction. I have no unpleasant memories whatsoever – I'm not even sure I had an accident on the motor bike and far from being afraid of them I'm just dying to get back to the bike. It's been very amusing and instructive seeing a hospital from the point of view of the patient. I shall soon be able to speak with authority on concussion – incidentally I only lectured my orderlies on it the other day!

Lots of love

RB

8)   Harewood House
                                                                       near Leeds

Dearest Darling Gwenda,
You wicked girl, how dare you ring up and spoil things, just as I was getting on so well with all my female attendants! Actually F had already put her foot in it by asking about you as soon as she saw me, so apparently we didn't pass entirely unnoticed in Cardiff [*where we had spent a year of our clinical training*]. I'm afraid poor appearance is still rather counting against her and the nurses have been grousing about her. The ADMS came to see me and was frightfully nice. I managed to persuade him that the head centre at Newcastle might not be the best place to send me so I wangled my way into Harewood (pronounced har-wood) House. This is the home of Princess Mary and part of it is being used as a convalescent home for officers. We have lots of glamorous part-time society VADs to hold our hands

sympathetically so you may find my picture in the Tatler or Vogue one day sitting with Lady de Vere or someone. I'm getting on fine but have not been allowed up yet except to wash and go to the lavatory on a wheelchair [*shades of Whipsnade: at a friend's 21st birthday party at Whipsnade we had hired a 'bathchair' and wheeled R around in it*] having persuaded them that my acrobatic feats of balancing on top of a bedpan were more strenuous then gentle defaecation in his Lordship's former private boudoir. The specialist is seeing me tomorrow and I shall probably be allowed up. My face is getting on fine but is still a little lop-sided and I look even more villainous than before. As soon as I'm allowed up I'll try to phone you. There's a chap here in the same room who puts my little episode completely in the shade. He's a paratroop officer and while on exercises he accidentally jumped from a plane at a height of only 150 ft (500 ft is the safe minimum). His parachute only just opened but he was concussed and had complete amnesia for no less than 5 days. The amazing thing is that during those 5 days he behaved perfectly normally sending a telegram to his wife and seeing her when she came. Yet later when asked to pay for the telegram he looked at it in blank amazement and didn't remember anything about it. This amnesia is certainly a funny business. I wonder what the electroencephalogram of a man like that would show? I can't help feeling that there must be an abrupt change of rhythm or form at the moment the amnesia ceases. Ask someone if it has been tried. I'm afraid I've rather mucked up the marvellous programme the ADMS had arranged for me. I should have gone on a tropical course to Liverpool today followed by other pleasant activities but I'm afraid I shall have to wait now. Still it's been interesting seeing hospital life as a patient. I've rather changed my views on nurses as a result. I think they do far too much work that could be done by unskilled cleaners and as a result they get no real medical work done at all, so it's not surprising that they sometimes appear inefficient to the houseman. Some of these here have rather odd ideas about sleep. They tend to wake you at 6 a.m. to tell you 'it's all right, you can go to sleep for another hour'. Then at regular intervals through the day just as you've made yourself comfortable and are dozing off they come and say 'Poor thing, you do look uncomfortable' and proceed to tidy up the bed, so that it takes you another two hours to get comfortable again. If you should be rash enough to actually fall asleep at any time you will be sure to have a thermometer thrust into your mouth and you will wake to find a nurse firmly grasping your pisiform and looking grimly at an egg-timer. If you look at your chart when she's gone you will be relieved to find that they've cured you of the heart block from which you were suffering that morning, and are at present struggling with one of your bouts of paroxysmal tachycardia [*abnormal slow and fast heart rates; I'm afraid we did not believe in pulse rates recorded by nurses*]. At 10 p.m. they wake you up to give you your sleeping draught but after that, apart from shining a light in your face every hour to see that you're asleep, they leave you alone.

When are you starting your PM stuff? [*I was in a trainee job in which I rotated between chemical, pathological and bacteriological labs*]. I thought you were to do it now. I've been learning to do tenotomies on corpses, as being an armoured division most of our casualties are expected to end up in grotesque attitudes which we are expected to straighten out. I hope you enjoy the course at Birkbeck. I don't know if they've still got the Library there – it used to be pretty good. Don't forget the Patent Office is almost next door. Let me know the names of your lecturers [*in my spare time I took a chemistry course in Birkbeck College*].

Lots of love,

RB

PS. In case you've forgotten, I love you.

9)   Harewood House

Dearest Gwenda,

Very short as am rushing to catch the post. Afraid they've done the dirty on me and are making me stay in bed 3 weeks. It's an army routine for all cases of concussion. Afraid this makes phoning impossible. Also if you feel you have to come down, next week end would be better, as I may be allowed up by then. Best if you came Saturday and stay overnight. There's a very good Inn in the village and I may be able to book a room for you there. Otherwise there's a good bus service to either Leeds or Harrogate (both about 7 miles). Of course will share expense. Let me know about trains & c in good time so I can make arrangements. Am getting on fine – no headaches and no epileptic fits so far!

Love

RB

PS. You blithering old fool of course it wasn't the Doctor who was burbling your name, it was me. Apparently I gave a very methodical list of people to attend the funeral!

10)   Harewood House

Dearest Gwenda,

You certainly excelled yourself in your last effort! Sister brought me a dirty piece of paper and gingerly sniffed it 'It doesn't look like anything interesting' – I think she thought it was a begging letter. However when I saw the envelope was stuck down with an old stamp and the address was tucked away in a corner, written half in ink and half in pencil (very decorative) I knew it was only my old Gertie in one of her attacks. The contents were also up to her old standard. I'm afraid I haven't been able to fix up anything definite at the Inn yet. It's rather an exclusive place and apt to be full, so they don't like booking for odd nights in advance. However I think it's quite likely that they will have a room or if not will be able to get you fixed up in the village. If the worst comes to the worst you will certainly be able to get in at Leeds, but the village would be better. There's a very good bus service from Leeds every 20 minutes right to the gates. The last bus leaves Leeds about 9 p.m. Do try to get an early train – do you think they'll give you Saturday morning off at the lab? If I can I'll meet you at Leeds but I rather doubt it. I was allowed up for a short time yesterday and am being allowed up progressively so I hope to be pretty active by the weekend. I shall try to ring you as soon as possible so be near a phone. I think about 11 a.m. is the likeliest time, so don't waste the precious 3 minutes. Will ring as soon as I know more about the accommodation problem. Look up the trains and try and give me an idea when you're coming – don't leave it too late because of the blackout. Don't forget towel, soap and identity card and don't turn up disguised as a sack of potatoes as I shall probably have to introduce you to the Colonel. I'll try to show you round the place. They have a lot of very old and valuable pictures in all the rooms and there is a ruined castle in the grounds. It should be quite interesting and anyhow I'm dying to see you. Don't spare the expense as I'm not spending a penny and I get paid as usual! If you're stuck at Leeds for any reason don't hesitate to take a taxi – it's about 8-10/- to here and we won't have much time together as it is.

By the way, darling, before I forget, could you possibly bring me some cash – say £5 for me – I shall let you have a cheque when I see you. I hope you're enjoying Birkbeck but I don't like the sound of these earnest discussions with young men – you'll be inviting them home and feeding them tinned fruit next [*a luxury in wartime!*]. I can see I shall have to do a lot of courses after the war to catch up with you. Your conversation will probably be far above my head. Still I shall be able to tell you how to construct a latrine for 10 men – if you ever want to.

Incidentally I don't know why they don't call in an army field hygiene section at Watford to deal with the fly problem. It's right up their street and I guarantee they'll clear the whole thing up in 48 hours. I don't want to sound superior but from all accounts the civilian MOHs are all right for things like measles and scarlet fever but are quite lost with things like these, which the army has been dealing with for years. I visited a Field Section at Scarborough and was most impressed. Most of the chaps had their DPH and some had been MOHs in peace time. They all admitted that they knew nothing at all about Hygiene until they joined the army. I'm afraid they had a wholesome contempt for bacteriologists (don't tell Miles) [*my boss, Professor of Bacteriology at UCH*] who are always digging up some silly little theoretical point which has never the slightest use in practice. They say that with experience one can dispense with bacteriology altogether. On one occasion a lot of civilian research people were playing about for a couple of weeks trying to trace an epidemic at a camp. They did this at their own request and out of politeness the Colonel gave them every help. However he got fed up in time and sent for the Hygiene Section secretly. Within two hours of arrival they had traced the cause and rectified it! I'm afraid that in the face of that one I thought it better not to tell them I was interested in bacteriology! The army certainly has an awkward way of making you wonder how much of what you learnt is any use. I should be quite glad to swap one of my degrees for some of the sergeant's practical knowledge. Incidentally, coming back to the hygiene business, you know that as a result of civilian service most colossal precautions were taken every time there was a case of meningitis. Practically everyone was swabbed and contacts were isolated resulting in great loss of time and man power. Nowadays none of this is done as we know it doesn't matter in practice. I think there's going to be a really interesting store of practical knowledge released at the end of the war. Some of the army pamphlets have certainly changed my ideas on things and I wish I could tell you about them.

Did you see AV's* letter in *The Times* about the falling birth rate? . . . It was the usual stuff about England being a third rate power by 1970 but of course he had to include a graph! I expect Rushton will bring out the mathematical theory soon. Anyhow we'll show them how to solve the problem practically won't we? – I wonder if our figures will fall on the graph?

Professor A.V. Hill.

I hope your Mother is quite recovered by now. Poor darling, you must have had a nasty time, but I'll try to make it up.

Lots of love,

RB

PS. Will write, phone or cable further details before Saturday.

PPS. What a pity they don't run a spelling course in Birkbeck.

[*I had a job in the 'Emergency Pathological Service' at a base hospital for UCH, in Watford. Note that we worked Saturday mornings in those days!*]

11)   Harewood House

                                                             October 1943

Dearest Darling Gwenda

Have just got your letter. Am so glad you arrived safely – have been worrying all the time about you. You've no idea how lonely I felt when you left, in fact I very nearly had one of those weeping attacks myself. Still we both have to pull ourselves together. Don't forget your performance in the job, especially with Miles [*my boss, Professor of Bacteriology, UCH*], may decide our future to quite an extent, so don't let things get you down. I felt so bored the day after you left that I went to bed directly after dinner. The sisters discovered me there and immediately started chipping me saying it was all reaction after the good time I'd had in the last two days. They were certainly right about that. I'm afraid you're going to have to have a bit of a blow. Apparently our house is being sold soon . . . [*his parent's house in London where we were sometimes able to meet; the old folks were by now in Oxford*]. Still there is a bright side to it . . . as I shall probably try to get leave to attend to my belongings. You wouldn't like to take some of my books would you? – though I suppose you haven't any room. If this materialises I'll try to make it a weekend and let you know in advance. I've just had a day in Leeds. It's much bigger than I thought. They have a magnificent modern University library, as good as, if not better than, any in London, and it was a treat to browse over some of the recent journals. There's another library at the medical school and I must try and have a look

21

at it before I leave. That's one of the advantages of being in uniform, it acts as a free pass to anywhere.

Incidentally I am going back to the Field Dressing Station so write to me there.

8th Field Dressing Station
Filey
Yorks.

I've been listening to some more of the gramophone records. I've definitely reached the conclusion that symphonies are not a patch on concertos, so keep your eyes open for some likely ones.

I'm afraid I've missed yet another tropical course. I was due to go at the end of the month but it was cancelled yesterday. However, it looks as if I'm definitely booked for it some time and it would be better to have our meetings spaced out properly.

I'm afraid there's not much news but will let you have a better letter next week, when I get back. The Free French officer here created quite a sensation yesterday by bringing a lovely French tart (not the edible kind) to tea. The old Colonel's eyes nearly popped out of his head. She certainly looked more like a paint factory than a woman.

Lots of love and thank you for a lovely weekend. I hope you have got everything straight at home. [*My Father had bought a little house in Watford for my Mother to come home to after the operation.*]

Love

RB

PS. Whom were you 'dosing' and with what, all the way to London?

[*My job was a trainee in pathology which included bacteriology, chemical pathology and morbid anatomy under Prof. A.A. Miles.*]

12)   8th Field Dressing Station
                                                       Filey

13.10.43

[*After my visit to Harewood House – a very happy time during which future plans were discussed.*]

Dear Mrs B (née Briggs),

It seems ages since your last letter. The post seems to take a long time – your latest letter has just arrived. I'm afraid the delay is going to be increased as we're rather isolated. It's quite ridiculous asking me to enfold you in my arms every night as I've got you there all day long as it is. In fact things are getting pretty bad as I can scarcely think of anything else. The idea of settling down with you seems too marvellous to be true and I spend all day planning things. I can't think of a single reason why we shouldn't be happy together. You know I would like to have everything settled right now if we were free but as things are at the moment, even apart from my possible misfortunes, I feel it would be so much more wonderful to wait until we could enjoy everything fully. We would both feel we had done something to deserve it, instead of taking the easiest way out. In any case it would make almost no actual difference as I simply can't imagine being any closer to you spiritually than I am at the moment. You can certainly tell anyone you like of our intentions. I know my people are in no doubt about them, and I'd love you to meet them as soon as we can fix it. I'm flattered by what you said about wanting a home before anything else, but you needn't think you're going to get away with it as easily as that. I just wouldn't know what to do with a wife who did nothing but mope at home while I was away. All my dreams are based on our working together (with 2 or 3 short gaps I hope!) and I shouldn't be happy if it were otherwise. I always thought even years ago that although you were keen on your work you were really less 'feminist' and more 'feminine' than most of the other girls. I've always felt that most girls were driving towards unhappiness by insisting on a career. The ideal solution is for husband and wife to work together as we shall, but this could scarcely be universal. We'll have to try and fix up our Jean Margaret temporarily [*name for a future daughter*] in the same way. I still like the idea of a secretary-collaborator to some promising scientist, she would have to learn a lot of languages too to translate papers. [*We had already decided on children's names, Robin Geoffrey for a boy, Jean Margaret for a girl.*]

By the way the technique with the electron microscope seems to be improving. One of the recent numbers of the *Journal of Bacteriology* has a couple of papers showing some most remarkable pictures, and the quality was quite good too. Some of the spirochaetes seem to have small lateral flagellae as well as a definite cell membrane and chromatin bodies. The most amazing pictures however showed bacilli being attacked by phage particles (which incidentally are shaped like this =O). You must get hold of the journal and see for yourself. Ask Miles if he's seen them – I think he was rather sceptical last year. Once the technical side has been conquered I'm sure the EM would solve the problem of antigen-antibody reactions –

incidentally there's a good review by Pauling in Phys Rev. I had a good look through the journals in Leeds. The medical school library was well up to the standard of their university library – just as good as UCH in fact, with all the journals easily accessible. It made me quite homesick to go into a medical school library again and see the young men in their dirty flannels and the girls poring over books with their hair over their faces and eyes nearly popping out of their heads – just like you used to be in fact!

I got a lift into Leeds from Lord Harewood himself (husband to Princess Royal), I was walking down the drive when his car pulled up and he asked if he could help me. I sat next to him and even shared his travelling rug. He talked to me all the way about his estates here and in Ireland (I was told afterwards that he never dared to go over there and they had actually burned down one of his houses!). He seems to own most of Leeds including the slums. However, they don't seem to treat their own servants very well. They actually had the nerve to tell them that they could not go out for a fortnight but had to knit for the troops instead. I wonder how much knitting Princess Mary (Princess Royal) did?

I managed to get an afternoon in Harrogate. It's rather a snobbish place but is quite nice really. There is one part in which there is nothing but antique shops.

I got back on Saturday night. They are quite a jolly lot here. The chief is Major McArthur, a Scot. There are two captains, Alderson and Booth. These are Doctors. There is one Dentist, a Quartermaster and a Stretcher-bearer officer – 7 officers in all. Alderson is from Newcastle; his wife is also a doctor. I think he is a very clever and efficient chap but he has become rather discouraged by inaction. He has been in the army since the beginning of the war and went through Dunkirk. There is never a dull moment when he is around and he is a first rate mimic. He has already christened me 'Cedric'. On merit he ought to have been promoted long ago but he is one of these people who doesn't care what he says to anyone and more than one Colonel has felt the sharp edge of his wit. Booth is another Scot. He is 39 and used to be a research chemist, working on cellulose. I expect all the present research posts are held by people who did a year's classics at Oxford, or by newly qualified Doctors who failed their exams 6 times. The Scots are certainly an amusing lot. I've been thrown up against a good many recently, and if any people can claim to have national characteristics it is the Scots. Their sense of humour is very remarkable and takes some getting used to. On several occasions I've heard them make remarks in all seriousness with no trace of humour and it's taken me some time to realise they were being funny, they will sit with wooden countenance while everyone else is roaring with laughter.

All the officers are married except me and they keep telling me to do something about it. Every few months they have a party to celebrate some new 'arrival'. There's usually a wife and a squealing infant somewhere around the mess.

After the luxury of Harewood things are pretty spartan. I share a room with Alderson and George Walker, the stretcher-bearer officer. There is no furniture and no heating. We have to keep our clothes in our suitcases. After a night on my bed I felt I should welcome a nice billiard table with a lovely soft brick as a pillow. Still I'm getting used to it and it's a healthy life. If we're lucky we get a bath twice a week, otherwise we wash and shave in ice cold water. Mrs D's will be a luxury after this – especially if we could share a double bed. [*Mrs D – our lovely black landlady in Bloomsbury.*] Incidentally our house will not be sold for at least another month so don't despair yet.

All my love

RB

13)

8th FDS
Filey
Yorks

Oct.

Darling Gwenda,

You are a wicked girl and I'm going to give you a round ticking off. I know it seems a long time since we saw each other last but do try to remember that I have only been back at this unit for exactly one week. Also, so far, I have been very much a passenger, partly due to my ignorance and partly because I have not felt up to it physically. To tell you the truth I've felt almost continuously dizzy for the last ten days and at one stage I felt like packing up. Fortunately and to my great relief I've felt very much better the last day or two and am rapidly getting back to normal. However as you can imagine I've not been pulling my weight and must have given a very poor impression. I don't think things would be improved if I had a visitor only 2 weeks after rejoining. Also this is not at all a suitable place for someone to come for a weekend from London. Scarborough itself is not a very good place to get to and the communications between Scarborough and Filey are atrocious. You would probably spend half the time travelling. Even when you got here I couldn't get off till Saturday afternoon and would probably have to stay in Sunday morning also. We can't just go out when we like here and if I go out it means someone else will have to stay in. Also I'm medical orderly officer this week. It is better for most of the other chaps here. The wives of 4 of them live within 70 miles of here and don't have to waste a lot of time travelling. Also they can get permission to sleep out with their wives. You have got a wrong impression about the ease of getting leave. The true facts are these:

We are allowed, at the discretion of the CO, *not* as a right, 7 days leave every three months. In addition we can take one 48 hrs leave and one 36 hrs leave in between. A 36 hours leave is useless to me as I couldn't get to London in the time. Even the 48 hrs is going to be a bit of a rush. It is true that in most regiments one can often 'stretch' a 48 hrs leave into 72 hrs and perhaps even wangle an extra leave or two – things are easier where there are a lot of officers. However, our CO, though extremely lenient in all respects, is extremely conscientious and strict as regards giving leave. There is no question of stretching our leave. One of the chaps has even had to forego his 7 days leave. I've painted a gloomy picture on purpose but I don't think it's going to be so bad; but you must be reasonable and give me a chance to settle down before I start asking for favours. We could probably best get over the 36 hr leave problem by my getting leave and spending it with you here, so that we could be together nearly all the time instead of a couple of hours only. As I've already told you if our home is going to be sold I shall have to collect some things and will certainly be granted leave for that.

All I ask is that you believe that I want to see you as much as you do me and leave the arrangements to my discretion. After all this is the army, not a holiday camp, and I alone can judge the most suitable times to get off. If I take too many liberties I can see myself losing my 7 day leave. It won't help matters if you send me telegrams asking me to arrange things at short notice either. Nor is it particularly easy for me to phone you. We have only one phone and while I am speaking to you a lot of important messages may get held up. For example, the CO was waiting to use the phone today – that was why I was so anxious to ring off. Please believe me that I am not trying to make difficulties where none exist. When I've been here a little time I shall be able to arrange things better but you must realise that so far I've been nothing but a liability to this unit and the army too and I can't afford to take liberties.

Be a darling and try to be patient. I know you're having a rotten time and there's worse to come, but try and think of the wonderful time we're going to have together when it's all over. It will be nice to think we've earned it and took our medicine without complaint. I've never admired people who wangled their happiness regardless of everything else and we should try to be a bit better than that. I know you think I'm being hard and unsympathetic but I'm only trying to be sensible and it affects me as much as it does you. Please don't be miserable about this. It makes it so much harder for me when I think of you moping at home. I should be so much happier if you were putting your heart into things and taking our joy as it comes instead of snatching at it. I love you so much that I could be happier thinking of you from afar with a clear conscience than having you by my side with a guilty conscience.

Do trust me darling,

all my love

RB

14)   8th FDS

                                                    16.10.43
                                                    [*his 27th birthday*]

My Darling,

Thank you for your lovely cake. It was really rather wicked of you, especially as we are well fed and I've no doubt you could do with the rations at home. Still, I thought you wouldn't be able to resist the temptation, being a silly old darling. You just wait till I have the chance to pay you back!

These married men are very funny. Anyone would think this is the women's lounge at UCH instead of an officers' mess. They're always talking about their wives and what they're going to do on their next leave. The little stretcher-bearer officer George Walker was reading a letter from his wife the other day, when he suddenly burst out indignantly, 'I'll teach her to go to dances when I'm away!' – quite oblivious of the fact that he goes to one himself every week. This leads to a general discussion on the dangers of having Americans stationed near one's wife – I hope there are none at Watford! Captain Wright, the Dental Officer has been very funny. For the last 3 days he has been expecting a letter from his wife telling him whether she is coming for the weekend. Every day he has been hanging around waiting for letters to come in, and his face has been getting longer and longer. He kept asking everyone what to do and one of the chaps advised him to try and make her take notice by not writing to her himself. Another said he should make her jealous next time he is out with her by remarking on the good looks of all the girls they passed in the street. The whole thing reminded me very much of what you told me about Betty A . . . being consoled about Tom S . . . He kept himself from writing for 3 days then broke down and wrote, followed by a wire to his Father. He got a snooty wire in return from his Father, saying his wife had already written twice that week! So it seems that the GPO is responsible after all and his face is all smiles now.

The men here are a scream. We had a salvage drive a few days ago, sending them out in small parties to bring in what they could and offering small prizes. They hadn't been out 10 minutes before we had the Police down on us. Later on one party brought in a whole automatic cigarette machine which they had uprooted bodily from its concrete foundation outside a garage a couple of miles away. The joke was that one of the officers went down to the garage to try and pacify the proprietor. When he got there the proprietor had not noticed anything amiss and came out all smiles and said, 'I hear you're holding a salvage drive, it's a jolly good idea and I think other units ought to do the same.' Suddenly he caught sight of the empty space where his machine had once stood and he turned pink! That particular party did not get the prize.

They tell me that the men are amazingly resourceful. Some time ago as part of their training they were driven to a lonely spot about 90 miles away in quite unknown country and in closed vans so they did not know where they were. All their money was taken away and they were told to make their way back individually. The officer in charge then drove straight back towards the unit. When he was within 5 miles of it he suddenly came upon one of the men waving his arms and asking for a lift! The fellow had actually got there 10 minutes before he had. On another occasion they were sent out blackberrying with only their mess tins to collect the fruit in. They brought back 128 lbs of berries and a magnificent collection of pots, pans, buckets and household utensils. It seems that they had been using their sex appeal to good purpose.

Your letter and photos have just arrived. Once again it's very wicked of you but very nice. Unfortunately the chaps are congratulating me with having 3 different girlfriends!

Incidentally, talking of girlfriends, the unit has been 'adopted' by a girl-guides rangers troop. They are very good and send us parcels of comforts but I rather suspect they are 'hopeful' as they write us letters and enclose photos. I'm afraid they've picked the wrong unit as far as the officers are concerned. It's my turn to answer their letters soon and I don't know what to write.

I didn't write anything about my work last time as I wanted to find out more about it. I'm simply appalled at the responsibility that's been thrust upon me. If I ever hear some young medical student saying that his talents will be wasted in the army I think I shall brain him on the spot. I'm profoundly thankful that I did an HS [*house surgeon*] job but I wish to goodness that I knew some surgery. As you know, all Field Medical Units are divided into 3 sections – Reception, Treatment and Evacuation. I have been put in sole charge of treatment. This involves mainly resuscitation, treatment of shock and blood and plasma transfusions. In addition I shall have to do a certain amount of operating of a life-saving nature – mainly amputations, control of haemorrhage and open wounds.

My equipment is simply fantastic. I have a fine portable operating table and a magnificent set of operating instruments including everything from a myringotomy knife to an amputation saw. I'm afraid I don't know the names of half the instruments. I have a steriliser, 4 gowns, 12 pairs of rubber gloves. Of course most of the surgery will be antiseptic rather than aseptic! I have 30 sets of transfusion apparatus and 4 complete BLB outfits. The drugs are equally staggering. I have 50 ampoules of pentothal and pints of chloroform and ether. In action the Dental Officer gives the anaesthetics. Of course we have M&B by the ton [*a sulphonamide; these were pre-penicillin days*] and almost every conceivable type of drug to be given hypodermically – strychnine, adrenaline, morphine, digitalis etc. All this is quite apart from the ordinary dispensary, so altogether we have enough equipment to run a hospital – I can see now why the capture of a medical unit is such a serious blow. The dentist says that his equipment is equally lavish – he can do fillings, repair dentures and deal with maxillo-facial wounds. It seems wicked that men's lives should be entrusted to the most junior MO but after all it would be wrong to risk experienced surgeons in a forward area. There are 4 doctors in an FDS. The CO is purely administrative as this has obviously to be entrusted to the most experienced man. Reception and evacuation are obviously of supreme importance too – a bottleneck there would be fatal. Thus treatment, the most purely medical part, has to be left to a junior. It's true that 50% of the cases we get will be moribund but even so it's a great responsibility as one will literally have saved the lives of any cases which recover. You can see that there's not much room for incompetence. It's true that there isn't much to do until the fighting starts but the least one can do is read up something on the subject. Let me know if you happen to come across any books on resuscitation and treatment of severe wounds. I rather think Hamilton Bailey's *War Surgery*

Vol. 1 contained most of what I want. If you get a chance you might look at it and refresh my memory as to its contents. Of course I don't know if I'm going to stay here for long but I think that next to an RMO job I've probably picked about the best going, even though it's very frightening.

The work here is rather different from an RMO's. In addition to taking turns at acting MO to the men and training them medically, we have also to train them as soldiers and look after their administrative side – just like the ordinary officers in a regiment.

It's certainly good experience for me though I see it must have become rather boring for the others. The trouble is that the whole unit has gone over its training dozens of times and it's very difficult to find anything new for them to do. We are about 1.5 miles from Filey which is a dull little place with 2 cinemas. There are no ATS around but there is no lack of dances as there is a big WAAF camp near here. Some of them are rather wild and it's not safe for a man to go out after dark!

Am longing to see you already but I don't think there's much fun for you coming down here. The nearest place you could stay is 2 miles away across the fields and I can't get off much in the day time. It's different for the others as they get permission to sleep out with their wives. Mrs Alderson has just come down here, she is rather nice. She did medicine at Newcastle too. Apparently Alderson did not approve of her when they first met at College as he told her she ought to be at home darning her brother's socks instead of wasting her time at Medicine! It looks as if he's going to be the housewife of that pair as he is our catering officer and has just been on a special course. All he talks of now is how to cook the various cuts of meat. They seem to have solved the separation problem quite well as she spends all her time doing locums near him, taking a holiday when one is finished, then doing another.

I'm glad you've told your Mother and she doesn't mind. I'm afraid it must be rather a blow to her from the religious point of view but I'm sure she'd put your happiness first. At least she knows it isn't just a sudden infatuation. Your parents' attitude has always worried me a good deal, as it would be simply horrible to cause them any pain, but I feel a lot easier now. [*My parents came to love him. It had been hard for both sets of parents as they came from different backgrounds – R's Russian Jewish, mine English dissenting Protestant. R and I had come happily to a common ground which did not change through the years. The two mothers and fathers were in reality very similar in outlook and values and would have been happy together. Sadly my Mother died . . .*] Well I'm afraid it's been rather a stodgy letter but I don't need to tell you how much I love you nor how much I miss you.

Love

RB

PS How's Janet? – you'll have to go and get some coaching from her.

15)   8th FDS

                                                             21.10.43

My silly old darling,

I've just got your letter and I hope you've got mine by now. I think you will understand why this weekend would be inconvenient and also the difficulties about phoning. But do please rest assured that I shall do all I can to fix things soon. Above all don't talk rot about my not wanting to take my leave when it's due. All the same dear, you've no idea how depressing it is to me to hear how badly you are taking things. I know it's difficult – I feel the same myself and your news of air raids increases my anxiety. When I remember that it's only two weeks since I saw you, though it does seem ages – I find it difficult to believe that your misery would be relieved for any length of time by your coming down here. If nothing else will convince you please try and think that it would make me proud and happy if I thought you were facing up to things bravely and sensibly. We can't go on exchanging miserable pleading letters for the rest of the war, can we? It won't do either of us any good and our work will suffer. Honestly, if you go on making me feel that I'm being unnecessarily hard I shall get so worried that I'll crack up. I feel it's better to be frank now and get the business settled once and for all before the rot sets in. I know it's no great comfort to remind you that some people have been separated for 4 years, but you know it's highly probable that the whole thing will be over in a few months and our suffering will be nothing compared to other people's. Could you derive any pleasure from imagining I'm near you? I always think of you when I do anything and I think it helps me to carry on – in fact (don't misunderstand me) I scarcely feel that we're separated at all. I'm glad you think that your parents are resigned to our marriage. I'll certainly try and correct the unfortunate impression I made on them last time. My Father's English is apt to be a little wonderful at times but he's quite used to all of us laughing at him so you mustn't try and suppress your giggle . . . [*R's parents had been born in Russia. They married in Odessa where their first son, Max was born. Then*

31

they moved to Warsaw where Jo was born. Still later they moved west and, via Sweden and Antwerp, arrived in England in 1914. R was born in London in 1916.]

I'm glad you've made it up with Janet. Don't forget I've got a soft spot for her too. Did you tell her about us? I expect she knew long ago really. Incidentally what was it she said and what advice did she give you? I'm dying to hear. I'm enclosing your comment on what she said about me. At first I thought it was written in Greek but then I realised it was your own wonderful spelling of 'hear, hear' or did you mean 'there-there'! I'm beginning to get a little more into my stride here now, I've been on a couple of route marches without any trouble and the dizziness has practically gone. Incidentally I noticed the other day that Soma Weiss gave a very good definition of dizziness, distinguishing it from vertigo: I had been very puzzled trying to describe my own sensations. They did not fit in with my own ideas of vertigo. I was trying to think of whether I was still and things were spinning round me or vice versa.

Actually I felt neither. Weiss defines vertigo as a sense of external rotation, dizziness as a sense of something revolving *inside* the head. I then realised that he had described my own sensations perfectly. It's a very simple distinction but like so many simple things very difficult to describe.

I'm sorry you couldn't find the paper on Phage, I should have taken the reference. It would be worth looking up the Quarterly Cumulative Index. I think it's one of the most remarkable papers ever published.

I notice that they have an EM at Woods Hole Marine Biological Station and have been using it to examine the axioplasm of giant squid nerve fibres. It would be marvellous if we could spend some of our long vacs at various marine stations. I see the Naples one is still intact. It might be rather interesting to work on fish viruses especially if we can get a portable EM or perhaps each lab will have its own by then.

I'm learning quite a bit about artillery. I had to go out with a heavy anti-tank regiment and stand by while they fired at moving tanks. Also we have some enormous coastal defence guns near here and I've become quite friendly with the commander.

Well I'm afraid I must rush to get this posted. Do take what I've said to heart but don't let it make you miserable rather than the reverse. Try and think of the lovely time we're going to have in only a few days time. I want to see you happy and well-fed, not thin and miserable.

All my love

RB

[*Some time about here we had a day in Oxford where I was introduced to R's parents. They were very sweet and kind and I took to them at once. His father felt my winter coat at once and said it was not warm enough! Since they were born in Russia his standards were more severe than ours!*]

16)

8FDS
Filey

Dearest Gwenda,

Thanks for your letter and photograph which I shall add to my already extensive portrait gallery of you. You always look like an old hag whatever you do, so I suppose it must be natural. I'll try and get one of myself as soon as possible but you know that it isn't easy for me to get into Scarborough – the bus services have been reduced even further. You will be pleased to hear that first reports from home on you are favourable. They were certainly impressed with your friendliness. Am very glad about your Mother's attitude, it certainly takes a load off my mind.

My cold is almost completely better now. I had to arrange and lead a route march myself yesterday as I was the only officer available. I managed to get permission to get the lorries to take us out into the country while we went on a circular route. We went along the Derwent Valley and across the moors. It is magnificent country and it would be lovely to go there together. The men are apt to yell at anyone they see and it's sometimes very embarrassing. We passed one large estate and saw the Lord of the Manor all togged up in a fur coat and carrying a gun, followed by his gamekeeper. One wag yelled out, 'Yah, poaching'. I thought the old boy would have a fit. Some of the remarks they shout at girls are rather dreadful and I'm sure you would go your usual beetroot colour if you were anywhere near them. Once when they passed a good-looking young woman wheeling a pram some of them called out 'That's a nice baby. Isn't he like our sergeant!' Woe betide any girl that passes on a bike, especially if it's windy. Of course most of the girls don't mind but some of them do. The Quartermaster told me that he was once on a march when they passed a pretty girl with a big dog. 'Beauty and the beast – it's a beautiful dog.' The girl went crimson, stepped out into the road and gave the wag a resounding slap in the face! Everyone laughed at him after that. The Quartermaster was once himself the victim of the men's wit. It was while he was still a sergeant-major. He was home on leave and taking his baby out in a pram. He passed a long line of several hundred men of another unit on a march. One wit began singing 'Kiss me goodnight sergeant-major' and this was taken up all along the line. He vowed never to take the baby out again after that. Incidentally he told me that although he has been married 15 years he only went into a woman's clothes shop for the first time last week and even then he had to have the dentist to accompany him and give him courage. He has never even gone with his wife while she bought a hat – so remember that next time you drag me into a shop. He seems to have a real phobia about shop girls as he will not even buy himself a pair of socks or a shirt if there is a girl behind the counter. God knows what he would do if he were examined by a woman doctor!

Glad to hear that Whitfield [*student in our year*] is still flourishing though I can't imagine why he should speak well of you. Wolfe told me that he was getting a little religious recently but he was never starchy or bigoted. I should think his children would look priceless. It would be interesting to see if they inherit his amazing ability to waggle his ears.

The two war surgery books look rather good. I've been reading a bit of the stuff and a lot of it is quite helpful and practical. It makes a good deal of difference reading such things for exams and being faced with the possibility of actually doing things oneself. I've already discovered a lot of things that I would have done wrong. Have you seen any result of sulphonamide treatment of burns? Everyone here seems to be carried away with enthusiasm for it. I can't help feeling that it's largely part of the sulphonamide craze. I still think that if I had a bad burn myself I'd have it treated with gentian violet – certainly as a first aid measure. It's funny though, I've had a lot of cases of impetigo among the engineers – they are a very neglected lot – and my predecessor had been treating them with sulphonamide cream. I said to the orderly that I didn't think sulphonamides were much use in impetigo. I had to eat my words as several cases showed a very marked and rapid improvement, so it does seem to work in some cases. I've got a bad case of chronic lichen planus which seems to be spreading to the arms. You ought to be an expert on this. [*My Father had it for years.*] Can you give me a list of alternative treatments – he's already had everything, including x-rays at some time or another, but I want to try and stop the spread. I'm getting a lot of skin cases here – I've got a beautiful ringworm of the axilla which has responded dramatically to iodine. Well dear, I hope you are getting into your stride at Shrodells. Take things easy and stop worrying about me – I hope you are quite reassured about the tanks (incidentally there's no sign of them yet). Everything seems to be too marvellous to be true. Regards to your parents.

Love

RB

17)

My own darling Gwenda,

It was really very sweet but very wicked of you to send me that toffee. I very nearly sent it back. You really must not waste your coupons on sweets for me – or food of any sort. You know very well you need it at home and I am by no means starving here. Thanks for the books. They seem to contain a lot of useful stuff. Do please let me know as soon as you need any books from Lewis's and I will return them.

My cold is very much better, after two days in bed. I feel very guilty as I seem to have spent more time hors de combat than working in this unit so I have a lot to make up.

The mess is very much less crowded now as the CO and Alderson live next door and only eat breakfast and sometimes lunch with us. Alderson is as mad as ever. I nearly died of laughing watching him hurl insults at a suet pudding the other day. He held it on the plate at arms length and yelled at the top of his voice. The gist of his remarks seem to have been that he had had it every day at school and now it was following him about in the army. I really think he expected the pudding to answer him back! The dentist is as gloomy as ever but cheered up when he got permission for another 36 hours leave. He was full of admiration for one of the men who went away on 36 hour leave taking no fewer than 10 contraceptives from the canteen and then returning to give a pint of blood! Incidentally I'm afraid I escaped that owing to my cold.

As I told you I now have to look after a big batch of engineers. All their inoculations are out of date and I'm busy doing them all. I can never understand why none of them go septic as the sterilisation of needles is by no means thorough and one needle serves to inoculate several men.

I've got an interesting case of a man who was wounded while lifting mines in the Middle East. He got a lump of metal in his head which the surgeon was unable to remove. The idiot told him about this but told him not to worry until it gave him trouble. Now he's getting headaches and poor memory. The case is complicated by a history of epilepsy and mental instability in the family.

I am so glad you enjoyed it at Oxford last Sunday. It's certainly not necessary to write to them about . . . I do hope your Mother is reconciled, as it appears from what you say. I should hate to do anything without your parents' consent.

A big hug and kiss

RB

18)   8FDS
                                                                    Filey

                                                                    Tuesday

Dearest Gwenda

Have just got your dreadful letter. You really are scandalous but is sounds marvellous. The only thing is I hope it doesn't get around – your people would be shocked. Mrs D is a scream [*our dear landlady in Bloomsbury, who had made some nice but unsophisticated arrangements for our stay there one weekend!*]. I expect after this I shall arrive at King's Cross at 1.50 p.m. (afternoon) on Saturday. I may be late but try to meet me by the bus stop directly outside the station.

I met George Clark [*UCH friend*] at a clinical meeting at an EMS hospital near Bridlington. He is in the same corps but a different division. He is with the tanks, lucky devil, and I bet his wife doesn't pester him about it. Actually he is trying to get into a Field Ambulance. He is stationed about 20 miles away and we are going to try to meet when I come back from my leave. The clinical meetings are held every month and are pretty good. We had an interesting discussion on infective hepatitis.

We had a first class concert by the men the other day. It was really exceptionally good and would have put most shows to shame. The main item was a sort of pantomime based on the Sleeping Beauty, but modified to suit local conditions. It was very well written and acted and kept everyone in fits of laughter. The amazing thing was that the whole show was remarkably clean contrary to general expectations.

I had to take part in these landing exercises. They went off quite well. We had to climb down scrambling nets into small boats and then from the boats up the side of a ship which took us for a sea trip. It wasn't too bad but fortunately the weather was good. I had to go down last into the little boat and I climbed away merrily without bothering to look. Suddenly I turned round and to my surprise saw the top of the boat about the level of my chest and everyone staring at me open-mouthed. Another step and I should have walked into the sea!

I attended a court martial the other day for instruction. It was very interesting and very fairly conducted. The man was charged with being absent without leave for 2 years. Actually it turned out that during those 2 years he had joined the Merchant Navy and sailed in an oil tender fuelling the fleet. He had taken part in the Malta Convoys and the North African invasion. He had just returned from the battle of Salerno when he was arrested. Of course he was guilty of desertion but I don't think he will be punished.

Must stop now if I want to catch the post.

Can hardly wait till Saturday.

Love

RB

19)

8FDS
Filey

Monday

Dearest Gwenda

Hope you got the parcel and my letter by now and are taking it sensibly. Please don't send me anything in future without asking me first as it makes things awkward. Whatever gave you the idea that my Mother's comments were not at all favourable? On the contrary they were all very favourable and she was particularly impressed with your friendliness. She always sends you her regards in her letters, so don't run away with any false ideas on that subject.

We had to go to a lecture by the corps commander, given to all officers in the division. He was rather impressive. He had been a divisional commander in Libya for 3 years and now has charge of the corps containing our division and 2 others. He is remarkably young, about 42 but seems to have been knocked about a bit having lost several fingers of one hand and with one dud leg. He told us that his initials were AFH and his men used to nickname him 'all f.....g hurry' because of his insistence on speed and preparedness. Our own CO seemed to be stimulated by the lecture for the next morning he made us parade in full marching order, which includes large and small packs, blankets, respirator, helmet, revolver and various other things worn over the great coat – the whole weighing a mere 90 lb. After the parade we heaved a sigh of relief and prepared to take everything off when he suddenly gave the order: 'Load and prepare to move.' We had to collect all our stores and kit and load it on to lorries just as if we had been given an emergency order in the field. It was a terrible sweat and at the end he went round criticising everything.

I met Peter Deller at the lecture but only had time to pass a word of greeting. However we saw each other yesterday at a demonstration and film on VD at the headquarters of a field ambulance. One of the first things he said was 'How's your wife?' That shook me for a moment but I replied unblushingly, 'My future wife, you mean,' so you can see that I am not keeping it very secret and you could also imagine the amazement it would cause if it were announced in the magazine. I think that he genuinely believed we were already married.

Your gossip spy service seems to have let you down. He told me that Jo B had her baby at the beginning of the month. It's a girl and she had to have a Caesar for foetal distress. Fortunately 'Uncle' [*a favourite obstetrician at UCH who would later deliver our son*] was looking after her and he's supposed to be very hot on Caesars. She is quite well now. One of the field ambulance MOs is Jimmy G who was an obstetric HS when Jo B was on the list. He has the reputation of being the dirtiest man in the division and he certainly seemed to be pretty busy yesterday. I don't think UCH has a very good reputation for that sort of thing. The film we saw was rather disappointing. We had been told in advance that it was one of the best films ever produced on the subject. Actually its only use seems to be to serve as an introduction to the MO's talk. It was meant for civilians and gave no actual information about VD. There's no reason at all why it shouldn't be shown to mixed audiences. By the way, why not suggest to Miles that he should make a short instructional film on bacteriology applied to hygiene, showing how diseases are spread! I'm sure it could be made very simple and would be very helpful to many of the men. A lot of this cross infection stuff would probably make good material. You never know, you might become a film star.

We went for a route march to the famous Flamborough Head. The head itself is rather disappointing but the surrounding cliffs and rocks are interesting. There are a lot of big caves which we intend to explore when we have more time. I'm repainting my bike and hope to get about a bit when the weather clears up.

Poor little George Walker's plans always seem to go astray. He went on a gas course last week in the Lake District. He has some relatives near there and arranged to get his wife up for the weekend. They were looking forward to a nice night together when a party of friends suddenly descended and demanded accommodation. The men had to sleep in one room and the women in another, so poor George and his wife were parted!

All my love dearest and let's hope we'll never be parted again.

RB

20)   8FDS
                                                                           Filey

Dearest Gwenda,

You've no idea how glad I am that you've told me the true reason for your unhappiness. I had a feeling from your letters that you were in a bad state of nerves and now at last you've told me why. Please don't hide your worries from me again as it has a bad effect on me too. With regard to what job I get, do try to remember that I have absolutely no choice in the matter. Neither the expression of a preference nor the possession of special qualifications count for anything at all. The only way to get the job you want is by graft and I'm not going to use that. There are dozens of people who have been applying to be sent abroad for the last 3 years, with no response. Much as I admire the army's good points I'm afraid your remarks about placing people in jobs best suited to them is simply laughable.

So you see that even if I tried to get into the tanks it would be largely a matter of luck, even if there were a vacancy. If by some fluke I should get into the tanks try to remember that they are not really as dangerous as they seem. Remember that they are widely spaced out and the fighting is not so concentrated as it is with infantry. Also tanks rarely fight at night. In any case the employment of an armoured division is quite different from an infantry division. The whole division is thrown in en bloc and the fighting is intense but of short duration. There is no front line and all units are equally exposed. In other words it doesn't much matter where I am. However as you are so worried I promise I won't go flying into danger – I've got too much to live for now. I don't entirely agree about the useful medical work but it's quite impossible to overestimate the effect on morale that a good RMO could have. I really believe that he could alter the whole course of the war in some situations. I promise you that I won't try for anything special but if I do happen to be given a job which you consider dangerous try and realise that it may actually be less dangerous than my present one – appearances are often deceptive. Also be thankful that I am not an airman or in a submarine or some poor infantry officer who never had any say in the matter. Always remember that we are incomparably luckier than most people in this war (and after it!).

Now let's turn to pleasanter things. One of the reasons that I didn't want you to come this weekend is that the division has been doing embarkation and landing exercises and I was detailed to stand by. I will let you know more about them later. I've also had time to make further enquiries about travelling. If you leave about 6 p.m. on a Friday you could manage to stay here until about 7 p.m. on a Sunday before going back. Of course it's a terrible journey and the trains may be full at York. Someone just told me that it's better by Hull. Will look this up in detail and let you know. The only snag is if anything turns up at the last minute. If it does I'll have to phone or cable you. It's possible that I may get leave myself soon – I'm nearly due for my 7 days. I think they usually take a few days off at Christmas at Schrodells? [*The hospital where I was working at the time.*] The standard of things at UCH doesn't seem to be improving. They'll soon have BB [*an awful duffer*] back as a registrar. I see that Illingworth-Law has become a surgical registrar at The Royal Northern. What's going to happen to Stella Luty? Is she still at Stanborough's? I wish you had some more friends at Watford. It would give you something to do instead of moping about me you old fool.

There are some quite interesting rock pools around here. I haven't found anything very interesting but there are thousands of empty razor-shells (solon). This is a bivalve mollusc of extraordinary shape with a long muscular body like a snake. There are a few at Plymouth but not so many as here. The sands here are magnificent – flat and firm and stretch for miles. We do PT on them.

I had a magnificent case of 'Raynauds' the other day (in a man), Tom [*Lewis, cardiologist*] would have loved it. He had severe attacks while I examined him. One interesting feature was that though his fingers were all ice cold, his palms were hot and moist.

We have been laying in a good store of prophylactic packets as it's rumoured that a big batch of Free French ATS are coming near here. The local WAAF are bad enough but these are said to be terrible. There is a chance that I shall have to look after them for a bit as we act as MOs for several isolated detachments in the neighbourhood. Well dear that's about all for the present. I will try to write oftener as you seem to need it, being rather feeble, but a nice old darling just the same.

Love

RB

PS *No* dressing-gowns!

PPS No motor cars for the boys, but insist on motorcycles.

[It saddens me to remember that I persistently urged R to try and get a hospital job, as people at UCH thought he should, or indeed a job in an army research establishment. Four of our close friends had gone to a research station at Lulworth and never saw 'active service' at all. We had been a bright set at UCH – the outbreak of war had brought many back to clinical medicine who had been doing research and R was among the best (a galaxy of professors came later from the group including my R). I felt that his talents were being wasted and felt sure, like many others (my own Mother in the First World War included), that he would be killed. I suppose I would not actually have said that the clever should be saved in preference to the less able but I believed in the deployment of talent and not in heroic sacrifice. He was right that I was undignified (see below) but I think I did what I was impelled to do. Where I know I was wrong, was in not accepting his right to his own decision. It was clear that he felt he had to fight against Hitler. He wanted to play his part and felt privileged that he could do it without violence but by helping to save lives. I think he felt I did not support him. For years after the war I felt that I had lost his respect to some extent. Yet in middle life I once asked him this; he replied with surprise, 'Oh no'. Perhaps he felt that this was the female role. I hope so.]

21)

8FDS
Filey

My own darling Gwenda,

I'm afraid I'll have to start this letter with a lecture. I know it's very tempting to arrange a code like the one you suggested to let you know when I'm going overseas but a moment's thought should make you realise that it's quite out of the question. In the first place I am not allowed to disclose such information to anyone and the use of codes is expressly forbidden. There have recently been heavy penalties imposed on officers for breaches of security and as officers' letters are not subject to the same strict censorship as the men's it is specially up to them to set an example. I know that at first sight it seems quite harmless to let you know that a move is imminent but you know how hard it is to prevent things slipping out – even in all innocence. A thoughtless remark might give the whole show away. I don't even know if we are going to get embarkation leave. In any case if I were sent overseas it would not necessarily mean that the unit had gone and vice versa. I am afraid that the only way you will guess that I have gone is by the fact that my letters are overdue. I know it's unpleasant but it's the same for everyone.

Anyhow so far as I know we are not moving in the immediate future so don't let it stop you from making arrangements to come down here if you can manage it. Let me know at least one week ahead.

I'm busy learning French for the invasion. I've had a number of sessions with the Channel Islander I told you about and it's amazing the difference it's made. At first I could hardly think of the simplest words but now we hold quite long conversations with only occasional halts. I had not realised how difficult the French 'u' can be – even worse than the 'r'.

I had a terrific day on Wednesday. I suddenly got a message to stand by at a physical endurance test on the moors. I was provided with no less than 3 ambulances and stretcher-bearers, and had to set up casualty collecting posts. The test was pretty awful. Teams of 10 men were told to make for a certain point about 12 miles as the crow flies across the moors. The country was simply frightful – mainly heather, bogs and hills with mud everywhere. At the end there was a very steep ravine with nothing to hang on to. The teams carried rifles and ammunition and had to shoot at targets at the end. Any team arriving with less than 10 men was disqualified. Altogether about 300 men took part. Fortunately there were no serious accidents, though plenty of minor ones. However, one complete team and a large number of stragglers were missing at the end of the day. We shone lights across the moors and waited till 11 o'clock at night but they did not come, so presumably they spent the night on the moors. There was one amusing incident. One man from a team arrived at a check point in the middle of the course and said that he had been left behind by the rest of his team. The team had not reported so he went on. An hour and a half later his team turned up! He finished the course long before the others even though he had no map.

We are in the middle of a series of gas exercises at the moment. We have to carry our respirators around all the time and are likely to be sprayed or gassed at any time of the day or night. We even have to sleep in our respirators.

One certainly sees extraordinary cases in the army. One man grazed his leg slightly and it swelled up to double its normal size, though his temperature is normal and the leg is practically painless. Another had developed a peculiar fluctuant swelling in front of the ear – possibly a preauricular gland, but again no temperature or evidence of sepsis. My collection of skins is increasing. I have what I think is a cement dermatitis of the hands. One man had a peculiar rash on the front and back of the chest. I couldn't think what to give him so I put some zinc paste on. The rash went in 2 days!

I've still no idea what it was.

I'm glad you've told Janet about us, but I don't think I'll take her advice just yet [*it was probably that we should have a baby straight away!*]. Has she offered to put us up while I'm on leave?

Do try not to quarrel with your Father. It all seems very trivial but I know things must be rather trying for you.

How's Birkbeck?

All my love dearest.
I am longing to hold you in my arms.

22)   8FDS
                                                               Filey

                                                               Thursday

My dear darling old idiot,

I hope by now you have received the pot of marmalade which, despite your wonderful accompanying note on the back of a railway ticket, I felt bound to return. You will be pleased to hear that at least you gave the quartermaster a good laugh when he saw me unwrap it. Whatever gave you the idea that I am short of jam? Only yesterday someone was remarking on the enormous amount of jam we ate in the mess and that we ought to cut it down. Honestly if I wanted to I could have 50 slices of bread and jam at every meal. You can imagine my amazement when I saw what you had sent, especially as I know that you were particularly short of marmalade yourself. So please don't be annoyed at my returning it – it's only sensible and it's quite wasted here. I could never eat it. The quartermaster said that he was being driven nearly crazy with unwanted gifts that his wife insisted on sending him. He had a big box full of them and takes them all back when he goes on leave. We both agreed that women are crazy, so let that be a warning to you. Incidentally I don't want any arguments about the Mars bars – you know I hate them and you like them and you've provided a convenient packing [*he sent me Mars bars with the returned marmalade!*]. By the way have a good look at that marmalade – it seems to have a mosquito in it!

I've just had an amusing session with some NAAFI girls whom I had to examine to see if they were fit for overseas. I had to examine them in the FDS and someone began to barge in by mistake. One of the girls let out a loud shriek and they were all overcome by fits of giggles. One of them was so nervous after that that her knees were literally shaking and her pulse went up to 120! The manageress who acted as a chaperone told me that one of her girls had been rejected for the ATS on the grounds that she had one of her fingers missing and would be unable to fire a rifle! You women doctors again! – they'll be insisting on girls having their breasts amputated like Amazons next. Anyway I won't let them amputate yours – am just dying to hold them again.

Don't you think you had better wait till after Xmas before coming here? In any case it's no use coming here unless you can get Saturday and/or Monday morning off. What are the chances? I could probably get Saturday afternoon and all Sunday off. I don't like the idea of your travelling at night – it would be much better if you could get Monday off. Remember the weather is liable to be cold and wet.

The medical work at the moment is quite tiring. After a busy morning yesterday I had to go and see a long and rather dull film about the field ambulance in war and I'm afraid I slept almost right through it – I hope no-one noticed.

All my love sweetheart. I can hardly wait to hold you in my arms again.

Yours

RB

23)   8FDS
                                                                             Filey

Dearest Gwen,
So sorry about the weekend. I'm afraid I'm on duty this weekend and wouldn't be able to get out. If you could give me a week's notice I could change it, but not once it's published. I suppose you couldn't manage next weekend? If not, early January would probably be best. I don't think they'd grudge you an extra day off then, as they mostly take several days off at Xmas. Don't despair. It's only 3 weeks till January and only 5 weeks after that until I get another 10 days leave! I hope you got the book on Japan. I'm afraid I should have returned it long ago but to tell you the truth, one of the officers borrowed it, forgot that he had done so, and it's only now turned up again. So sorry about the delay in letters. I got a bit rushed last week and couldn't manage it. Also, if I write on Friday you don't seem to get it until Monday.

We saw a very good film today. It was called 'The Nazis strike' and is one of an official series of American films. I don't think they are released to the public but if they should be, they are worth seeing. This particular film gives an excellent summary of events leading up to the war, starting with the march into the Rhineland and ending with the conquest of Poland. After the film we had a very good lecture by a Professor Jessop on 'Conditions in occupied territory'.

With regard to your buffer problem, I think you are making it unnecessarily complicated. Tables exist showing the correct ratio of salts to give a buffer at a given PH (I think Clark gives one in his book). Then calculate the concentration to give an equal tonicity assuming full ionisation in the case of Na or K salts – the error is small. I daresay you could calculate it all out exactly if you knew all the activities, but no-one ever does.

The CO has his wife and little boy aged 14 months next door. I'm getting plenty of practice at playing with children as he often comes into the mess and usually leaves it in even more of a mess than before. He has urinated on the floor on more than one occasion. The dentist is rather dandy and fussy about his clothes but the young devil managed to upset the jam all over him much to our amusement. I hope you'll be able to see young Robert as he's rather a good looking baby, though not as nice as ours are going to be.

Goodnight darling. I'm afraid I must go to bed early as we're having a route march tomorrow. I dream of you every night.

Love

RB

24)

8FDS
Filey

Sunday

Dearest Gwen,

I hope you weren't too disappointed about the weekend. It was a great pity as the weather was quite good. I suppose you can't manage next weekend. If not we'll have to leave it till after Xmas. Incidentally, young woman, I've not had a letter from you since that miserable little note asking if you could come, which arrived on Wednesday.

I had a very good day on Friday. The DDMS arranged a study day for all the MOs in the Corps. I ran into Meara, Brian Warren and Witt. Meara, who has grown an enormous black moustache, is in a field ambulance. He is in a Scottish division and wears a pom-pom. Brian Warren was absolutely priceless – the complete guards officer. His accent has become more la-de-da than ever. His wife seems to be better now. I don't know if you remember Witt. He was the bright boy of the year ahead of us at College. He has been in the army two years and is the RMO to a unit near Hull. It was a very interesting day and we are going to have more of them. The corps commander spoke to us on what he considered to be the role of the RAMC. He left no doubt in my mind that by far the most useful job was that of RMO. He said that even during a campaign, war was 90% boredom and 10% sheer fright and the RMO can do an immense amount of good work during periods of boredom.

We had a first class talk from a colonel who had been in charge of a CCS in Libya and Tripoli. He was a surgeon and knew what he was talking about. He emphasised that the job of forward units was 'treatment for evacuation' not 'treatment for treatment'. Some wounded had to be transported 1700 miles and many of them needed resuscitation every few days. The latest thing in transport of fractured femurs is to enclose the whole limb in a padded plaster, and then put on a Thomas' splint. They had two complete CCSs and an advanced surgical centre laid out in the grounds. The CCS is a very big thing and can hold 50 beds and 200 stretchers. They have a physician and 2 surgeons and an x-ray apparatus. It's all housed in big tents. The nearest they ever got to the front was 15 miles and fortunately they were never bombed in daylight. Another CCS was bombed purposely by the Germans after we had shot down one of their hospital planes which was found to be carrying cameras. He said it was a great pity that there were no nurses with the CCS any more, though he caused roars of laughter by his unfortunate choice of words in protesting against 'the stripping of the nurses from the CCS'. They did have a few sisters attached to them during one quiet spell and he said it made an immense difference to the patients. After a few weeks in the desert everyone got an intense craving for civilisation and the sight of women pottering around and arranging flowers worked like a tonic. Box told me exactly the same thing happened in the last war. It's amazing how even a huge thing like a CCS has to move during a battle especially during a retreat. In 50 weeks they had to make 50 moves. Incidentally I also met Herepath again. He's with one of the CCSs in the corps. The last lecture of the day was by a Brigadier who had been in charge of supplies and administration in Libya. It was certainly a profitable day.

Alderson is quite crazy. He spent most of his time on the way to the conference making most horrible faces and gestures out of the windows of the car. One girl on a bike was so astonished that she nearly fell off. He pulled especially wild faces at WAAFs as we were all nearly killed by a crazy WAAF driver who decided to overtake just as we were passing a tank. We drove onto the grass verge but she was quite unconcerned. I'm sure that people thought that we were escorting a lunatic, especially as there is a red cross on the car.

Well darling that's all for the moment. I'm sending you a few hankies for Xmas so that you won't have any excuse for pestering me whenever we're out.

Love

RB

[*The weekend at Filey finally materialised at New Year. We had a lovely time and some cold walks. We planned to marry as soon as possible. However, when we arrived back at my boarding house, the landlord told us he would lock up at 9 p.m. and not allow me in thereafter. Nothing would shift him – he must have had a sadistic approach to young couples (see later), so we had to sit demurely on the sofa until R had to depart!*]

25)   8FDS
                                                                        Filey

                                                                        5.1.44

Dearest,

I hope you had a good journey home on Monday and arrived in time. Do tell me about it. It was a pity our lovely time together was marred by that last parting but I hope you didn't quarrel with the wretched man any more. It wouldn't do any good. I love you more and more every time I see you. I'm glad we had a chance to talk things over together. I'm going to write to your Father as you suggested and you must sound them on the question of the ceremony. Actually I rather fancy my leave is going to be mucked up for various reasons and there may be a chance for us to meet somewhere to get married. Anyhow I shall know in a few weeks.

I've been busy trying to balance the books during the last few days. I've got them straight at last and am anxiously awaiting the result of the audit. Don't be surprised if I get sent to prison for embezzlement.

You will be interested to hear that we may have passed a murderer during the weekend. The body of an RAF sergeant was found on the golf course the other day, with the head brutally smashed in. There are no clues so far.

The CO came back on Monday night looking very fed up. Apparently he had gone all the way up to Scotland for a course, only to be told that it was all over!

I hope you managed to get the biscuits back all right. I'll try to get some more when I come on leave.

There's not much news at present but I hope to have something more interesting soon.

All my love darling,

RB

PS Has the other UCH Mag come? If not, I'll send you mine back.

26)   8FDS

                                                                       Sunday

Dearest Gwen,

Sorry you had such a bad journey back via Hull. They tell me it's most unusual. However I hope everything was all right at the lab. Things have gone back to normal last week. I spent a lot of time vaccinating and inoculating several hundred men and have just had my own first typhus inoculation. Apparently the Germans have been testing out the efficiency of 6 different types of Typhus vaccine on prisoners purposely infected with Typhus. They find that the Cox type of vaccine is about the best. There seems to be a real scare on about the danger of Typhus on invasion. I've just been to a clinical meeting at York Military Hospital. It was quite interesting. Hamilton Patterson is one of the graded medical specialists there. It was a bit of a shock to realise that I had been sending him cases. I suppose he's quite competent but rather young to be a medical specialist. Did you see Lewin's recent article in the *Lancet*? I see he's only a Lieutenant, which is as it should be. [*Both were UCH doctors.*] Alderson has come back in one of his manic phases yelling and swearing. However he soon quietened down when I gave him his inoculation. He's having some trouble next door as young Robert insists on defaecating all over the place. He's in rather an awkward position as he has rented the bungalow and the Major is only a sub-tenant but he's hardly in a position to tell the Major what to do.

James Booth was a scream when he had to audit my books. He simply can't add at all and never got the figures to agree. At one stage he announced that I was 10d out and was just settling down to a whole day's work to check over the Canteen books when I added up a few of his figures and found the missing 10d. Alderson says he can never understand how a man like that ever managed to get an honours degree in medicine. I think it must be the Scotch system – all book learning. The other day a chap came to me with a lump on the back of his hand which I diagnosed as an insect bite. I painted it with iodine and left it alone. The next day I had to go away and James took the sick parade. When I came back I found to my horror that he had incised it! He got nothing out but of course the thing is now secondarily infected. I'm getting really interested in skins – in fact I may even apply for training as a specialist in dermatology (!). One of the engineers has a simply superb pityriasis rosea. What's the best treatment? At the moment I'm giving him Ung. Picis Carb and treating it on the same basis as psoriasis. Is there anything better? I want to get it right as he says I'm the first MO who's ever diagnosed it and has a rather poor opinion of doctors. I had a very good example of the importance of treating the scalp in seborrhoea. I had a man with seborrhoea of face and chest. The chest cleared up with simple zinc cream. The face improved at first but then relapsed. I then left the face alone and gave him a hair lotion containing spirit. The face is now clear. I can see that treating skins must be great fun. You have such a definite indication of how the treatment is working and don't have to rely on symptoms alone.

Well dear I'm afraid I still don't know about my leave, but don't worry, we'll fit it in somehow.

Love

RB

27)   8FDS

                                                                    13.1.44

Dearest,
I hope that my letter to your Father has arrived by now. I'm afraid difficulties

are mounting up at the moment and I doubt if I shall get leave until March. I'm afraid the CO has no say in the matter at present. It looks as if I'm going to spend most of the time sleeping in the snow under a hedge, but I should think March is pretty safe. I may not know until very short notice. If your parents are quite reconciled I'm quite willing to get married quietly by ourselves, perhaps in London. I doubt if my parents could come as it's rather a strain travelling, although, great news, my Mother's eye seems to be improving slowly at last. Darling, I'm afraid it would have to be a really exceptional emergency to force me to go through a ceremony in church [*I can't imagine this was ever seriously suggested as I also would not have contemplated it*]. It's against all my feeling and as you know it's one of the aspects of religion about which I feel quite strongly. Also you must realise that it would certainly hurt my parents. Holding independent opinions is one thing, but conforming to the outward ceremonial of another religion is another matter. You know I don't set much store by these things but I should feel a hypocrite and turncoat. Actually I somehow feel that your Mother won't be all that much upset – as long as she knows what we really feel about it.

You can make any arrangements you please about the registrar – as you say it doesn't much matter if it lapses after 3 months. By the way, what is a 'special licence'? I have a vague idea it's one allowing you to marry somewhere where you haven't been resident. Anyhow dear, find out all you can and I'll stick by any arrangement you make.

Incidentally I wrote to my Mother about getting married. She replied that she agreed it would be nicer to be married when everything was over, but she didn't mind at all and didn't want to interfere with any plans we made.

Janet is really dreadful – I'm glad you disillusioned her about not being able to manage it first time . . . [*Comments on contraception and various friends getting married.*]

I had a terribly interesting time yesterday. Booth and I went over to a big aerodrome to see a demonstration of rescue apparatus. Fire fighting is quite a problem. They used to have a man in a complete asbestos suit and mask. He had to be very fit and took 3 months to get used to wearing it. The risk of pneumonia was very great. Nowadays they just wear a mask and a fire resistant jerkin and just take the risk. The rescuers often get burned themselves and two of them were severely injured not long ago by exploding ammunition. We saw a demonstration of parachutes and rubber dinghy. The dinghy folds into a small pack of a little bigger than a service respirator. It's inflated by a small CO_2 cylinder attached and the package contains a collapsible mast and a sail – with full instructions for steering on the sail, written in English, French and Polish; there's also a hand bellows and bailer, a number of distress signal lights, apparatus for mending punctures and emergency rations. The airmen wear a 'Mae West' lifebelt, so-called because of the shape of the bosom, and this too has a number of pockets containing all sorts of useful things – even some fluorescein for staining a patch of water to make themselves more visible. The small dinghy contains a built-in hood so that only the pilot's face is exposed. The big new dinghies even have a small motor and heating apparatus. Incidentally the Mae West contains a rubber hot water bottle containing a chemical powder which remains hot for 5 hours when a little sea water is added. It's all exceedingly clever but on the whole I should prefer not to land in the sea in this sort of weather. We went over all sorts of planes – Spitfires, Mosquitoes, Lancasters, Stirlings etc., and were shown the very best way of getting people out of a burning plane. It's remarkably difficult to get into a plane. The only thing to do is to break the bullet proof glass – this as a rule can only be done with an axe. Even then there's precious little room even in the biggest bombers and the members of the crew are very isolated from each other. It was a bit of a shock to be shown over some planes by a young chap with the DFC and DFM and to be told that one of the Mosquitoes with 5 planes to its credit was his own plane. All the pilots are very young but surprisingly they don't bother much about keeping fit. Most of them spend their spare time drinking and playing cards and going out with women. They are terribly pampered and live in the lap of luxury. We saw drinks in their bar that had long disappeared elsewhere. They can get as much milk as they like and if sick get extra milk, eggs and butter. We had a first class lunch with choice of dishes. All the same they deserve all they get as the life must be a terrible one. The crashes can be devastating. The MO told us of one crash not long ago in which the bodies had completely disintegrated and the bits were scattered over ½ a mile. They didn't know how many were in the plane – there was some doubt as to whether someone had gone up as an extra. They spent a whole day collecting fingers but eventually the only way they could tell was by finding 5½ pairs of great trochanters [*protuberance on the thigh bone*], so presumably there were 6 people. In some high speed fighter crashes the plane may bury itself 18 feet into the ground. In one Mosquito crash a plane buried itself in marshy ground and all they could recover was one hand and a leg. The relatives insisted on a proper burial so they had to send the hand in one coffin and the leg in another! The adjutant at the station had an appalling burn of the face – the whole face was scarred and all his eyelids were everted, presenting a red rim. In the afternoon we visited another aerodrome and saw some gliders. It was a great pity the weather was bad as otherwise they would have taken us for a flight.

Well dear, don't rush things at home, let it sink in gradually. I should think it's quite likely that I will have left here by March and, who knows, perhaps I may be nearer Watford.

All my love darling

RB

Letter to G's mother

28)   Field Dressing Station
                                                         Filey, Yorks

                                                         15.1.44

Dear Mrs Briggs,
Thank you so much for your letter. Yes, I'm afraid I have changed my mind. I must confess I still have certain misgivings, which I have explained already, but the main thing is Gwenda's happiness. It would certainly be very difficult for her if I were sent overseas for a long period – though I hope this won't happen.

I do want to thank you for your attitude regarding the ceremony. I know how you must feel about it and it must be a great disappointment. However, it would only be hypocrisy on our part to do anything else and that's not exactly the best way to start a married life. We do regard the step as a sacred one and I'm sure you will agree it's the spirit of the thing that counts, not the actual surroundings. I'm also glad you want it small and private. I've always felt that marriage is a personal and rather solemn affair and tends to be spoilt by too much excitement – there's plenty of time for celebrations later. Of course we'll have it near home if you want it.

I'm afraid the arrangements are rather in the air at the moment but I think March should be all right.

Kindest regards to Mr Briggs and yourself.

Love

Robert

[From Christmas 1943 we were planning our marriage. No clear date could be fixed because leave was likely to be cancelled at short notice. The

division was on rigorous training in Yorkshire in January/February 1944 and 'incommunicado'. We were anxious not to hurt our parents because we ourselves were 'humanist' and would not have a religious wedding.]

29)   8FDS

Feb. 1944

Dearest,

Have just returned from the wilds and got your letters. Have just heard my leave has been provisionally fixed for March 3-12, starting on a Friday, so if all's well Saturday March 4th will be the great day. You needn't worry about my not wanting it. You know very well I do. I must confess I'm still a little worried about the possibilities but I do believe you when you say it would be better for you. I suppose it's female psychology. So please don't worry any more but go ahead and make arrangements. I think we ought to have it in Watford – I've already told your Mother we probably would, and we must try to please them as far as possible. All the same try and make it as private as possible with the minimum of fuss. I don't think your parents will mind. I do want you to come down to Oxford for a couple of days afterwards. I feel rather guilty about spending only one day last time and I feel we owe it to my people, especially as they probably won't come to the ceremony – I'm trying to dissuade them. Anyhow Oxford is as nice a place as any and we could go and see Lewin and Weddell [*2 of our teachers*] – I wonder if Weddell will get the Anatomy chair at St Mary's – he's done awfully well in the last few years.

It's very sweet of Janet to make that offer and I don't see why we shouldn't accept. Don't squabble too much about the rent – after all we wouldn't want any ourselves if the positions were reversed, would we? We can always make it up in other ways – presents for the kids for example. I'll write to Janet at once. [*Our friends Janet and John Humphrey gave us a room in their house in Highgate, where we could spend leave.*]

About volpar [*contraceptive gel of this time, used with a diaphragm*], I don't think there would be any danger in using it to the extent that we shall be able to. I imagine that the only possible danger would occur after very prolonged use, so don't worry about it.

I suppose I'll have to answer your aunt's letter – I'm glad you told me it was your aunt as there was no indication of her sex in the letter and I thought it was your uncle!

For heavens sake try to avoid any more of these things and also presents. You are lucky as no-one will write to you extolling my charms.

A few 'don'ts' to end up with:

1. Don't be worried if you don't hear from me for a few days. We're not allowed to give away our location on exercises but you can go on sending letters to Filey until I tell you otherwise.

2. Don't keep asking me if I've got another job.

3. Don't keep running down my present job.

4. Don't ask me for another leave before March. It's impossible at the moment.

All my love you silly old darling

RB

PS Do I need a birth certificate for marriage?

PPS Horror, have just lost Janet's address. Send it me again.

PPS Have just been ordered to proceed on a week's VD course starting March 1. However with great sacrifice I managed to get it changed – you see what I'm prepared to give up for you!

30)   8FDS

Dearest Gwen,

The expected delay in the post has now happened and I've only just got your letter. I've not been able to write as we were supposed to be cut off. However, everything is now all right again except that all the Coldstreams are supposed to be killed. Apart from a spot of dive bombing we've come through unscathed. I'm glad Prof. Miles was decent about your holiday. I'll write to thank him. I wrote to the Ram [*Miss Ramsay my old headmistress and a dear friend*] long ago. If you want to take Friday off I'll try to travel up overnight to give us more time. As I mentioned last time I'm going to try to wangle an extra few hours and will let you know as soon as possible. If I travel Thursday night you had best meet me at Lewis's [*medical bookshop, Gower St*] about 10 a.m. Friday but will let you know later. Have just heard from Max that he's trying to fix me up at the Great Western Hotel on Friday night. That should ease the travelling problem. The taxi sounds a good idea.

Get everything taped for me would you? I'm glad you got such good seats –
I thought they were further back last time you wrote [*seats for a play for all
to go to after the wedding*]. How did Ruth know about it? You <u>must</u> send
me her letter [*UCH friend*]. I'm dying to see it.

Do you think it would be a good idea to contact the food office people
about changing your identity card? You know there is always liable to be a
bit of a queue at these places, especially on a Saturday morning. I'm sure
they'd fix it for you if you explained that you had to get away at once. If you
said you'd be in between 10.30 and 11 they'd probably do it at once when
you came. [*R was worrying that I would not get rations as all documents,
including ration books had to be altered with change of name on marriage!*]

Let me know as soon as you get a ring from Oxford. I hope they won't be
too late.

That's all for now dear.

Love

RB

31)   c. Feb. 1944

Dearest Gwen,

I'm returning your letters [*letters from relatives and friends after we had
announced we were going to be married*]. Some of them are certainly rather
amusing but I expect you want to keep them. By the way who is the fellow
Robert Barham that you're running about with? [*An aunt put this name by
mistake.*]

Don't think about a Physiology job. I think pure Physiology is rather a
dead end and very poorly paid as compared with more medical jobs. You
can always do Physiology even in a hospital. Anyhow you're well set now
and it would be pure madness to give up your present job however tempting
the offer. Don't send any more wires now and don't ask me to ring you. We
are not allowed to carry money or use the public services. I've written to my
brother but I expect he'll take about 3 weeks to answer, so it's not a bad
idea to ring him. About 9 a.m. is the best time. Hitchin 1110. Let me know
about St Pancras and Oxford as soon as you can.

Test out the divan properly before you buy it. Does the price include
mattress etc.? [*I had bought a second-hand divan for £20.*]

We had one of Monty's informal talks the other day. It was delightfully informal – it only took about 3 weeks to prepare and it only meant getting up at 4 a.m. but as the newspapers say, 'Monty won't stand on ceremony'. Anyhow, you'll be pleased to know that he said we would win the war.

Darling, I've just thought, don't ask for Friday afternoon off. I won't get in till 2 p.m. and after I've had lunch I've got to do some shopping – it'll be the only opportunity I shall get, so I probably won't get to Watford before 7. I think you ought to pluck up courage and ask Miles for Saturday to Saturday off, as soon as possible.

You haven't told me if you're taking cod-liver oil yet. Also, have you given up Birkbeck?

Goodbye for the present darling, don't worry if letters get a little erratic.

Love

RB

32)
                                                                    8FDS
                                                                    Filey

                                                                    Feb. 1944

Dearest Gwenda,
I'm glad you're thinking about the arrangements. Here are some of the things we shall have to fit in:
1. Some time with your parents – the lunch and theatre sounds good.
2. A couple of days at Oxford – you ought to get leave from the Lab – I think it's justifiable especially as you didn't take any time off before.
3. Some time in London – to fit in at least one visit to Janet and a night with my brother.

We can get married on the Friday or Saturday, whichever you prefer, but find out what time the registry office shuts. We could then take your parents out on the same day. My parents will almost certainly not be coming as the travelling is too strenuous. Now when shall we go to Oxford? Shall it be on the Sunday or Monday? Sunday would be better as Father would be home. If we had the ceremony on Saturday, we could book somewhere to stay in London on Saturday night – preferably an hotel near Paddington. Suppose we stay Sunday, Monday and Tuesday at Oxford. Where are we going to stay the rest of the time? We should have plenty more time to take your people out. I should think my brother could meet us in London on the following Saturday. Incidentally my Father suggested that he would like to come over to the ceremony. I doubt it, but I'll write to him and see what he says. I imagine he would prefer to meet us some other time. I shall have to leave on the Sunday by the 10.15 train (night). Let me know what you think of this rough outline.

Have just this moment heard I'm going on a blood course at Bristol tomorrow morning. Alderson says it actually ends next Friday and I needn't come back till Monday morning. With luck I ought to be able to get to London by 1.30 p.m. on Friday afternoon and needn't leave till Sunday 10 p.m.!

So we'll get our weekend in after all. What shall we do? Shall I come straight up to Watford? Can you put me up on a camp bed? *Don't* ask for Saturday morning off – though you might be able to leave early. I don't want anything to prejudice your chance of getting a week off in March. I could easily come along to the lab and see Miles or go to Lewis's. My Mother has just written me saying Father is at work on a ring for you.* I'm very much afraid it may be a very spectacular affair worth a small fortune and I'm writing him about it. It's rather a pity as he's probably putting all his soul into it. I'll try to get a plain wedding ring your size instead. I've written to Jan thanking her. I'll leave all the arranging of the room to you. If you like I could get some of my best books out of store and put them there. They could borrow them. Well dear, let me know quickly about next weekend. Write direct to Army Blood Supply Depot Bristol (will wire you if that's not the correct address).

Love

RB

PS You *don't* write too often by any means. I've become quite a standing joke with the office staff as I keep poking my head in every five minutes asking if there are any letters. They must think I'm soft!

33)   8FDS

Dearest Gwenda,
Have just got your letter and one from my brother. He also sent the enclosed

---

R's father was a working jeweller.

cheque toward expenses! Could you put it in your account or keep it till I come? The nearest bank seems to be about 50 miles away. He says he will try to come to Watford and to Oxford and asked if I could book him in a room in London. I suggested that as it would probably have to be in Watford it might be best if he stayed in London on Friday and Saturday nights and suggested that he should write to the GWR Hotel Paddington. However, as I know he's quite hopeless about arranging things except at the very last minute I would be glad if you would keep in touch with him and see what he's doing. I'm sorry to lump all this on you dear but it's quite impossible for me at the moment and I don't want anything to go wrong. Would you mind letting him know how to get to the place and if possible the best trains? He's far too lack-a-daisical to be trusted to do it for himself! My Mother has suggested that it would be nice if we had a nice lunch at the hotel when we got to Oxford. I think the price is OK, so confirm it and also please order a table for 5 for lunch (about 12.45) – my Father wants to pay for the lunch. They will meet us at the station. If the Randolph can't do lunch, write to the Mitre – though the Randolph will almost certainly manage it. I'm really terribly sorry to give you all these 'orders' but I'm afraid it's the only way. At the moment I'm surrounded by a sea of mud and I've just lost my collar stud! Incidentally I don't suppose you've ever had to put a wringing wet collar on? It's not a pleasant experience. However, we're infinitely better off than the infantry.

It's OK about the bed and about the stay at Janet's. What about bedclothes? Did Miles himself give you 10 days off? I'd like to write and thank him. Let me know. I don't suppose Holborn Registry could fix it. Our stay at Mrs D's might qualify us. Try and book *My Sister Eileen* [*West End play*], I've heard it's very good indeed. For God's sake warn your Father not to make a speech or any toasts at the Hungaria. It gives me nightmares to think about it.

I can't think of anything else at the moment. Time's getting short and we must make our arrangements cut and dried. Let me know <u>exact</u> details of everything from now on.

Love

RB

PS Will try to get Mother to post a plain gold ring to you. Your other ring's ready! [*I was lucky that R's Father managed to get a 22 carat gold wedding ring; most girls in wartime had to be content with 9 carat!*]

34)   8FDS
                                                                    Filey

                                                                    end Feb. 1944

Dear Mrs Briggs,
Thanks for your note. I've just got back from my polar expedition and can
write at leisure. I'm glad Gwen is taking her medicine faithfully; it should
do her a lot of good. I'll certainly see to it that she gets some relaxation
while I'm on leave. It's only a week now before the great day and I'm
feeling quite nervous. I'm afraid the Hungaria is rather gaudy but it's
difficult to find anywhere nice nowadays and it's nice to have a bit of a
splash once in a blue moon.

I would like to say how much I appreciate your broad-minded attitude. I
know very well that this is not what you have always hoped for, and I
appreciate it all the more. Please believe me when I say that Watford
Registry office will be as sacred to Gwenda and myself, in our own way, as
the finest cathedral in England.

Love

Robert

Regards to Mr Briggs

35)   8FDS

Dearest Gwen,
Have just got your letters. As you say, there's not much chance of the MRC
getting me out of this unit and even if they could I'm afraid the type of job
I'd ask for wouldn't be very much to your liking. Anyhow, let's take things
as they come.

I've been asking about the income tax and on the whole I think it would
be better to keep everything separate at the moment. What happens is that
the army pays me 4/- a day (i.e. about £70 a year) extra on marriage. I can
do what I like with it and needn't pay you a farthing if I don't want to so you
had better behave yourself. This £70 is free from tax. In addition I get an
increased personal allowance on my income tax – £40 I think. So you see
that the benefit is all on my side. I don't think your income will be affected.

This sounds pretty straightforward and there is probably less opportunity for errors to arise. Actually they say that it should come to the same whichever way we work it.

I'm afraid it's no use hoping for a weekend before March as it's impossible to plan ahead for more than a couple of days at a time. To make things more difficult our CO's partner is ill and he has been granted special leave to attend the practice. James Booth has just gone on leave but gave us two Haggis's before he left. I'm afraid I wouldn't go out of my way to eat it though it's quite nice. The dental officer's Father and Mother-in-law came down to Filey last weekend. They were even less fortunate than we were! They stayed at Greycourt [*B & B where I had stayed*] but found themselves locked out at 10 p.m.! They banged on the windows but no-one came so they had to sleep in the same place as the dentist and his wife. I think the chap must be a bit dotty. I had an interesting call last night. I was dragged out to see a deserter under police arrest. When I got there I went inside to be met by the deserter's wife saying that the man had escaped taking a razor with him. I expect he's after my blood.

Do you know any hotels at Oxford? The Mitre is the best known but is probably very expensive. Can you get a directory of hotels? Probably one of the Station type would suit us best – there's probably one at the GWR or LMS hotels there.

Tell me what advice Harry gave you [*Professor Himsworth, our Professor of Medicine*]. I'm getting my share of advice here too. They've been telling me all about the feminine wile of crying. George said that on one occasion when he went on leave his wife met him at Manchester and went back to Warrington with him without saying a word. When she got back she burst into tears. It then came out that she had thought he wasn't writing as often as he should. She had gone all the way to Manchester and back merely for the pleasure of remaining silent!

Don't buy a ring. If you know the size or can send a cheap one that fits you I'll send it to my Father and get one from him. It will be much cheaper and we shan't get rooked. Wedding rings are just plain gold aren't they? You'll have to do without the £200 diamond engagement ring. I'm afraid your parents are going to think I'm awfully mean but I prefer everything plain and anyhow everything now has 100% purchase tax on it.

Your mould extract sounds interesting. I wonder if it produces excess PABA, or perhaps it alters the sulphonamides chemically. Try incubating it with sulphapyridine and see if you still get the colour reaction. Have you identified the mould yet?

By the way, you say that we have to give 1 day's notice. Does that literally mean 24 hours? If so I shall have to travel on Thursday night. Or would it be all right if only you gave notice?

There may be a chance of a tropical course coming off soon and if possible will try to get it in London.

All my love

RB

PS I suppose your horrible feminine vanity insists on an announcement in the papers or in the UCH mag – just to make the other girls jealous. If so I want just plain MB and no parents names and addresses.

36)   8FDS
                                                       Filey

                                                       26 Feb. 1944

Dearest Gwenda,

Back at Filey at last and have just had a hot bath and change of clothing (I haven't had my trousers off for a week!). Have some good news for you. The extra day has materialised. I shall leave here Thursday morning arriving King's X at about 2 p.m. If you can meet me conveniently at the booking office do so, otherwise I'll come on to Watford in the evening (hope I can stay at your place). I'm glad you've fixed up my brother for Friday night. Do you know if he's got fixed up for Saturday in London too? – he must book – you can't leave things to chance.

I feel uncomfortable about accepting the certificates (National Savings) from your people – it must represent a considerable part of their savings and we don't need the money. However, I suppose they would be hurt if we refused. Don't forget what I said about using our funds for any family expenses. Darling, you really are getting quite naughty about this job business – I know you mean it for my own good, but do you really think I'm going to sink so low as to write crawling letters to people? You know what I'd think of anyone else who did that. It's nonsense to talk of my being pushed into jobs I would hate – I can't think of many jobs I would dislike and in any case I'm very unlikely to be shifted from the division. These exercises have given me a good idea of the sort of stuff I'm expected to do and I can assure you that no-one would be wasted in a job like that. In addition to our function of resuscitation we very often have to act as the headquarters of a field ambulance in which case I should be responsible for the earliest real surgical care of thousands of men. I know that my experience is quite inadequate but at the same time if I didn't have the job some complete idiot might get it. Please don't do any more canvassing on my behalf. If I do get any offers I promise I'll consider them, or at least point out the sort of thing I'd like but the approach must come from above, not from me. I know it's hard for you even though I can't agree with you, but do try to behave with some dignity. I'm sometimes afraid that you are so carried away with your concern for me that you may do something quite desperate such as writing to people yourself. Anyhow, let's hope this finishes the question. Be patient dear and see what turns up.

Well as you say in a short time we shall belong to each other for ever – not that I feel any different now. In fact this will probably be the last letter I shall address to 'Miss G.R. Briggs'. It's been nice knowing her but I hope it will be even nicer knowing 'Mrs B'.

All my love dearest

RB

PS Please thank everyone who sent us presents. Do you think I'm supposed to write to them too? Don't forget about notices in *Telegraph*,

Robert and Gwenda , March 1944

BMJ and UCH mag. What about those incredible wedding cards? Has the ring arrived yet?

[*We were married in Watford on 4 March 1944, a cold bright sunny day. The taxi man said 'Ah, one of Monty's men' and charged double ('wedding') rates. We went together by tube to London where we met again my parents and R's brother Max, also Marianne (Austrian refugee girl who had come to live with my family) and Janet and John. At the Hungaria restaurant in Haymarket we had, for wartime, a splendid lunch at 5/- a head – the maximum charge allowed at that time. The London hotel where we had booked the night had been bombed a couple of days before, so we proceeded to Oxford and stayed happily at the ancient coaching inn, The Golden Cross, moving next day to the Randolph Hotel. We had a good time with R's parents and also visited Graham Weddell, who had taught us anatomy at University College. He had subsequently got a job in the Oxford Anatomy department under the famous anthropologist, Wilfred Le Gros Clark. Graham was serving at a head injuries hospital and was very pleased to see us. 'You're just the kind of chap we want in our department after the war,' he said to R. 'We need a biophysicist.' I had been reluctant to spend precious time visiting Graham but had, I am thankful to say, acquiesced! In the midst of the northern European campaign, R was invited to apply for this job – and on his first leave, May 1945, he got it! So does the course of life depend on chance! After 2-3 days we returned to Watford to see my people. We called in at my lab on the way home. Anxious friends gathered round and said, 'Your father is much better now.' So we learned that he had been taken dangerously ill on our wedding night but no one had wished to tell us. So we did not go on to London but stayed the rest of our week at the little Watford house. There was no room for us so we slept on the floor! And my dad recovered slowly.*]

37)   8FDS

                                                14 March 1944

My dearest wife,

It's lovely to be able to call you that at last – you know how I've always wanted to be able to call you that, even if I had some doubts as to the best time for it. It's marvellous to feel that we really are together now and that I've got someone definite to come home to. You needn't worry about my not wanting to take short leaves as at the moment I feel very much like going off without telling anyone! However, things have been happening in my absence. Our old CO was granted leave to go back to his practice and we now have a new CO – Major Rogers. I think he comes from Mary's. Of course it's a terrible blow for Alderson, who had taken it for granted that he would be promoted and had been going about saying what he would do when he was CO. It seems a deliberate insult to him as this new man has only just been promoted to Major. He's making a lot of changes but it remains to be seen whether they are all good. I think he intends to tighten up the discipline here which would be a very good thing. I don't know what Alderson will do. In a way I'm glad he's not CO as I think he is temperamentally unsuited to be in complete control of a unit. He would be quite competent as a 2nd in command. How is your Father getting on? Let me know as soon as possible. Did you see John Humphrey's article in the BMJ on March 4th? It's a pity we missed it as we might have said something about it.

That's all for the present, dear. Don't forget to fix things with Carter Patterson [*removal firm*]. Let me know if you hear from the income tax people at all.

All my love dearest,

RB.

CHAPTER III

Waiting for D-Day, collecting old books

38)

8FDS

March 1994

Dearest Gwen,

I'm glad to hear your Father is now getting up a bit. You haven't told me much about him – I hope you're not keeping anything from me. I'm rather surprised about Gough's path. It merely shows what a gap there is between a good GP and a hospital doctor [*GP in Watford*].

I'm sending the forms for our joint account. I don't really see what advantage it is at the moment, but I suppose we might find it useful occasionally.

I can't say I share your disappointment about the MP. [*R did not want us to try for a baby but I did; I don't think we were trying at this stage. After a few months he changed his mind and agreed but our meetings were rare and brief*]. Still you'll have another chance in April!

You'll roar when you see me. We've just been issued with our new caps – they are just like cook's hats and everyone looks idiotic, but I suppose we'll get used to them.

I'm really rather pleased at the moment as I've just proved that a certain set of curves in all the wireless books are quite wrong. I think they've all copied them from one another and no-one's bothered to check them. They all work out the maths using unjustifiable approximations, saying that the full treatment is too difficult as they say. The results are most interesting and if I get them verified it might be worth sending a short note to some journal. Of course there's probably a flaw or else someone's done it already – but it certainly hasn't reached the text books.

By the way, dear, I don't know what your plans for your Father are, but if they involve any expense at all don't hesitate to tell me. A holiday might do him good. Has the woman helped to ease the strain on you?

It's rather amusing about Mrs M. You'll have to write an article on the

'Big Breast syndrome'. There's not much risk of your getting it!

Love

RB

39)   8FDS

Dearest,

Have just got your letter. Glad to hear your Father is improving. Let me know how he gets on. Very pleased to hear you are getting a woman 5 days a week. I'm very sorry about getting cross on the train. We mustn't cut it so fine next time. I had to stand all the way and then go on a route march as soon as I got back. Still, as you say, it was worth it.

Anyhow I've got some good news for you. I'm going on a gas course at Salisbury from April 10-22 (Monday to Saturday). The CO suggested that I might like to take the opportunity to see my wife. I shall get at least one week-end out of it and with luck two or even three, so keep those three week-ends free. He may let me travel up on the Saturday. The course starts on Monday and I shouldn't be surprised if we have Saturday afternoon and Sunday free. The course ends on a Saturday and possibly I shall be allowed to remain in London on Sunday. Have just been to a clinical meeting in Driffield and bumped into Cyril Rubin, who has been stationed at the aerodrome there for the last 6 months! He was most shocked when I told him about Asher [*a close student friend just killed in Italy*]. He had applied to go to Italy especially to be able to contact Asher. I also met Philip Henderson again. We had quite a good talk on penicillin by Bigger's assistant. He said as regards the mode of action, in large concentration it seems to kill the bugs, but in low concentration it prevents them multiplying. It is going to be used as a routine local application for wounds, mixed with a sulphonamide powder. Darling, will you please let me have, <u>by return of post or by telegram</u>, the name of the registrar who married us (i.e. the signature on the marriage certificate). I need it to claim the allowance.

I love you more than ever.

Yours

RB

40)   8FDS

Dearest Gwen,

I'm afraid I've got a bit of a blow for you (and for me too). My course has been changed from Salisbury to the Lake District! It's such a pity after all the arrangements we've made and all the wangling I've been doing. However, don't despair, they may change it again.

I'm glad the x-rays on your father don't show anything. It must have been some localised lung infection – I don't see why you say it couldn't have been lobar pneumonia – surely the x-ray signs would have disappeared by now – 3 weeks?

Did you see the announcement about us in the *Lancet* (March 11)? Did you send it or did they copy it from the BMJ? The new CO seems a good chap. The last one was quite pleasant but I don't seem to get on very well with the Scots sense of humour. The present one likes a good laugh. He's young and athletic and our physical training is being tightened up. I've just come back from a marvellous 5 mile run! His wife and 9 month baby have come down here. Right at the beginning of the war he was suddenly ordered to Gibraltar at 1½ days notice. He rang up his future wife and she said 'Right, I'm coming down tomorrow and we'll get married. Get everything ready.' (Just like you!) He had no option about it. He went out to Gib and she tried to follow, but wives were not allowed. Apparently it was quite all right to live in sin, or to have your fiancée out there but wives were banned as they were the responsibility of the army. She went up to the War Office and told a heart-rending tale about a newly wed bride who had only seen her husband for 1½ days and the usual flood of tears etc. and a dear old Colonel told her that there was nothing to prevent her going to Spain and slipping into Gib incognito. She went along to the passport office and by great good luck and exercise of feminine wiles managed to see another dear old man who got her a passport right away. She went to Paris by air and thence to Spain. Then the fun began. She used to go into Gib every day and meet her husband but apart from a few close friends no-one knew their relationship (or so they thought). Actually the ADMS found out and told them that as far as he was concerned, he knew nothing. However, it came out eventually and he was officially reprimanded and his wife had to leave.

I'm returning your paper on penicillin. I see that paracolons produce indole. Actually I see no reason why the reacting substance should not be an enzyme to produce Liesegang rings, but there doesn't seem to be much evidence of the enzymic nature of penicillinase. It seems just as logical to assume that 'penicillinase' is some substance which forms an inactive compound with penicillin, and that different bugs produce it (or contain it) in different amounts. All Harper's statements on pages 4 & 5 can be explained on this basis. What substance (apart from things like concentrated acids) are known to interact with penicillin? And do they occur in bacterial metabolism?

Well dear, don't be too down-hearted about Salisbury. Things may not be as black as they seem.

Regards to my in-laws and all my love to you, my darling.

RB

[I was working in a bacteriology lab at Watford and one thing I had to do was to test organisms for their sensitivity to penicillin. It was still in very short supply for civilians and only those seriously ill with 'sensitive' bugs received it. Later, R was to be dismayed and infuriated to find that there was insufficient in the army for front-line MOs, whereas the Americans had plenty. Thus our wounded men had to wait for it until they got back to a CCS or hospital – often a serious delay.]

[The next letter was from our dear friend Janet Humphrey. She and John had offered us a room in their home to go to when R had leave. In it we had a divan bed and three bookcases (which Jan had given us) full of books. Marvellous, it was home! We must have had one night there on our 'honeymoon'.]

41)   81 Highgate West Hill
                                                              N6

                                                              March 17th 1944

Dear Gwenda,
Thank you for your letter and for the enclosed cheque. I have accepted the money you sent this time for your rent as I think you would rather I did but in future, please don't be so regular in payment because I feel unhappy about charging the exorbitant rent of 4/- per week for an unfurnished room which would not otherwise be let – nobody would want it – and it is greatly to our advantage to have your beautiful bed to let people sleep in sometimes so please don't pay too often as the last thing I want in the world is to make money out of you. As for the records, that is a lovely idea, and though I

object in principle there is nothing I would like more than you to buy records for us. I think that I will get the Beethoven violin concerto which I have always wanted to possess. We thank you and Robert and hope to retaliate with a wedding present to you before long. (Now that I come to look at your arithmetic again it seems that you have paid £1 for the food consumed in this house. Now that is ridiculous so I am taking it that you have paid the rent for the five weeks on from May 3rd that is to the middle of June.)

Now to stop talking about money matters we *did* enjoy having you two and I am ever so much looking forward to your next visit. Tell Robert that I have been upstairs looking at his books and sitting in your chair and really enjoying it – getting right away from the busybody-ness of this household!

I'm so glad your Father is all right. I wonder what it could possibly have been.

I am always hoping for the very best luck for you to be together almost as much as if it was myself-sort of interest, because I know you are bound to be so happy together and so good for everybody.

Much love from

Janet

42)   8FDS

Dearest Gwenda,

Am returning Janet's letter. How's your Father? What do you think of the idea of our sending them both away for a holiday as a present? The snag is that there aren't many places to go now the South coast is out? Still, find out how the land lies. [*South coast was banned in the run-up to the invasion.*]

We had an inspection by the King the other day. As with Monty it was quite informal and only took about 10 days' preparation. Spontaneous cheering broke out at a pre-arranged signal. The penicillin phenomenon you described is very interesting. It is almost certainly due to Liesegang rings [*I must have observed organisms growing in rings round a trough of penicillin*]. I think Liesegang's original experiment was to put a drop of silver nitrate on a gelatin gel containing Pot dichromate. As the $AgNO_3$ diffused, a number of rings of Ag chromate were deposited at increasing intervals. You can get good rings in agar with lead chromate. If the experiment is done by putting the gel in a test tube you get a number of strata. Some people think geological strata are really a Liesegang phenomenon. You might try getting strata with penicillin and staphs. As Miles said, it looks as if staphs produce something which combines with penicillin making it harmless. Liesegang rings of this harmless compound are deposited as the penicillin diffuses and staphs can grow there. The production of the rings depends on the gel and on the concentration of the reacting substances, so it's a little tricky. It would be interesting to grow staphs in broth and see if the extract will neutralise penicillin. Do staphs produce penicillinase? It's possible they may do in small quantities (or perhaps penicillinase is not really an enzyme at all). It would be interesting to try out this effect with B.Coli or some other bug which is known to produce penicillinase. I imagine B.Coli is not <u>completely</u> insensitive to penicillin and you might get these rings, though as I said the concentrations are tricky.

By the way, dear, my course starts late in the afternoon of Easter Monday. I needn't leave London till after lunch. Do you think you could get Monday morning off? I'm beginning to doubt if it would be worth meeting in the middle week-end. It all depends on how late we have to work on Saturday. However, I'll see when I can get there.

All my love dearest

RB

PS Just remembered penicillin acts as an acid and forms salts. Hypothetical combining substance may therefore be an alkali – e.g. An organic nitrogenous base (doesn't B.Coli produce indole? – sorry I've forgotten all my bacteriology). It seems worth thinking about.

43)   8FDS
                                                                                         Filey
                                                                                         Yorks

Dear Mother-in-law,

I understand that you are feeling neglected and I've got to write to you. It isn't that I haven't wanted to write, but the trouble is, that I can never think of anything to write about. I'm sure that you wouldn't be the least interested to know that I spent all today at shooting practice or that we went for a 5 mile run yesterday (I'm so stiff that I can hardly move at the moment – if I drop anything I have to get someone else to pick it up). I suppose Gwenda has already told you that my gas course has been switched from Salisbury to the Lake District. It's a bit of a blow but to compensate for it I think there's a chance that I may get my next leave rather earlier than I expected, as my last one was postponed on account of an exercise. Anyhow I'll be able to do more work on the course without Gwenda around – don't tell her I said so – she'll be furious.

How is my Father-in-law? I hear he's getting on very well and the x-rays were very satisfactory. I do wish he'd go away for a holiday, but I suppose he's quite made up his mind.

I'm glad to hear you're getting a woman in 5 days a week and she helps with the shopping. It must make an immense difference.

Well that's about all I can think of at the moment, I've used up most of my love ration for the month on Gwenda but I think I can just spare a little for you and Mr Briggs.

Your obedient son-in-law

Robert

44)   8FDS

Dearest Gwen,

I hope the weather improves before the week-end – it's been so lovely up to now. I chose Carlisle as I have to go through it anyhow to get to Penrith. I go via Leeds so I don't expect we'll meet. The CO will let me leave early Saturday morning and I can get to Carlisle by 2 o'clock in the afternoon. The best thing for you would be to get one of the two trains about 9 o'clock Friday night from St Pancras, getting into Carlisle about 6 a.m. You could then go to sleep for a few hours until I come. If you leave Saturday morning you wouldn't get to Carlisle till about 6 in the evening. I think we ought to visit some of your relatives if we have time – they'd be very annoyed if they heard or if we bumped into them by accident. I'll try to buy a pork pie for Sunday lunch if we go out anywhere. I suppose nothing will deter you so it's no use my arguing.

I've written to Harry thanking him. I met Meara again yesterday at a corps study day. We had a good talk on VD. Apparently the incidence of late neural and vascular complications is far higher than I thought and NAB seems to make them come out earlier. He told us about a boy of 23 who died from aortic aneurysm. In any case 1/3 of all cases of Syphilis cure themselves if left alone. The ordinary 'interval' treatment of a number of courses of injections at 1 week intervals doesn't seem to be good enough. At the moment they are trying 30 day treatment – daily injections of Mapharside. It looks as if penicillin may be the answer. The figures for the Anzio beachhead are pretty amazing – 25% of all cases are new VD! They have a special travelling VD clinic in Italy and it's badly overworked.

Well dear, let me know quickly what you have fixed up.

All my love

RB

[*We got a weekend at Carlisle (where my Father, and I had been born) before R went on his gas course in the Lake District. We had a marvellous whole day's walk along Hadrian's Wall and to Housesteads on the Sunday, but we couldn't get anything to eat. Back in Carlisle, we tried a pub, but I was turned out as Carlisle had state pubs which would not admit women! We were at a very cheap 'commercial traveller's' hotel which served only breakfast so we went to bed starving!*]

45)

> Officers' Mess
> Glenridding Wing
> Army School of Chemical Warfare
> Glenridding
> Penrith
> Cumberland

Dearest Gwen,

I do hope you got home all right and weren't too tired. We were very lucky to have such a nice time and I hope we shall go on being lucky.

This certainly is a wonderful spot. We are in the Glenridding Hotel and it's very comfortable. The food must have improved as it's quite adequate for me. The only snag is that we have to do PT at the unearthly hour of 7.15 a.m.! The course promises to be interesting. Today we saw a demonstration of various gas weapons. It was quite spectacular as they fired mortars right across the lake at a spot high up on the opposite hill. We had another dose of that wretched DM stuff. Most of the fellows held their breath but like a fool I tried to be conscientious and took a good gasp. I haven't recovered from it yet. There are 2 or 3 RAMC people here, one of them was at Crookham with me. I'm in a room with a lot of Tank officers, one of them in the Welsh

Guards in my division. They are quite a good crowd. The chap who was at Crookham with me is a lucky devil. He's stationed with a CCS at King's Langley! I offered to change with him. I went for a walk along the lake tonight and saw your Hotel Patterdale. I must try to get out on the hills on Sunday.

All my love dearest

RB

46)

Officers' Mess
Glenridding Wing
Army School of Chemical Warfare
Glenridding
Penrith
Cumberland

Dearest Gwen,

Just got your letter. I guessed you were probably waiting to get the full address but a made-up one would certainly have found me.

The course here is quite interesting. They pay a good deal of attention to details, especially regarding the training of men to look after themselves. We make protection against gas an individual responsibility, but the Germans go in for special gas troops. We are split up into groups under a sergeant instructor. They are extremely good and specially chosen. The officers are very good too and some of the lectures are very amusing. Our sergeant told us a very funny story about the ATS. He was once asked to give some ATS a little gas practice. He let off a generator of DM gas and told the girls to march past in file. Now it's a part of the drill that when the senior member of the party smells gas he shouts 'Gas!' and everyone puts their respirators on. Of course this is only drill and in action every individual would take the appropriate action. Well the girls walked past the DM and everyone spluttered and coughed but no-one put their masks on. He thought there must be something wrong so he marched them through once more. By this time some of the girls were getting in a bad way so he called them away and asked 'Why on earth didn't you put your respirators on?' 'Oh but Sheila never shouted gas!' came the reply! I hope you are fairly well up in your own gas drill especially as regards blister and choking gas. It's not giving away military secrets that this would be a very good time for the Germans to start using gas. I'll have to give you some coaching.

Did you see that Lieut T.H.E. had resigned his commission on grounds of ill health? I wonder what's happened to him? I should think army life would drive him to an asylum, as it's impossible to avoid speaking in the army.

Well dear, that's all for the moment. Keep your fingers crossed for next week-end.

Love

Robert

PS Love you very very much

[*Postcard of Ullswater to Mr & Mrs F.R. Briggs*]

Having a good time. Isn't my wife writing to me any more?

Love

Robert

47)   Glenridding

Dearest Gwen,

Just got your letter. I'm afraid the week-end's off as you'll realise, but will try and fix one up as soon as possible so don't despair [*all leave was stopped*].

We have our exam this afternoon. The course has been quite good fun. Unlike most courses they aim at making you remember every single thing they teach, but it's a good way of getting vital information over.

I've had some fun here. The MO has gone off on a penicillin course and I've been doing sick parades. It's such a long time since I examined a woman that I felt quite embarrassed when the ATS turned up.

The most interesting thing has been a number of mild cases of blistering from mustard gas vapour. We have to go through heavily contaminated ground and also remain for sometime in a heavy vapour concentration. They very rarely get any casualties but just occasionally some get a few blisters.

We had a brain's trust on ASS and unfortunately I was put on it! Being a doctor I was inevitably labelled as 'Joad' and all my remarks seemed to be greeted by roars of laughter.

My student lesson went off quite well. I had a relatively easy subject – Protection against blister gas vapour.

It's possible that I may be able to see Arthur North tomorrow after all. I shall try my best.

I've not heard from Janet at all, unless she wrote to the FDS so I don't know what she's up to.

The use of living mould on gauze is not new but contrary to what you've heard, Bigger told us that neglible amounts of penicillin are produced.

Well dear, I'm sorry about the week-end. Remember what I said about being careful what you write and about not telling people anything unnecessary about my activities. Write to me in future at 8 Field Dressing Station, c/o A.P.O., England.

All my love dearest

RB

[*From now the location of units was secret. Censorship of letters by officers started. Presumably all leave was cancelled but as will be seen, we were lucky to get a few more brief meetings.*]

48)

Lieut R Barer
8 Field Dressing Station
APO
England

My own darling Gwen,
I hope you won't find letters are being too long delayed. I got the one you sent to Glenridding before the one you sent to the FDS, although it had to be readdressed. The exam went off all right but it was such a waffly paper and they have rather odd ideas on how it should be answered that it's quite impossible to say how I've done. I had quite an amusing time on the last night of the course. They had a celebration. One young tank officer seemed a bit merry but not obviously drunk. He went to bed early – about 11 p.m. and seemed to be fairly normal. The others went to bed about 12.30 a.m. A

few minutes later after they had turned out the lights we heard the tank man getting out of bed and crawling towards the window. We asked if he was all right and he said 'yes'. We then heard the sound of water falling on the floor near the window. I thought he was being sick. He crawled back to bed and we asked him again if he was all right. This time there was no reply so I put the light on and investigated. He was flat out – completely comatose and could not be roused. I went over to the window and nearly died of laughing, he had wanted to empty his bladder and had evidently mistaken the mirror for the open window! The urine had splashed all over the dressing table and dripped on to someone's open trunk below! This fetched the owner of the trunk out of bed pretty quickly. Eventually we all went back to bed again, after covering the beds with ground-sheets just in case he should take it into his head that someone's bed would be a good place to micturate. Actually I wasn't feeling too secure as there would have been an awful row if he died in the night and there was just one chance in a million that he might not just be drunk. However an hour later the others were asleep but I was still awake and I heard the chap getting out of bed again. Again I heard the sound of water splashing – this time from the direction of the wash basin, so I was no longer worried. In the morning I went over to have a look at the chap and found that far from using the wash basin he had micturated all over the clothes of the chap next to him! There was a big pool on the carpet too. The cause of all the trouble was now completely sober and remembered nothing of the incidents. It was fortunate for him that the course was over as he would never have lived it down.

Well dear, I'm afraid there's not much I can say now with this censorship. I've been doing a bit of censoring of the men's letters. It's very remarkable how unpleasant a job it is. One would think that it might be rather amusing but instead it's perfectly loathsome. Fortunately after reading a number of letters I can't remember who wrote what. I'm afraid that, compared with the men I don't seem to be a very ardent husband. Most of them seem to introduce some term of endearment every other word and to fill up the blank spaces with kisses. However I suppose it's the difference between the calm solid Anglo-Saxon and the ardent excitable Semitic!

All the same, dear, even if I don't express my thoughts on paper I think you really know what they are about.

All my love dearest – keep hoping – things are never as black as they seem.

Love

RB

PS I think I asked you to keep a book for me. I've now changed my mind and asked Lewis' to send it to me direct.

49)

Lieut R Barer
8 Field Dressing Station
APO
England

Dearest Gwen,

Thanks for your letter (of Wednesday). I hope you're getting mine regularly – I'm trying to write every day too. I'm returning your University Literature. I like the way the Graduate's Association say they are non-political and then enclose Graham Little's letter with theirs. I rather fear that many of these people are well-meaning stooges. As regards Mitchener, he's quite a nice chap with plenty of common sense and is not afraid to criticise officialdom when he thinks it's wrong. He's strongly against a state medical service – mainly on the grounds that it will put doctors in the power of officials.

I think Graham Little's letter one of the slimiest things I've read. He certainly seems to try to keep in with everyone. On the whole I think it's quite a good idea to have special University MPs. They do represent what should be the best educated section of the community. The number of MPs is too small to influence parliament seriously on any major issue but they serve a useful purpose in bringing up certain special questions for discussion. Frequently too these men are doctors, scientists and other types of specialist rather than professional politicians, who would not otherwise enter parliament. Certainly when entry to the Universities is by merit, not money, there would be even less objection to graduates being allowed a double vote.

You would have laughed if you had been here last night. We had an ENSA concert and one of the actresses sang sentimental songs while staring fixedly at one member of the audience. I was in the middle of the front row and suddenly she looked at me and sang 'Oh Robert, Oh Robert, how you can love!' There were roars of laughter from the men – I expect one of them had put her up to it. They are still going around singing the wretched song this morning.

I've just heard from Mother. The watch and bracelet are on the way. You'll soon look like a Rajah's wife with all your jewels. I'll have to get you an enormous pearl necklace. [*Grandpa's watch and bracelet were, and are, beautiful*]. Glad your Father is better. Thank your Mother once again for the pen – it's working fine.

All my love dearest and lots of hugs

RB

PS Let me know how my letters are arriving.

50)

Lieut R Barer
8FDS
APO
England

Friday

Dearest darling Gwenda,

Just got your letter of Tuesday today. I'm enclosing a couple of snaps; one of the officers and one of the sergeants. Keep them for me will you? I'm afraid I look pretty awful.

We had a most inspiring talk from our divisional general. He looks a most meek and mild little man and on previous occasions when I've met him he was always very pleasant but always gave the impression of being rather feeble. However he was said to have a very good record in action and I can well believe it now. He gave us a most interesting account of the way things are going and what we expect to happen and then went on to our particular role. He was absolutely magnificent and we all went away feeling full of confidence and eagerly awaiting our big chance.

We heard a very amusing story. An old Frenchman was evacuated over here with his goat. On his arrival he caused some consternation by saying that he didn't know he had brought his goat – he thought it was his wife! As the quartermaster said, 'All the married men laughed, but the single ones didn't see the point.'

Well, dear, I'm afraid there's nothing more to say at present. I'll try to ring you next week but you must realise that all the phone lines are very much in demand at the moment.

An enormous hug and great big kiss

RB

51)

Lt R Barer
8 Field Dressing Station
APO
England

Dear Mother-in-law,

It was very naughty of you to send me such a nice surprise but it's very welcome all the same. However did you get it? I've been trying to get a decent pen for months, as my present one leaks [*shortage in wartime!*]. This is the first letter I've written with the new pen so you will be able to judge for yourself how it affects my handwriting. It feels beautifully smooth.

I do wish you could let me do something in return. I know it's a matter of pride not to accept things but do remember that Gwen and I have never been in a position to do things for anyone and it's a new and exciting experience. Gwen tells me you have a new woman but doesn't say how often she's coming. Do try and get her at least 5 times a week. Remember it's partly for Gwen's benefit too and for that reason I insist that we must pay our share.

How is Mr Briggs? Gwen wrote that he had a bit of a chill. I hope it's cleared up by now. Give him my regards and tell him that I enjoyed meeting Mr and Mrs North [*cousins in Penrith*]. They seemed a very nice couple.

Love

Robert

52)

Lt R Barer
8 Field Dressing Station
APO
England

Dearest Gwen,

It was terribly nice of your Mother to send me that pen. It's working splendidly and the nib suits perfectly. I'm glad you've got someone from the Labour exchange. You didn't say how often she's coming. Do try to get your parents to accept a reasonable weekly sum from us for her services.

How's your bank balance? If you're short, let me know and I'll send you a cheque. I'll let you have a cheque anyhow to buy us some more certificates. How's your father? You'll obviously have to be careful with him – no more football matches! [*He was crazy about matches and had, perhaps, caught his 'cold' at one just before the wedding.*]

Have my people sent you the watch yet? The latest atrocity is that my Father is making you a gold bracelet to go with the watch! It's no good trying to stop them though. Have they sent the photos you ordered? I expect they'll take another 2 months! Isn't it about time the new UCH mag came out! I don't suppose you get a chance to go up to UCH. Is DW chief Surgeon yet? What did you think of all those articles on penicillin by the Barts people? A little disappointing I thought. I suppose the trouble is that they really haven't got enough of the stuff to use really effectively. I thought it was terrible the way they had decided not to accept any more cases of staph septicaemia. It's carrying science a bit too far – I wonder what they'd do if one of the team got a staph septicaemia?

Well dear, that's all for the moment. Will try to write often but don't worry if letters are delayed. I love you more and more each day.

RB

53)   Lt R Barer
                                             8 Field Dressing Station
                                             APO
                                             England

Darling Gwen,
Sorry about the delay in writing – it was quite unavoidable. Hope letters will be a bit better now, though there's very little indeed to write about. The pen is fine and the nib suits me splendidly – I wouldn't dream of changing it.

I didn't quite understand what you advised Nancy to do [*Nancy Hayward, an Australian friend at my lab who had been 'stranded' five years in England. She was an expert on gas gangrene organisms and ran courses for army officers.*] Did you tell her to wait for the chap or not? Anyhow why does she want to go back to Australia? I thought she was doing something on this gas gangrene team.

Your Father and Mother sent me a letter each. Please thank them and tell them I'll reply as soon as I get a chance. They don't say anything about helping to pay for the woman. I do wish you'd come to some agreement with them.

Your remarks on Madame Curie (a film) are certainly amusing. I'm sure that at the time no-one ever dreamt that Radium could either cause or cure cancer. It's a pity they can't make films more accurate. There's quite enough interest in most people's lives without being ultradramatic. I think *The Magic Bullet* – the life of Ehrlich was about the best I've seen of that type, but as it was not highly dramatic it didn't make a great hit with the public.

Well dear, that's all for now.

All my love darling

RB

[*During this period troops were concentrating in Southern England in preparation for the invasion of Normandy. I found out where R was in a strange way. We got permission to attend a great friend's funeral in Brighton. As we emerged from the station I saw a military convoy entering the train – on the trucks was the 'EYE' sign – the Guards Armoured Division! After the service I wandered round the town asking servicemen the location of 8FDS – I actually found the Guards Armoured Divisional headquarters and discovered that 8FDS was some miles away in the countryside. Of course my informants were seriously breaching security – 'Careless talk costs lives'.*]

54)

Lieut R Barer
8FDS
APO
England

Sunday

Darling Gwen,
Thanks for your offer of Hugo's but I already have them with me. However do you happen to have Hugo's German reading simplified? That would be useful.

Talking of books I picked a bargain yesterday. It was really very funny. I had been thinking for days how much I should like a copy of Biedermann's *Electrophysiology*. It's a classic work written in 1896, in two volumes.

81

Many of the diagrams are still copied in the modern textbooks. Katz (Bernard Katz – later Nobel laureate) used to use it a lot. Well I walked into one junk shop and the first thing I saw were these very two volumes – in excellent condition, price 3/6 for both! I also picked up two other things, a copy of T.H. Huxley's *Elementary Physiology* 1881, price 9d and W.B. Carpenter's *Animal Physiology* 1864 price 1/6. Huxley's book is not very remarkable but is useful as showing us the ideas of that period. The other book is really most remarkable. It might almost have been written today instead of 80 years ago. It's a sort of textbook of comparative anatomy and physiology, written with a clinical bias. The diagrams are excellent and some of the ideas are remarkably modern. When I send it to you be sure to read the introductory chapter which deals with public health and also pleads for a wider knowledge of physiology. I'll bet you'll never guess what was the main cause of infant mortality about 1800. It was actually tetanus neonatorum! – I wonder if Miles knows that. The book contains a wealth of information about all forms of living creatures, including plants and even delves into pathology. The style is modern and the language is not at all stilted. Carpenter must have been a remarkable man. He was MD FRS FGS FLS and describes himself as Registrar of the University of London. It's a pity the book does not give references but he does mention the 'recent work' of Claude Bernard on the liver and Davy's contribution. Some of his remarks on nutrition are interesting. Apparently it was well known in 1860 that sugar or starch alone or gelatine alone will not sustain life. He knows that various salts are also essential – phosphorus for nerve and bone, sulphur, calcium and iron. It was known that hens deprived of calcium laid eggs with very weak shells. The use of iron in the treatment of anaemia was apparently well known. I wonder who first discovered that? Most interesting of all are his remarks on the value of cod liver oil – especially in TB. He seems to regard TB as a result of disordered metabolism – the contents of the blood not being able to form normal tissue but being deposited as tubercles which set up inflammation, 'good food, active exercise, pure air, warm clothing and cheerful occupation . . . at a sufficiently early period' would save many lives.

I'll probably be sending the books off in a few days. I hope you don't think it's extravagant of me, but after all they only cost 5/3 all together.

So Janet's guessed too has she? I expect you've been dropping hints to everyone without realising it. [*I don't know what this referred to.*] It'll be all over UCH before long.

Did you manage to get to the Phys Soc yesterday? Let me know if you met anyone we know.

I realise that I'd left your watch behind soon after I'd left. It's a pity but

I'm not so sure about trusting it to the post. On the whole I think you had better try to get it done locally.

I saw 'Madame Curie' yesterday. It's pretty laughable isn't it? I'm quite sure that even geniuses don't behave like that. Their mathematical conversion was sheer rubbish. Still it was quite amusing.

It's very sad about your friend at Liverpool, but you needn't worry – nothing like that will happen to <u>us</u>.

All my love darling

RB

55)

Lieut R Barer
8FDS
APO
England

Dearest Gwen,

Thank you for Hugo's reader which arrived today. It looks quite useful.

I have sent off all the books at last. Let me know when you get them. By the way don't take any notice of the prices marked. I got those 2 books on microscopy for 9/- the pair though they are marked 12/6. I got them from a dealer, not a junk shop so naturally the prices are higher. I think they are worth it though as a good deal of the work seems to be original. I'm getting your letters pretty regularly now but they tend to arrive two at a time! Don't bother to send me a dictionary – in fact, dear, please don't send me anything at all unless I ask for it specifically. By the way, I sent back Bailey's *Surgery of Modern War* to Lewis'. Unfortunately I said it was from me but I believe it was on your ticket. I don't suppose it matters. Get a book out for yourself. Don't let it lie idle.

I think Florey probably deserves his knighthood but I can think of many more deserving scientists than Fleming. After all he didn't exploit his accidental discovery and it seems wrong to honour a man for one startling discovery while there are dozens of men who have done excellent work involving real thought for many years – A.V. for example. It's bad luck about Eva [*Marianne's sister, who had collapsed with a complete heart block*]. She certainly doesn't look as if she could tackle anything yet. What are you going to do about her?

Please let me know about insurance as soon as possible. Will try to ring you later.

All my love dearest Gwen.

RB

56)

Lieut R Barer
8 Field Dressing Station
APO
England

Dearest Gwen,

It was a great treat being able to drop in like that wasn't it? I must try and persuade some more people to go to that hospital.

You really mustn't be upset over your disappointment. Everything will be all right in the end and I'm still hoping we'll have another chance.

With regard to the insurance, I've talked it over with Inky who's insured with the same company and I think that our arrangement was OK, namely to have an endowment policy for 15 years, at £1500.

This works out at about £104 per year, approximately £15 of which will be refunded out of income tax.

The only snag at the moment is whether we can pay for it immediately. I think I have approximately £100 in the bank, assuming my pay cheque for last month has come in. I've not heard from the bank, but I'll write to them again. In any case we shall be able to afford it next month. If we both get our increase in pay (mine is due on July 31st) we shall be able to afford it easily with plenty left over for savings certificates. I don't want to touch any of the certificates at present.

Well dear, there's no news I'm afraid. Thank your parents for me would you? Your Mother certainly seems to know the sort of food I like!

All my love dearest wife.

RB

[*R had suddenly appeared at our house in Watford when taking someone to hospital – we had a brief time together at Janet's. We took out a life insurance (£100 p.a.) but, sadly, we could only afford it for three years. The outlay was locked up for fifteen years – a big sum for those days!*]

57)

Lieut R Barer
8FDS
APO
England

Thursday

Dearest Gwen,

Still no letter this week. I shall have to ring you up if none come today.

Strange coincidence last night. We went down for the evening to one of the field ambulances and I met Ruth Cyrlas-Williams' brother who's only been with them a short time. He was at Charing Cross. He told me that Glyn-Hughes, our DDMS whom you've heard about, has a daughter who is a nurse at UCH. She used to be at Ashridge and he knew her quite well. One day her Father came to see her and she asked him (Colyer) to take him in to lunch. At lunch Glyn-Hughes asked him if he would like to join our division. He knows quite a lot of the people at UCH. John Wylie, Rabinovitch etc. He said Ruth took things pretty badly at first but has now settled down and has a job at the Birmingham fever hospital [*her husband, a UCH graduate, was killed in North Africa*]. I also met a chap who served in the same field ambulance as the people at the depot. It was quite an interesting evening but rather spoilt by the excessive amount of liquor drunk. James vomited all over the side of the car coming back and Alderson was as mad as usual. Being driven late at night at 70 mph by someone whom you know to be under the influence is quite an experience.

Well dear, that's all I can think of for now. Hope to ring you later today.

All my love

RB

PS Have appointed you as my proxy to vote at Parliamentary Election at Watford.

58)
Lieut R Barer
8FDS
APO
England

Dearest Gwen,

I do hope you got home all right and managed to get some supper. Everything went smoothly at my end.

We certainly had a lovely time, didn't we? – but not nearly as lovely as we're going to have in a few months time.

Seeing you has put a new zest into me – I was getting rather fed up, but now I've been getting down to the job of brushing up a little German – I expect I shall have ample opportunity to practise it soon.

With regard to the income tax, in my claim I put down last year's earnings as £300 for you and £254.10 for me – £554.10 in all. Have you heard from the bank yet dear? They seem to be very slow.

Give my love to your people and tell them I'll write them a separate letter as soon as I can think of anything to say.

Will try and ring you up tomorrow.

All my love darling

RB

59)
Lieut R Barer
8 Field Dressing Station
APO
England

Dearest Gwen,

Your letters seem to be coming through a little better now. I hope you're getting mine too.

I haven't been able to find any more books yet. I discovered one place but the owner was an expert and knew what to charge. He showed me a magnificent great tome on surgery by Fabricius, written in German in 1630. It was full of fine woodcuts. Apparently the idea of internal metal splints for fractures was used even then! It looked very fine indeed but he wanted £5 for it. I should think it's worth even more but I don't think it's justifiable to spend all that. I've been reading a little of Darwin. It's very interesting but I don't think you'll like him as he makes disparaging remarks about the mental powers of women! He attributes many of the sexual differences to natural selection.

I'll be sending you the other books soon. Let me know as soon as any arrive.

Well, dear, I'm afraid there's no news as usual. Give my regards to your people.

Love

RB

60)   Lieut R Barer
                                                       8FDS
                                                       APO
                                                       England

                                                       Sunday

My own Darling,
I've heard from the bank at last and find I have a credit of £104, so if you could pay in £5 or £10 we can easily cover the cost of insurance. I've still not had my marriage allowance yet but I'm expecting it next month. Let me know as soon as possible what you want me to do about the insurance. We now have a very interesting addition to our library. I picked up two old books on Microscopy, both by Henry Baker FRS written in 1754 and 1764 respectively. They really are first class and in a very good condition though the covers are loose (I think you had better leave them now but we'll try and get them repaired by a good bookbinder – if I think it's worth it). He states that the microscope was first invented about 1620 – these were actually single lenses. He gives a very interesting account, with diagrams of early microscopes including that of Leuwenhoek (about 1680). He constantly refers to Leuwenhoek's work. Much of his work appears to be original, and is beautifully illustrated. He shows a perfect picture of the scabies mite, together with a very interesting account of the disease. He attributes the discovery of the mite to a Dr Boonio, who described the burrows and eggs. He points out that since ointments only kill the mites and not the eggs 'it is advisable to continue the ointment for some days even after the cure seems perfect.'

He makes interesting and accurate observations on the blood and its circulation (e.g. in a frog's web) and puts in a strong plea for microscopical examination of the blood in disease, 'Would our learned physicians . . . be induced to take this method into their practice it is reasonable to believe that in a few . . . the causes of disease would be better known' – prophetic words! He makes interesting remarks on the history of intravenous therapy – pointing out that the stomach can destroy drugs before they get in the blood. I think it would be worth looking up a zoo book to identify all the animals he describes as some of them appear to be the original description. In particular I think he describes Vincent's organisms in the teeth!

I wonder if this chap was the Baker who founded the Bakerian lecture. He appears to have had a good reputation and was given the Copley medal.

Well dear, must rush to catch the post.

All my love, RB

61)
Lieut R Barer
8FDS
APO
England

Monday

Dearest Gwen,
No letter today. I suppose it's got delayed. I'll be sending you some more books I've picked up. I've got hold of Darwin's classics *The Origin of Species* and *The Descent of Man* 1882 in very good condition. They really are immense works. It seems hardly possible for one man to have such vast knowledge. The other two books are rather a surprise. I found what appears to be a brand new copy of *Life-Outlines of Biology* by J. Arthur Thomson and Patrick Geddes 1931 in two volumes, hidden away in the floor of a cupboard in an old junk shop. This is not a 'popular' work but a very good scientific discussion of biology in relation to the other sciences. Like Thomson's other books it covers a very wide range. It is quite modern and should remain a useful reference book for many years. It contains a very excellent bibliography. I remembered after I had bought it that you have some of his books and I wondered if this was one of them, but I rather doubt

it as this seems rather more advanced than what you would have had when you did biology. However all four books cost only 12/6 altogether and Thomson by itself is probably worth far more. Do let me know, dear, if you think I'm being too extravagant. It's my main source of amusement at the moment and I do try to buy books of some real interest. It would be lovely to have a really fine reference library of our own and some of these older books contain a good deal that none of the modern books do. They seem to have had so much more time to think about a subject than we have today, and did not overburden themselves with mere facts. I think this is quite a good time for finding these books as a lot of people have been moving from bombed areas and have been getting rid of their 'junk'. If you come across anything you think is worth buying please do so. I'll be sending these books in a day or so.

You'll be glad to hear that I've had my TAB, TT and Typhus vaccination, so I should be pretty immune by now. I wonder if all this stuff confers any nonspecific protein immunity?

I had a letter from the chap I used to coach in matric mechanics at Stanboroughs. He returned a book I leant him, so I'll be returning that book too. He got through his matric, by the way.

The news about Rome is good isn't it? Perhaps things will move really soon and we'll be able to settle down to a life of ease at Oxford! – won't it be lovely?

All my love dearest Gwen

RB

PS Chapters in Thomson and Geddes listed.

62)   287225 Lieut R Barer
                                                8FDS
                                                APO
                                                England

                                                Thursday evening

Dearest Gwen,
You'll notice that I've put my number at the head of the page. I want you to address all letters to me in future – it's just an added safe-guard.

I was sorry to hear about your Mother [*alas, a recurrence of her breast cancer*]. I hope everything turns out alright.

Glad you got the books safely. Have a good look at them and let me know what you think. I'll try and pick up some more.

Saw a rather striking film the other day called *The Moon and Sixpence* based on a novel by Somerset Maugham. It is actually supposed to be the life of the great painter Gauguin. It was a remarkable psychological study. He started off as a perfectly respectable stockbroker, married 17 years with 2 children. His life was perfectly ordinary and he seemed rather dull but quite happy. Suddenly, at the age of 40 he left his family flat and went to Paris. A friend of his wife went to remonstrate with him, thinking he had gone off with another woman. However, he found him quite alone in a squalid hotel and was told that he (Gauguin) had just got tired of his wife and wanted to paint! He argued but it was useless. Gauguin just seemed devoid of any social conscience whatsoever. Months passed and the painter's money went. He lived in a filthy garret and never sold any pictures. However, one Dutch painter recognised his genius. Gauguin became ill through starvation and this Dutchman sheltered him and his wife nursed him. When Gauguin got better he worked in this artist's studio and continued to live with him, uninvited. All the time he was atrociously rude to everyone, showing no gratitude and treating his benefactor's paintings with contempt. Eventually matters came to a head and the Dutchman asked him to leave. To his astonishment his beautiful English wife said she would go too! The Dutchman was broken-hearted but he loved his wife madly and eventually left himself, leaving half his money with her. Gauguin and the woman lived together for some months, then Gauguin deserted her and she committed suicide. The Dutchman returned to his home and found that Gauguin had left one of his pictures, a portrait of the dead woman. His first impulse was to smash it, but he recognised it as a masterpiece, wrapped it up and took it back to him. The latter didn't seem in the least bit interested and said that he had finished with it and didn't want it. He wasn't in the least bit bothered about the suicide and said that he had only needed her to practice painting nudes! The Dutchman then invited him to come and live with him in the country in Holland, but he rudely refused saying that he was going to Tahiti (in the south sea islands). He did go there and for the first time appeared to attain happiness. He actually married a native girl and had a child. He painted some of his best masterpieces there. Eventually he died of leprosy. It's a remarkable story and most gripping. I wonder what the psychological explanation was? At one stage he seemed to be devoid of any human feeling. He never even tried to sell any of his pictures. You must try to see the film or read the book (there is a Penguin edition).

Well dear, I'm afraid there's no real news. Regards to your people.

All my love dear one

RB

63)
287225 Lieut R Barer
8FDS
APO
England

Dearest Gwen,

Just got your letter of Saturday. I'm afraid the post is very liable to be delayed at present, but I'll try to phone you when possible. I share your scepticism about Max but I hope it's true for all that. He told my Father that he was attending various clinics in London. I'd forgotten about the photo otherwise I would have reminded him about it.

I've got a few more interesting books which I shall send. The best is *The Hand* by Sir Charles Bell (1837) – the Bell of Bell and Magendie. It seems quite interesting and covers a very wide range of topics – in fact everything but the hand. I've also got another of Darwin's books on 'Expression'. It shows Darwin as an anatomist and physiologist as well as a keen observer. By a coincidence he says that the best book on the subject was written by Bell. Incidentally I think I have only sent you one of the two volumes of Darwin's *Descent of Man* – I think it's in two volumes and I can easily get the other, so let me know which it is.

Another interesting and unusual work is *Floating Matter of the Air* by John Tyndall, the great physicist who like Helmholtz was also a doctor. You may remember that he invented a method of sterilisation called Tyndallisation. He refers to this in a letter to T.H. Huxley at the end of the book. The book is especially interesting as he was contemporary with Pasteur and Lister (1881) and makes many references to them. The first chapter is called dust and disease and should be rather interesting. I wonder if Miles has read the book? Finally I've got *Notes on Nursing* by Florence Nightingale. It seems quite good and she certainly seems to flay old fogies. I also saw another copy of Baker's *The Microscope Made Easy*. They wanted 10/- for it alone so I did quite well to get the two for 9/-. These four new books cost me 9/- altogether too. I've seen a whole lot of really beautiful old medical books but they are more expensive. That man Carpenter seems to be pretty prolific.

I saw a 1st edition of a book on microscopy by him but they wanted 42/- for it!

Well, dear, I'm afraid there's no news.

All my love dearest

RB

64)   287225 Lieut R Barer
                                                             8FDS
                                                             APO
                                                             England

                                                             Tuesday

Dearest Gwen,

We certainly were lucky this week-end weren't we? I hope everything will be OK next Saturday but at the moment there are certain difficulties. However I'll let you know later on. I expect it will be all right.

I did a little more book hunting today but without much success. The promised medical books I told you about turned out to be a text book on nursing! However I've been promised some more by someone else – I hope it materialises. He's got a lot of very old stuff but he won't let me get at it. The only thing I got was a very nice little copy of Dante's *Inferno* for 1/-. It's one of the Oxford classics series (modern). It's got Italian on one side and English on the other. I saw a beautifully bound copy of Galsworthy's plays in a junk shop but they wanted £2 for it!

How is Marie getting on at her new job? Has she got the sack yet?

Well, dear, I can't think of anything else to write about so I'll just end as usual by sending you all my love.

RB

[*This probably refers to a lovely weekend in a pub at Mayfield in Sussex in beautiful May weather. I spent one night alone in the pub in some anxiety – very merry Canadian soldiers were shouting outside my window 'I want a . . .!'*]

65)   287225 Lieut R Barer
                                             8FDS
                                             APO
                                             England

                                             Wednesday

Dearest Gwen,
I think you will find the letter situation much better now. I got one of yours
written Monday today. I had a great day for books today. Bought four in all
for the total sum of 7/6.

One is a virtually unused copy of Michael Foster's big text book of
Physiology 1879. It's an excellent work of 700 pages and is a valuable
guide to the beliefs of the time. Some of the omissions are most interesting –
no reference is made to any of the endocrine glands. On the other hand there
are many references to the work going on at that time. Claude Bernard's
work on glycogenesis is well dealt with. The discovery of visual purple by
Boll (1876) and Kuhne's (1877) work on it is well described. It's interesting
to note too that practically nothing was known about the spleen (I doubt if
we really know much more today). They had a vague idea that it controlled
pancreatic secretion and its function with regard to red blood cells was
hinted at. Next on the list is a very interesting old book on *Diseases of
Women with Child and in Child-Bed* by Francis Moriceau (of the Moriceau-
Smellie-Viet manoeuvre) and translated by Hugh Chamberlen, one of the
'forceps' Family in 1718. It's a most remarkable work and shows how little
the subject has altered. Moriceau describes a hook for puncturing the head
but Chamberlen in his preface says that he has a better and safer way of
removing an impacted head but as his father and two brothers are alive he
cannot give it away (if you remember they kept their forceps secret). The
book deals not only with normal and abnormal obstetrics but also with
diseases of the new born e.g. Infection of the umbilicus, napkin rashes,
imperforate anus, D&V, hernia etc. etc. also with diseases of the puerperium
including breast troubles. There are a number of good woodcuts.

The other scientific book is called *Nature and Man* by W.B. Carpenter –
the chap I told you I was interested in. About half of it is devoted to his life
story, the other half consists of a number of his more philosophical essays.
He certainly was a most interesting man and a study of his life and work is
really a study of the whole development of biology in the 19th century. His
first paper was written in 1836 at the age of 24 'On the Structure and
Functions of the Organs of Respiration in the Animal and Vegetable
Kingdoms'. A list of 293 of his main papers and books is given in an

appendix. His writings cover an immense range – natural history, geology, plant and animal Physiology, Neurology, Psychology, Microscopy, Embryology, Oceanography and Medicine. He wrote an article on the germ theory of disease in the British Association report 1883, which we must get hold of as it's just at the most interesting period. It's strange how the coincidences crop up; two books influenced him profoundly. One was Lyell's *Geology* (we must get that obviously) and the other was Herschel's *Preliminary Discourse on the Study of Natural Philosophy* which I showed you last week-end and for which I payed 3d! He says of the latter that he derived more benefit from it than from any other book except the bible. At that age of 32 he was elected FRS and appointed Fullerian Professor of Physiology at the Royal Institution. He lectured at the London Hospital and lived in Stoke Newington. In 1847 he was appointed to the lectureship in Geology at the British Museum. In 1849 he was appointed to the chair of medical jurisprudence at University College. In 1852 to the principalship of University Hall – a remarkably varied career! His friends were interesting – Carlyle, Emerson, Paget, Darwin, Huxley, Sharpey, to mention only a few. He comes out strongly in favour of Darwin, and indeed some of his own earlier writings were on a very similar theme. His influence on the teaching of the period seems to have been immense.

His remarks on women students may amuse you. He came into contact with them as a student at Edinburgh. He wrote in a letter to his father (1835) that scientific pursuits were carried out 'to an extent which even I think hardly feminine; such as geology and practical chemistry in classes – a row of young ladies performing experiments all at the same time, like a company of soldiers going through an exercise'. I wonder what he would say if he were alive today! It's a pity that his work is not better known today. The only reference Foster makes to him is that he was responsible for the idea that the Corpus Striatum is mainly motor and the thalamus sensory. I think that his work is well worth studying; it seems to be a very good commentary even if not very original.

My final purchase was a copy of Ibsen's plays *The Doll's House*, *The Wild Duck*, and *The Lady from the Sea*, price 6d.

Well, dear, I think you'll like these books when you see them. It really is great fun collecting them and one learns an immense amount.

All my love dearest

RB

66)

287225 Lieut R Barer
8FDS
APO
England

[*Presumably D-Day 6 June 1944*]   Tuesday

Dearest Gwen,

I've only just got the letter you wrote on Friday. I hope mine aren't taking so long.

Well, you will have heard the news by now. Things seem to be going well at the moment. Let's hope it takes less time than anyone expects.

I'm very amused to hear about Mrs D. I hope she doesn't spill the beans to Marie!

With regard to your physics problem. I think where you have gone wrong is in your formulation of Newton's law. You state that 'in an interval of time the T will fall by a constant fraction of itself'. This is not quite true. Newton's law states that the rate of fall of temperature is proportional to the <u>difference</u> between the T of the body and that of its surroundings (air).

i.e. $dT/dt = -K(T_1 - T_0)$

where To = air temperature

Taking out dt as 1/2 minute we get

$15.1 - 15.0 = -k (15 - To)$

i.e. $.1 = -k (15 - To)$

and if the temperature falls x^0 in any half minute after introducing the body, the temperature being T1, $x = -K(T_1 - T_0)$ where x and T_1 are given.

This gives two equations enabling k and To to be calculated and thence the required initial temperature can be found. Actually you should be able to do it all from one curve alone, using two points, but remember that you must find room temperature.

Glad to hear about your rise. You now earn more than me – in fact I'm just a 'kept man'. By the way when do you get your pay cheque? Remember to try and build up your bank balance a little in case we have to pay this insurance premium all at once. I still haven't heard from my bank.

I expect you'll be getting plenty of interesting bacteriology in a few days. It's queer to think that while I'm sitting here peacefully writing this the first casualties may already be on the way back.

All my love dearest

RB

PS Can you remember Max's address? I'm afraid I've lost the number!

67)
[From Miss E L Ramsay, headmistress of my school]

Walthamstow Hall
Sevenoaks
Kent

June 6th 1944

My very dear Gwenda,

I must send a note today to say that my thoughts flew to you at once this morning when I turned on the news at 12 o'clock – for I know the anxiety you are bearing. There is nothing to be said except that you are one of a great company – each helps the other and is helped. I do think of you constantly and with such pride. Yours is the hardest part but you would not have it otherwise.

Ever lovingly

E L Ramsay

[The Guards Armoured Division was not destined to land in the first days of the invasion – Mulberry harbour was required for landing large quantities of armour. Further delay followed the great storms which nearly destroyed the harbour and put the whole enterprise in peril. Thus it was the end of June before the whole division arrived in Normandy. There came a tremendous, unexpected and wonderful surprise – R appeared at the front door of the Watford house for a brief leave. We spent it in great happiness at Highgate.]

68)

> 287225 Lieut R Barer
> 44 Wilbury Road
> Hove
> Sussex

My dearest one,

You will now notice that I can use an open address once more so your letters should take less time.

I'm so sorry I was irritable and made you miserable. I love you so very much that it upsets me to see you looking unhappy and tearful. You always try to take on so much, darling, and at times it gets too much for you. Don't think I'm hard-hearted, dearest, but you mean so much to me that I can't bear to think of you putting yourself to such a lot of extra trouble and inconvenience for other people. I know you have had a trying time and unfortunately will probably have still more trouble with your Mother, but do try to take things as easily as possible. Don't imagine troubles before they come – they may never come. Above all you mustn't worry about me. At the rate things are going now the war may be over before I go overseas and we'll be in Oxford sooner than we expect.

I'll let you know about the week-end later. I'm afraid there's not much hope of your coming here – the police have refused permission. I'm still hoping I may be able to get away but it may be difficult.

All my love dearest wife.

RB

[*In my job we were testing bacteriological specimens. We had to test bacteria for sensitivity to penicillin, which was just becoming available but in very short supply. Only patients suffering from 'sensitive' bacterial infections could be treated.*]

69)

287225 Lieut R Barer
8FDS
44 Wilbury Road
Hove
Sussex

Wednesday

Dearest Gwen,

No letter from you so far this week. I expect one will come tomorrow. I'm afraid I still don't know about the week-end.

Our library is growing slowly. I picked up a copy of Lyell's *Student's Elements of Geology* for 6d. I also got a book called *Animal Mechanism* by E.J. Marey, Professor at the College of France 1874. I remember him from Physiology days. He formulated Marey's Law – something to do with the circulation – look it up in B&T or Starling. It seems rather interesting as it deals with the animal as a machine. He did a lot of interesting experiments on running and walking, also on flight. He got people to run with recording apparatus strapped to their feet and recorded the pressure changes. He also makes some interesting remarks about evolution.

I also got a book containing two lectures on evolution, one by Huxley the other by Weissman. Also a good copy of Humboldt's travels and memoirs and letters of Sir James Paget. The last three books only cost me 4/- altogether. The Paget book had one of his <u>original</u> letters in it – probably quite valuable (1867).

How is your Mother dear? Did you see the RMS discussion on stilboestrol in this week's BMJ? It's certainly worth trying.

All my love dearest. Don't be disappointed if the week-end falls through. I'll certainly be able to come some other day.

Love

RB

70)

287225 Lieut R Barer
8FDS
44 Wilbury Road
Hove
Sussex

Tuesday

Dearest Gwen,

Thanks once more for a lovely week-end, one of the nicest we've had, wasn't it? I think there may be a chance of another after all – will certainly try but don't be disappointed if it fails; the post is very good now. Hope you get this in time for your Birthday. Many Happy returns, you old darling. You're getting to be an old antique.

Yes, I had a spot of diarrhoea too, but it's all over now. It seems like the chop suey.

Got some more books! The two volumes of Huxley's life and letters and Karl Pearson's *Grammar of Science*, 1st Edition, 10/- the lot. It seems expensive but the Huxley books are cheap at any price. We need never have a dull moment while we have them. They are equally fascinating wherever one dips in. They throw new light on all the people we're interested in. Tyndall was his bosom friend – he refers to him as 'Tyndalides' and a lot of correspondence passed between them. Darwin, Wallace, Michael Foster, Carpenter, Sir John Lubbock, Romanes, Haeckel, Lyell, Pasteur, Bastion, Lonkester and dozens of others crop up all over the place. There's a very exciting account of the famous 'British Association' meeting at Oxford just after Darwin published his *Origin of Species*. The clergy, led by Bishop Wilberforce attacked it, but Huxley completely demolished his opponents. You <u>must</u> read that chapter, even if you've time for nothing else. Huxley's views on religion were quite unbigoted but he detested the influence of scientist clergymen, who stifled true learning. He fought them when he helped found the new London University constitution. You'll probably be interested in his views on women doctors. Miss Jex-Blake, one of the founders of the Royal Free, wrote to him when she was a student at Edinburgh, asking for help. The women students there had to be taught privately but the university refused to recognise their tutor (quite unjustifiably). Huxley expresses sympathy for her cause but agrees that it's bad to have mixed classes. He says he never lectures to a mixed class on comparative anatomy! Later Jex-Blake fails her exam and accuses the University of bias. Huxley examined her papers and found them not up to standard.

The story of Sir Richard Owen is very interesting. He appears to have been a great scientist but very unpleasant and unscrupulous. He quarrelled with Huxley but nevertheless Huxley wrote an appreciation of his scientific work. It was he who 'primed' Bishop Wilberforce in his famous speech attacking Darwin. Someone said of him that his sweetness was 'like sugar of lead'. His style is very boyish and amusing – not at all Victorian.

I saw a two volume life of John Lubbock (afterwards Lord Avebury) for 6/- but I didn't get it. I might later. He really was a remarkable man – a great scientist and politician. He was an MP, a chairman of the LCC as well as FRS. Karl Pearson's book is of course a classic – it's rather like Herschel's book – a general discussion of scientific laws and method. It has some good references. One is by Virchow 1877, on *Die Freiheit der Wissenschaft im Modernen Staat* – a sad commentary!

I saw a catalogue of books from a bookseller Thorp of Guildford and all at Berkeley in London. He's got some good stuff but rather expensive. He has a lot of books and papers from Tyndall's library including some of Pasteur's stuff. Pasteur wrote a commentary on Claude Bernard's work. We must visit Guildford some time!

Well dear, here's hoping for the week-end.

All my love dear one

RB

[*We were very fortunate to get one more weekend after D-Day and had a wonderful time at Highgate.*]

CHAPTER IV

First 100 battle casualties in Normandy, German wounded, assault on Hitler, French civilians

71)   From HM Ship, Maritime Post Office   287225 Lieut R Barer
      ON ACTIVE SERVICE   8FDS
                                                   APO
                                                   BWEF

Dearest Gwen,

Just a short note dear to let you know all's well. You can draw your own conclusions from the new address. I don't know how much I can tell you at the moment, but I think I can say everything went very well indeed and I didn't have to use my vomit bag.

I don't expect to get any of your letters for a few days so I won't have much to tell you but will write as often as I can.

All my love dearest

RB

PS Let my parents know will you?

72)   287225 Lieut R Barer
                                      8FDS
                                      Guards Armoured Division
                                      BLA

                                    Sunday 16th July

Dearest Gwen,

Yet another change of address – as you may know we are now to be called the 'British Liberation Army' though I'm afraid I don't feel much like a liberator at the moment. We are quite comfortable – more so than on most exercises and the feeding is adequate. There seems to be no shortage of dairy produce over here. I've not seen much sign of starvation so far and people seem to be dressed quite well. Life seems to be going on quite normally in many places and some of the shops are quite well stocked. I've not had an opportunity of buying any books yet but I expect to get some in Paris which I hope to visit shortly!

Well all my love dearest one; don't worry, whatever you hear.

RB

73)

287225 Lieut R Barer
8FDS
Guards Armoured Division
BLA

Wednesday 19th July

Dearest Gwen,

Had a great treat today amid all the fuss and bother – a whole pile of your letters suddenly arrived. Sorry to hear about your cystitis but I won't worry. You must get it cleared up <u>completely</u>. Don't hold back sulphonamides if they are really necessary – you know it's most important not to let it become chronic. Still I'll leave it to your own judgement.

Oh dear! You've sent me such a pile of correspondence that I scarcely know where I am. I'm glad you've started on Tyndall at last and are enjoying it. What I wanted you to do with penicillium was to repeat and extend his observation that the mould would not grow where pyocyanus was already growing. If this is correct, see if the mould will grow in presence of extracts of pyo. With regard to the visibility of light, a ray of light viewed from the side in a perfectly clear atmosphere is invisible, since no light impinges on the eye. The presence of dust particles (not molecules, which are too small) scatters light laterally and makes the path of the ray visible. By the way ask Miles if Tyndall's was the first reference to antibiotic action or did Pasteur notice it? Yes, Schwann does seem to be an interesting man. We must try and get the literature of the origin of the cell theory – particularly Brown on the nucleus and Brownian movement. I'm afraid most of the best work was German. I think I ought to be able to pick up some of the early French bacteriologists' work over here – Pasteur, Roux, Metchnikoff etc. The French also go in for a number of really big multivolume books – there were some really good ones on physiology in UC. I'll try

Claude Bernard of course and Marey, who seem to have been quite good.

We had some Canadian nurses round to our mess before we left England. They're a heavy-drinking crowd and I thought it was going to end up with a bed party. I was amazed to hear what a nurse earns in America. One of them used to run a flat and a car while nursing at the Columbia hospital in New York. Over here, as a junior sister in the Canadian forces she earns £35 per month tax free! – more than our CO in fact!! It makes one feel pretty sick when you remember that RAMC is very much higher than other soldiers' pay and yet a nurse can even outdo that.

Well dear there's nothing else to write about so far. I suppose you're listening to the news. I'll be able to give you more details in 2 weeks time.

All my love sweetest and do look after yourself

RB

[*I had indeed got a bad cystitis but, worse, I had been losing weight and feeling exhausted – so I had an x-ray which showed a small TB lesion at the left lung apex. My former boss and consultant at UCH, Andrew Morland, sent me into Stanboroughs base hospital, Watford, as a patient. I could not bring myself to tell R this for some weeks until all seemed to be going well. An added though joyful worry was that I thought I was pregnant.*]

74)
                                              287225 Lieut R Barer
                                              8FDS
                                              Guards Armoured Division
                                              BLA

                                              Sunday 23rd July

Dearest Gwen,
Just got your letter of Thursday. The post is very good indeed this way. I hope it's OK for you.

You really are very wicked just to say 'am much better'. You know very well that sort of thing won't satisfy me at all. Please give some details – are you up yet? Is the culture sterile? I'd also like to know more about Marie [*poor Marianne had been sacked from a new job; we did not know then, but the trouble was she could not type. She was developing a rare muscular wasting disease*]. She must be incredibly bad to do that sort of thing twice running. I'm afraid you'll have to resign yourself to the fact that she isn't going to make good in any but a very simple routine job.

Glad you're enjoying Verworn. It's full of interesting stuff like that you describe. I'm sure a lot of it had been forgotten and might well be repeated using modern methods.

I don't know what it was you referred to when you said I told you there was something interesting on the front page of one of the books, unless it was that letter of Paget's.

I don't know much about Hooker either. Huxley evidently regards him very highly. Isn't that big index of British Flora written by him?

Conditions over here have improved now and we are quite comfortable. The local children are picking up English quickly but I shudder to think of what our respectable post-war tourists will say when they hear every noun preceded by some particularly choice adjective!

Well darling that's all for now – all my love

RB

PS Wonder if you'd mind sending cheque for £1.11.6 to BMA for me? – last year's sub.

75)
                                    287225 Lieut R Barer
                                    8FDS
                                    Guards Armoured Division
                                    BLA

                                    Friday 21st July

Dearest Gwen,

Got two more of your letters today; hope you're getting mine. I didn't understand Tyndall's remarks about not finding bacteria in air either. He says something about bacterial germs (or seeds) – presumably spores – perhaps you could ask Miles about it.

Glad you are being sensible about your cystitis. Don't get up until it's quite clear – do what Joan Stokes advises and don't argue. After a few days of heat wave we have now had a cloud burst and are knee deep in mud. Our dug-outs are completely swamped and we've taken to sleeping above ground. Fortunately there isn't much shelling at the moment.

What do you think of the latest Hitler sensation? It certainly looks like the beginning of the end – even if they crush the present revolt it's a sign of disunity.

The mosquitoes here are absolutely vicious. I'm afraid I'm unrecognisable at the moment being simply covered with bites – I've had to give up shaving as I cut myself over the bites. Some of the men have their eyes almost completely closed by oedema.

Well dear, let me know how you are getting on. Don't do anything rash about the cystitis.

Regards to all

All my love dear one

RB

76)

287225 Lieut R Barer
8FDS
Guards Armoured Division
BLA

Tuesday 26? July

Dearest Gwen,

Just a short note to catch the post. Everything here is going on fine but I probably won't get your letter for a day or two so I won't have much to answer. I'm getting what I wanted at last and it's certainly an experience!

Do let me know exactly how you are getting on.

Love to all and especially you my darling wife.

RB

[*The first engagement of the Guards Armoured Division*]

[*Late June-30 July*
The Division was stationed in the Bayeaux area – from 17-20 July it undertook its first major action, Operation GOODWOOD. This took place east of CAEN and the main objective was to improve the position of the

Die Ansprache des Führers

Der Mordanschlag einer Verräterclique gescheitert

Aus dem Führerhauptquartier, 21. Juli 1944

Der Führer hielt heute nachts im deutschen Rundfunk folgende Ansprache an das deutsche Volk:

Deutsche Volksgenossen und -genossinnen!

Ich weiss nicht, zum wievielten Male nunmehr ein Attentat auf mich geplant und zur Ausführung gekommen ist. Wenn ich heute zu Ihnen spreche, dann geschieht es aber besonders aus zwei Gründen: Damit Sie meine Stimme hoeren und wissen, dass ich selbst unverletzt und gesund bin. Damit Sie aber auch noch das Naehere erfahren über ein Verbrechen, das in der deutschen Geschichte seinesgleichen sucht. Eine nur kleine Clique ehrgeiziger, gewissenloser und zugleich verraeterischer dummer Offiziere hat ein Komplott geschmiedet, um mich zu beseitigen und zugleich mit mir den Stab der deutschen Wehrmachtführung auszurotten.

Die Bombe, die von dem Oberst Graf von Stauffenberg gelegt wurde, krepierte zwei Meter an meiner rechten Seite. Sie hat eine Reihe mir teurer Mitarbeiter schwer verletzt, einer ist gestorben. Ich selbst bin voellig unverletzt bis auf ganz kleine Hautabschürfungen, Prellungen oder Verbrennungen.

Ich fasse das als eine Bestaetigung des Auftrages der Vorsehung auf, mein Lebensziel weiter zu verfolgen, wie ich es bisher getan habe, denn ich darf es der ganzen Nation feierlich gestehen, dass ich seit dem Tage, an dem ich in die Wilhelmstrasse einzog, nur einen einzigen Gedanken hatte, nach bestem Wissen und Gewissen meine Pflicht zu erfüllen, und dass ich, sobald mir klar wurde, dass der Krieg ein unausweichlicher war, und nicht mehr aufgeschoben werden konnte, ich eigentlich nur Sorge und Arbeit kannte und in zahllosen Tagen und durchwachten Naechten nur für mein Volk lebte.

Es hat sich in ernster Stunde, in der die deutschen Armeen im schwersten Ringen stehen, wie in Italien nun auch in Deutschland eine ganz kleine Gruppe gefunden, die nun glaubte, wie im Jahre 1918 den Dolchstoss in den Rücken führen zu koennen. Sie hat sich diesmal aber schwer getaeuscht.

Die Behauptung dieser Usurpatoren, dass ich nicht mehr lebe, wird jetzt in diesem Augenblick widerlegt, wo ich zu Euch, meine lieben Volksgenossen, spreche. Der Kreis, den diese Usurpatoren darstellen, ist ein denkbar kleiner. Er hat mit der deutschen Wehrmacht und vor allem auch mit dem deutschen Heer nichts zu tun. Es ist ein ganz kleiner Klüngel verbrecherischer Elemente, die jetzt unbarmherzig, ausgerottet werden.

Ich befehle daher in diesem Augenblick: 1. Dass keine Zivilstelle irgendeinen Befehl entgegenzunehmen hat von einer Dienststelle, die sich diesen Usurpatoren angeschlossen hat. 2. Dass keine Militaerstelle, kein Führer einer Truppe, kein Soldat irgendeinen Befehl dieser Usurpatoren zu gehorchen hat, dass im Gegenteil jeder verpflichtet ist, den Uebermittler oder den Geber eines solchen Befehls entweder sofort zu verhaften oder bei Widerstand augenblicklich niederzumachen.

Ich habe, um endgültig Ordung zu schaffen, zum Befehlshaber des Heimatheeres den Reichsminister Himmler ernannt und habe in den Generalstab Generaloberst Guderian berufen, um den durch Krankheit zur Zeit ausgefallenen Genralstabschef zu ersetzen, und einen zweiten bewaehrten Führer der Ostfront zu seinem Gehilfen bestimmt. In allen anderen Dienststellen des Reiches aendert sich nichts.

Ich bin der Ueberzeugung, dass wir mit dem Austreten dieser ganz kleinen Verraeter und Verschwoererclique nun endlich aber auch im Rücken der Heimat die Atmosphaere schaffen, die die Kaempfer der Front brauchen, denn es ist unmoeglich, dass vorn Hunderttausende und Millionen braver Maenner ihr Letztes hergeben, waehrend zu Hause ein ganz kleiner Klüngel ehrgeiziger, erbaermlicher Kreaturen diese Haltung dauernd zu hintertreiben versucht.

Diesmal wird nun so abgerechnet, wie wir das als Nationalsozialisten gewohnt sind. Ich bin überzeugt, dass jeder anstandige Offizier, jeder tapfere Soldat in dieser Stunde das begreifen wird. Welches Schicksal Deutschland getroffen haette, wenn der Anschlag heute gelungen sein würde, das vermoegen die wenigsten sich vielleicht auszudenken.

Ich selber danke der Vorsehung und meinem Schoepfer nicht deshalb, dass er mich erhalten hat, mein Leben ist nur Sorge und ist nur Arbeit für mein Volk, sondern ich danke ihm nur deshalb, er mir die Moeglichkeit gab, diese Sorgen weiter tragen zu dürfen und in meiner Arbeit weiter fortzufahren, so gut ich das vor meinem Gewissen verantworten kann. Es hat jeder Deutsche, ganz gleich, wer er sein mag, die Pflicht, diesen Elementen rücksichtslos entgegenzutreten, sie entweder sofort zu verhaften oder, wenn sie irgendwie Widerstand leisten sollten, ohne weiteres niederzumachen.

Die Befehle an saemtliche Truppen sind ergangen. Sie werden blind ausgeführt entsprechend dem Gehorsam, den das deutsche Heer kennt. Ich darf besonders sie, meine alten Kampfgefaehrten, noch einmal freudig begrüssen, dass es mir wieder vergoennt war, einem Schicksal zu ntgehen, das nichts für mich Schreckliches in sich barg, sondern das den Schrecken für das deutsche Volk gebracht haette.

Ich ersehe daraus auch einen Fingerzeig der Vorsehung, dass ich mein Werk weiter fortführen muss und daher weiter fortführen werde.

Leaflet of Hitler's speech after surviving assassination attempt

106

Dönitz an die Marine

Aus dem Führerhauptquartier, 21. Juli 1944

Der Oberbefehlshaber der Kriegsmarine, Grossadmiral Dönitz, richtete folgende Ansprache an die Männer der Kriegsmarine:

Männer der Kriegsmarine! Heiliger Zorn und masslose Wut erfüllt uns über den verbrecherischen Anschlag, der unserem geliebten Führer das Leben kosten sollte. Die Vorsehung hat es anders gewollt. Sie hat den Führer beschirmt und beschützt und damit unser deutsches Vaterland in seinem Schicksalskampf nicht verlassen.

Eine wahnsinnige kleine Generalsclique, die mit unserem tapferen Heere nichts gemein hat, hat in feiger Treulosigkeit diesen Mord angezettelt, gemeinsten Verrat an dem Führer und dem deutschen Volke begehend. Denn diese Schurken sind nur die Handlanger unserer Feinde, denen sie in charakterloser, feiger und falscher Klugheit dienen. In Wirklichkeit ist ihre Dummheit grenzenlos.

Sie glauben durch die Beseitigung des Führers uns von unserem harten aber unwiderruflichen Schicksalskampf befreien zu können und sehen in ihrer verblendeten angstvollen Borniertheit nicht, dass sie durch ihre verbrecherische Tat uns in entsetzliches Chaos führen und uns wehr-

los unseren Feinden ausliefern würden. Ausrottung unseres Volkes, Versklavung unserer Männer, Hunger und namenloses Elend würden die Folge sein. Eine unsagbare Unglückszeit würde unser Volk erleben, unendlich viel grausamer und schwerer als auch die härteste Zeit es sein kann, die uns unser jetziger Kampf zu bringen vermag.

Wir werden diesen Verrätern das Handwerk legen. Die Kriegsmarine steht getreu ihrem Eid in bewährter Treue zum Führer bedingungslos in ihrer Einsatz- und Kampfesbereitschaft. Sie nimmt nur von mir, dem Oberbefehlshaber der Kriegsmarine und ihren eigenen militärischen Führern Befehle entgegen, um jede Irreführung durch gefälschte Weisungen unmöglich zu machen. Sie wird rücksichtslos jeden vernichten, der sich als Verräter entpuppt. Es lebe unser Führer Adolf Hitler!

(Der Aufruf des Reichsmarschalls lag zur Zeit des Druckes noch nicht vor.)

Leaflet of Admiral Dönitz's speech after the attempted assassination of Hitler.

east flank of the Normandy bridgehead while causing as much damage as possible – thereby diverting attention from the Americans in the west, where the main breakout was planned. There were 300 casualties in the Division including 79 killed. The operation was ended by a storm but the Guards stayed in the area for a while to prevent a counter-attack.]

77)   287225 Lieut R Barer
                                               8FDS
                                               Guards Armoured Division
                                               BLA
To G's Parents
                                               Friday 28th July

Dear Mr and Mrs Briggs,
Glad to hear everything is going on all right at home. Gwen doesn't tell me much about herself, but I hope she's being sensible. Things over here are not too bad though we get a pretty fair share of excitement. The mosquitoes are perhaps our greatest bother. Some of us are quite unrecognisable. I was badly bitten at first but they seem to be leaving me alone now.

Sorry to hear about Marie and Eva. I'm afraid it looks as if M will have to be content with a simple routine job, unless she makes up her mind to improve. As you say, it's just as well about Eva too. I'm sure she would never have the strength to take on a job at the lab and you would all have a lot of trouble.

I'm afraid there's very little I can tell you about things over here. I've been to quite a few places some badly knocked about, but a few are quite untouched.

There's one thing I've found out since I've been here and that is you can believe very little the newspapers say – they love to spring on anything sensational, whether it's true or not. It's simply amazing the way false rumours get around. I think most of them are manufactured by men writing home to show off.

I've just had to censor one man's vivid description of French women snipers. I know he's not seen any and no-one in the original landings has ever seen or heard of one – despite the newspapers! That's all for now, hope you're both in good health.

Love
RB

78)   287225 Lieut R Barer
                                                 8FDS
                                                 Guards Armoured Division
                                                 BLA

                                                 Sunday 30 July

Dearest Gwen,

Got 2 of your letters dated 22nd and 26th today – they all seem to arrive piled up, but it doesn't matter as long as they come. I'm still alive and well, despite Rommel's efforts (I just heard a rumour that he's dead). You needn't worry about my not digging. My depth from the surface increases daily, though I fear my natural sloth may prove my undoing. Nevertheless I had the laugh on the others the other day. We got to a new site in the middle of a very hot day. They all started to dig but I said I'd do it later when it was cooler, a few hours later we were ordered to move again!

I saw the BMJ report on the commission on medical education. I see it's a very long thing so my original criticism may be invalid. I see <u>Oxford</u> is to <u>experiment</u> in <u>teaching</u>. This sounds fun, but I'm not so confident of getting a job there now – unless Weddell knew about it at the time. I saw the description of Cushing's library too. I don't think I'd like to do that at all – he seems to have collected umpteen editions of a few men's works – like collecting furniture instead of books. Glad you're reading Pearson. What are the four books he mentions? I think Herschel is one of them.

I'd be interested to know how M lost her 2nd job. Was it the typing again?

Do get this cystitis properly cleared up

RB

PS Always think of you when things get difficult. Won't be much longer now!

[End of July-mid-August
From the end of July to mid-August the Division took part in Operation BLUECOAT. The attack, from the Caumont area south-west of Caen, was designed to protect the American left flank. This was 'Bocage' country, an area of many small woods, fields, banks with high hedges and hills. Conditions were bad for tanks and communication. There was much

confused fighting and losses were heavy (249 killed and 1,115 wounded or missing in the Division). By 12 August, however, the Germans were attempting to retreat to a line beyond the Seine, having failed in their big counter-attack against the Americans who had broken out and were threatening the Normandy positions from the rear.]

79)

287225 Lieut R Barer
8FDS
Guards Armoured Division
BLA

Tuesday 1st August

Dearest Gwen,

No letters now for four days – but I quite expected that. Afraid I've not been able to write much either. All continues to go well – I think you can start looking for a home at Oxford. I have a number of souvenirs – German letters and newspapers which I may send if I get the chance. Found several German books too, but nothing very interesting.

Had an amusing incident the other day. Some of the lads decided they'd like some fresh milk for a change. So they went up to some cows lying in a field. They saw one which looked very fat and contented and started to prod it with a stick. The animal rose to it's feet with a surprised expression – more in sorrow than in anger and to their horror they observed it was a bull! They didn't get any milk.

Glad to say I seem to bear a charmed life. The other day, just by way of a change my truck decided to catch fire in convoy! The petrol tank was sizzling away nicely under my seat but fortunately all went well!

All my love dearest

RB

80)

278225 Lieut R Barer
8FDS
GAD
BLA

Wednesday 2nd August

Dearest Gwen,

Just received 2 letters from you and one from your Ma. All goes well still – very well indeed – I've had an interesting time with German wounded. They're a mixed lot – a few ardent Nazis but one or two really encouraging. One 19 year old boy with a chest wound and thigh wound said all the German soldiers know they are beaten but Hitler wouldn't give in. He looked forward to the end of the war and all he wanted to do was to go back to his work. His brother was killed in Russia. He said that they had entered this war enthusiastically but now all they did was to clasp their hands together (he made a gesture of sorrow). He hadn't had a wash for two weeks and seemed very appreciative of our efforts to help him. Our men are very good to wounded prisoners – they almost treat them better than our own! They always have a crowd round them offering cigarettes etc. We certainly are a soft-hearted lot. I find it very encouraging that a boy of 19, who has been brought up under Naziism should speak as he did – even their propaganda evidently had not addled his brain. I wish my German were better. He said he was one of the lucky ones – he had been called up at 18, but now most people were called up at 16.

The French peasants continue to do us simple acts of kindness. We woke up at one newly liberated farm to find the women and children going round solemnly putting bunches of flowers on all our vehicles. Sounds silly but it was very moving.

Have put my third pip up but official notification of Captaincy not through yet, so you'd better stick to Lieut on letters.

Well my dearest one, that's all for the moment. Things are going extremely well – there are definite signs of a rout developing. Our men are in great spirits while German morale is sinking steadily.

All my love

RB

81)   287225 Lieut R Barer
                                                        8FDS
                                                        GAD
                                                        BLA

                                                        Friday 4th August

Dearest Gwen,

Just got your letters of 29th and 30th, also one from your Pa. Thank him for
me would you? I don't like the way your staph is hanging on. Don't you
think a bit of sulph would help?

Everything continues well here. We have a travelling menagerie. First we
picked up a little kitten, who soon got into mischief. He put his head into a
tin of jam and got absolutely covered with it. Then he explored the cookhouse
and succeeded in getting one side of his whiskers singed off completely!

Then we got a tame albino rabbit, who resides quite happily in a box of
straw slung underneath one of the lorries. Next we got an odd looking
puppy, with a touch of dachshund about him – apparently one of the
unfortunate results of the German occupation! Our latest additions are two
ducks! We got them as a gift from a farmer whose horse had been hit by
shell splinters. We dressed the wounds with tulle gras and sulphonamide
cream and gave him 5 tabs of M&B by mouth – he lapped these up as if
they were sugar! The ducks are a bit of a problem. They're not really fat
enough for eating yet. After cooping them up in a slit trench for a bit we
drove them out for a swim in a pond. I'm afraid it doesn't look as if we'll get
them back!

Am enclosing a couple of American propaganda leaflets. Also a German
one issued after the attempt on Hitler.

All my love dearest

RB

82)

287225 Lieut R Barer
8FDS
GAD
BLA

Sunday 6th August

Dearest Gwen,

Still getting your letters regularly. I suppose you heard on the wireless that we've been going 3 weeks. I can tell you that although my address is the same I'm actually attached to one of the field ambulances. I'm glad as they're a good crowd and the work is far far more interesting. I've had some very good, if somewhat unpleasant experiences. Conditions are even more primitive than I ever imagined. Asepsis is quite out of the question. Nevertheless some extremely good work is being done by the RMOs. I suppose you have heard by now that Peter Deller had been wounded – I think he's all right. We've had quite a few French civvy casualties in – it makes things a bit complicated as some of them are women. We had a pathetic pair – brother and sister whose parents had just been killed and their farm destroyed. Some of the fighting has been incredibly bitter – prisoners say worse than in Russia. It's beyond understanding how these Hitler youths will fight on knowing that they have lost. The ordinary Germans hate these SS men. One of them called them '*schweinerei*'. He said the Germans got on quite happily with the Dutch civilians until the SS came. Then when the SS officers saw a nice house they would just turn the occupants out into the street. The Wehrmacht seems to be a remarkable mixture, Germans, Poles, Czechs, Russians, I'm sure once the SS have been cracked the rest will be easy. There are many things I'd like to tell you about the fighting but I'm afraid it'll have to wait. There's no doubt that truth is stranger than fiction as far as this business is concerned.

I'm getting on fine so far. I don't need anything so don't send me anything. I could do with a good bath – the roads are so dusty that we all look like bronze diabetics.

Sorry to hear about your Mother. I still think silboestrol worth trying as a measure of desperation.

My mother tells me we've been given £5 by some friends of ours – better late than never.

All my love dearest

RB

SAFE CONDUCT

The German soldier who carries this safe-conduct is using it as a sign of his genuine wish to give himself up. He is to be disarmed, to be well looked after, to receive food and medical attention as required, and is to be removed from the danger zone as soon as possible.

PASSIERSCHEIN

An die britischen und amerikanischen Vorposten: Der deutsche Soldat, der diesen Passierschein vorzeigt, benutzt ihn als Zeichen seines ehrlichen Willens, sich zu ergeben. Er ist zu entwaffnen. Er muss gut behandelt werden. Er hat Anspruch auf Verpflegung und, wenn nötig, ärztliche Behandlung. Er wird so bald wie möglich aus der Gefahrenzone entfernt.

Allied safe conduct leaflet for German soldiers

DIE NÜCHTERNE WAHRHEIT ÜBER KRIEGSGEFANGENSCHAFT

Deutscher Soldat: Wir versprechen Dir weder Utopien noch das Schlaraffenland, falls Du in Kriegsgefangenschaft gelangst. Aber — auf die folgenden Tatsachen kannst Du mit Bestimmtheit rechnen:

1. **„FAIRE" BEHANDLUNG,** wie es einem tapferen Gegner gebührt. Der Rang des Gefangenen wird anerkannt. Deine eigenen Kameraden sind Deine unmittelbaren Vorgesetzten.

2. **GUTE VERPFLEGUNG.** Viele Deiner Kameraden sind erstaunt, wie gut die Ernährung bei uns ist. Wir heissen mit Recht die bestgenährte Armee der Welt. (Manche Landser ziehen das deutsche Komissbrot unserem Weissbrot vor, aber über unseren Kaffee und die Zubereitung unserer Speisen hat sich noch niemand beklagt . . .)

3. **ERSTKLASSIGE LAZARETTPFLEGE** für Verwundete und Kranke. Gemäss der Genfer Konvention erhalten Gefangene dieselbe Lazarettpflege wie unsere eigenen Truppen.

4. **SCHREIBGELEGENHEIT.** Du kannst im Monat drei Briefe und vier Karten nach Hause schreiben. Die Postverbindung ist schnell und zuverlässig. Du kannst Briefe und auch Pakete erhalten.

5. **BESOLDUNG.** Gemäss der Genfer Konvention behält der Kriegsgefangene das Anrecht auf seine Entlohnung bei. Für etwaige freiwillige Arbeitsleistungen erhältst Du aber selbstverständlich Bezahlung. Für das Geld, das Du erhältst, kannst Du verschiedentliche Marketenderwaren kaufen.

6. **WEITERBILDUNG.** Sollte der Krieg noch länger dauern, dann kommst Du wahrscheinlich noch dazu, Dich an den verschiedentlichen Bildungs- und Lehrkursen zu beteiligen, die von Kriegsgefangenen selbst veranstaltet werden.

Und selbstverständlich kommst Du nach Kriegsende nach Hause

ZG.20

Allied propaganda leaflet

83)

287225 Lieut R Barer
8FDS
GAD
BLA

Wednesday 9th August

Dearest Gwen,

Got 3 of your letters today. You really needn't worry about my not taking enough safety precautions dear – my hands are all blistered from digging. I descend another few inches daily. Altogether I'm surprisingly comfortable. I'm no longer troubled by mosquitoes but the other night dozens of little frogs persisted in jumping on my head.

The second in command of the field ambulance – a very charming man told us a funny story about his son aged 11. They took their children down to some friends who own a model dairy farm in Devon. Their friends have a very buxom daughter of 20. They were all standing watching an electric milking machine at work when the boy suddenly asked 'can we do Joyce next, Daddy?'

There are a lot of things I'd like to tell you about things here but I can't just at present. Remind me to tell you a very funny story about a Sherman tank when I get back.

Sorry to hear about your Ma [*going downhill rapidly*]. I think there's a reasonable chance that I may be back in England in a couple of months and we could all meet then. It's rather an awkward journey to Oxford for your Ma just now. Glad to hear Janet's in Devon. Hope our room doesn't get messed up – all our valuable books too!

Well dear, take care of yourself.

All my love dear one

RB

84)

287225 Lieut R Barer
8FDS
GAD
BLA

Friday 11th August

Dearest Gwen,

So glad to hear about Max. He won't answer your letters but he'll go miles to see you. Anyhow I'm glad he was firm about your cystitis. I know it's not serious but it <u>must</u> be completely eradicated – especially if RG's on the way. I hope he is but you mustn't be disappointed dear if nothing happens – being ill in bed may account for it. I think it's a good idea about stilboestrol too [*for my Mother – some evidence had been found that it had beneficial effects on breast carcinoma*]. It can't do any harm – you can easily stop it at the first sign – and it may possibly do a lot of good. I thought Max would like the books. We must encourage him to go in for book-collecting instead of stamps. He'd probably go in for it on a more lavish scale than we could!

How long do you think I should write to Stanborough's? I don't want any of my letters to get lost. Wouldn't it be better to continue sending them home?

For heaven's sake don't worry about finances. My pay should have gone up by now and in any case I haven't spent a penny since I came over here – we should have tons. Anyhow I think the Ministry will go on paying you. Don't withdraw NSC unless absolutely desperate.

I've seen the BMJ's report on the questionnaire. It's not much use is it? – only 50% of doctors replied.

Did you read Adrians' lecture on cerebral localisation? I thought it was rather good. We'll have to read up some of his references.

Well dear, here's hoping you're out of Stanborough's soon [*actually I had to rest in bed for 4 months*]. Try and get out in the sun and fresh air and keep up Keplers etc.

All my love dearest

RB

85)
287225 Lieut R Barer
8FDS
GAD
BLA

Sunday 13th August

Dearest Gwen,

Just got your letter of Tuesday, afraid I can't tell you very much of interest at present. Now that I've dealt with several hundred casualties, British and German, I think there's no doubt that the RAMC is doing a magnificent job in the forward areas, under very difficult conditions. Despite everything there must be many thousands of people who owe their lives to their initial treatment. It's quite pathetic how grateful they are too. Time and again they make remarks like 'Thank God we've got such a medical service'. I think the treatment a man gets in the first few hours after wounding is most important. Admittedly it's mostly first aid – an occasional ligature of an artery or emergency amputation with no attempt at sterility is the most one can do. Nevertheless it's impossible to over-emphasise the importance of making the man comfortable and immobilising his injury so that he can stand the journey back to the CCS, usually 10 to 25 miles away across bad roads. Plasma too is very useful. It's amazing how they perk up after a couple of bottles. Intravenous morphia is a godsend. I had to dress a German tank man who had a compound femur and burns of hands and face. He had been lying in the field for 30 hours and was heavily infected. A shot of morphia allowed me to dress a most filthy burn quite painlessly. He was most grateful. One sees the most frightful wounds – a travesty of anatomy. One of the most remarkable and fortunate was a man brought in on his face with a wound in his back. He had a hole about 6" square. Half his scapula and a couple of ribs were blown away. At the bottom of the hole I saw what looked like muscle but when I cleaned it up it moved up and down with respiration. I was, in fact, gazing at the parietal pleura, with the lung moving up and down inside, apparently unharmed! Some of the RMOs are doing very good work. Quite often we don't bother to redress the man it's done so well. Most of the wounded are terribly good. They hardly ever complain. I think most of them are so glad to be still alive they don't worry about anything else.

Well I think I've seen all I want to see by now and a good deal I didn't want to see, so the sooner it's over the better.

I don't think it will last long but these SS people are beyond belief. I wish we could turn their fanaticism to more useful channels – I think perhaps we may.

All my love dearest

RB

86)

287225 Lieut R Barer
8FDS
GAD
BLA

Monday 14th August

Dearest Gwen,

I suppose you'll be listening to the news with bated breath. It certainly doesn't look as though I'll have to stay here over winter, does it? So you'll have to hurry up and get well. Then we'll go out and celebrate by buying up all the book shops in London!

I don't think I've ever told you about Bayeux and Caen. I've visited both and they're very different. Bayeux has been exceedingly fortunate and is almost undamaged. The cathedral is very beautiful and is intact. They have removed the famous tapestry but have a replica there. Caen on the other hand is even worse than the newspaper descriptions. The destruction is terrible and the town is virtually a heap of rubble. Nevertheless a few hardy French civilians hang on and manage to keep cheerful despite everything. It was quite a big place, bigger than Watford. Bayeux is the centre of the camembert cheese industry. We used to get a lot of the stuff but now we're forbidden to buy it as it's wanted for civilians. The French were very bitter about it as the Germans forced them to make such a lot of cheese that the quality went down.

Well all my love dearest, I've no real news at present.

RB

87)   287225 Lieut R Barer
                                                 8FDS
                                                 GAD
                                                 BLA

                                                 Tuesday 15th August

Dearest Gwen,

Just got your letters of 11th and 12th. Afraid I can't answer all your questions re: FDS for military reasons. However everyone at FDS is very well and very safe. The FA crowd is much nicer. They are mostly London qualified. The CO is a very good gynaecologist (MRCOG) and a charming man. I've been mostly at the ADS but I've had one or two hectic periods at a CCP. Heard a good story about one of the MOs who's now back in England wounded. He's the one I told you about who got drunk and fell asleep on the road and then walked in the wrong direction. When he was a student he was up in a small town in Scotland at a pub one night when he wanted to empty his bladder. He went outside but couldn't find anywhere so just did it in the yard. At that moment he was pounced on by a policeman. Now it so happened that this yard was the meeting place of 3 Scots counties, so the charge appeared formidable – 'committing a nuisance in that he did urinate in the 3 counties of X, Y & Z'! Judging by the fuss he thought he would get at least 5 years but the magistrate said he didn't want to blight his medical career and fined him 5/-.

I've seen Alderson once since the birth – it was about 3 weeks overdue and she had to have pitocin. Interested to see the cutting about Kisch, but I'm afraid it looks as though the only people to reap the benefit will be the Arabs. I think the Palestine problem will have to be settled once and for all one way or the other at the Peace Conference. Whatever the Arabs may have done 25 years ago I don't think their contribution (?) has been very great this time.

All my love

RB

[16-27 August
The Division rested and refitted. General Patton reached the Seine on 19 August, cutting off Normandy from Paris, which was entered on the 24th.]

88)
287225 Lieut R Barer
8FDS
GAD
BLA

Saturday 19th August

Dearest Gwen,

No letter for a day or two, so I'll just write a few lines to let you know I'm all right. As you probably know things have gone very well indeed and it doesn't look as though the war can possibly last more than a few more weeks.

I had to take a case for a PM to a base hospital during the recent quiet spell and found the pathologist had done the anaerobes course at Watford. His name is Gillespie and he was at Watford last X-mas. He remembered you. Definition of bacteriology by a Guy's surgeon 'a long tube with a little bug at one end and a silly bugger at the other'.

Interesting psychological point – at an exam students were asked to give the relations of the vagina. Analysis of the papers showed that all the men described it as running upwards and backwards, all the women as running downwards and forwards!

Saw Lorna and Stella's paper in the BMJ. Quite interesting but it seems a long way from reality out here.

All my love dearest

RB

89)
287225 Lieut R Barer
8FDS
GAD
BLA

Sunday 20th August

Dearest Gwen,

Have just got your letter with the good news and I needn't tell you how glad I am darling. I don't think there's any need to tell anyone just yet. I think there's very little doubt I'll be back in time. The war will certainly be over very soon, it's only a question of how long they're going to keep us in the army of occupation.

Thank Kenneth for his love, you can reassure him that I'm probably doing more good in a FA than in a hospital – half of them seem to do nothing at all except enjoy themselves.

What's the matter with Matthews? It sounds rather like spontaneous hypoglycaemia. I thought he had TB.

I went and saw George Formby during a recent quiet spell. He was quite good and went on singing his songs for hours. We could certainly do with some more relaxation like that. There's a good story going around about the German commander at St Malo. The telephone had been left intact and the Yanks were in direct communication with him. They asked him to surrender but he refused saying that a huge German army was coming to relieve him. They then offered him a safe conduct to go up in a plane anywhere he wanted to look for his army. They also said he could spend a couple of hours with his lady friend who they knew lived nearby. He accepted the offer, couldn't find the army and surrendered.

Well dear, that's all for now. Look after yourself.

All my love my dearest wife

RB

90)   287225 Lieut R Barer
                                               128 Field Ambulance
                                               BLA

                                               Tuesday 22nd August

Dearest Gwen,

Just got your letter of the 17th. As you see, you can now write to me at the 128 Field Ambulance – there'll be less delay. I'm not going back to the FDS if I can avoid it though I'm not officially transferred. I met Colyer the other day and told him his wife was very worried. He says he didn't think it could have been a fortnight – more like 10 days! So you see not everyone writes to their wives as often as I do. Oh dear! So you've told Mrs Bound. I expect it's all over the hospital by now and Sister Billings [*UCH obstetric sister!*] will come rushing up to put you on her books! I expect Mrs S has already congratulated you. You women can't keep secrets can you? Which

Ruth were you referring to, Kemp or Colyer? I suppose the latter. It's just as well really. Don't send me any papers as we get them flown over here and usually delivered the next day or day after. Incidentally I see that Sir Henry Wood died in Hitchin Hospital. I wonder if Max had anything to do with it? He died of acute jaundice, carcinoma I suppose – see if you can find out from Max.

Well look after yourself dear and take <u>plenty</u> of vitamins.

All my love dearest

RB

91)

287225 Lieut R Barer
128 Field Ambulance
BLA

Wednesday 23rd August

Dearest Gwen,

No letters today, but hope the new address will speed things up. Things are much the same here, still going well, with lots of rumours flying about. I'm afraid there's no real news. I had a very mild bout of the gastroenteritis flying about here but am perfectly all right now. I think a good deal of it is due to the local cider which is very sour and strong. I'm going to avoid it in future. We've been sampling some of the local wines too. The General himself brought us a couple of bottles as a mark of his appreciation. It appears that the CCSs and base hospitals have been sending back specially good reports on the way our patients have been arriving. It certainly is very important to fix up a really good splint or plaster as the journey back of 20 miles or so over bad roads to the CCS would be very shocking to a man with a fracture.

Psychological cases – which are labelled 'exhaustion' – are very common in battle. I think in most cases the cause is seeing one's pals blown up. One man we had was in a very bad way – so terrified that he tried to climb up the chimney of a farm house – like a hysterical dog. Sometimes a man will go on fighting all day under appalling conditions and then break down during a quiet period.

There have been many fantastic acts of bravery but I'm afraid few of them will be rewarded. One of the tank RMOs has got the MC. I think they should all get it. Their difficulties have been enormous at times.

All my love dearest

RB

92)

287225 Lieut R Barer
128 Field Ambulance
BLA

Friday 24th August

Dearest Gwen,

I've only just received your letter and bank statement posted on the 16th! I'm glad they've started paying the allowance at last. It'll come in useful. Still, as you say, we still have £80 and next month's pay (captain's I hope) is due in a week, making it well over £100. Have you heard whether your pay goes on while you're ill. I think it does. What do you think of the news? I'm very glad the French are playing such a big part in their own liberation. They are showing up remarkably well. Passing through a ruined township the other day we were inundated with gifts – apples, cider etc. although the people seemed in none too good a state of nutrition themselves.

I think you'll like *Flatland*. It's one of the best books for explaining the idea of dimensions and is an excellent introduction to Einstein.

You don't tell me why they're still keeping you in hospital. Have you still got a temp or isn't the urine clear yet? Give my regards to your parents.

All my love dearest

PS We're in the midst of our first Maternity case!

93)   287225 Lieut R Barer
                                                   128 Field Ambulance
                                                   BLA

                                                   Monday 28th August

Dearest Gwen,

Just got one of your letters written on the 18th – the one with the news about
Janet. The post is rather chaotic as I've had several later ones before that . . .
What are they going to call this one? Does she say if David or Huxley are
over here? – I might be able to meet them.

By the way I hope you told Max about RG?

While I remember, when the time comes, will you combine our two
Lewis' subscriptions – there's no point having two – it's cheaper for one big
one. Max shares mine at the moment. I think he has about 3 vols and I have
3. I don't know if he wants a separate sub or if he wants to continue sharing.
I think you and I could manage on about 6 books between us.

All my love dearest

RB

94)   287225 Lieut R Barer
                                                   128 Field Ambulance
                                                   BLA

                                                   Tuesday 29th August

Dearest Gwen,

Hope you're out of hospital by now. Have you had any sulphonamide?
Don't refuse it if it's necessary – you've been ill a month as it is. <u>Please</u> let
me know the exact state of affairs.

Afraid there's no real news. However I'd better warn you that the post
may be delayed during the next few days, so don't get alarmed. Please let
my Mother know if there's a long delay.

There are some bright sparks in this unit. One man was asked how he
would treat a man who had had his arm blown off. He replied without
hesitation 'I'd dip ee in boiling vinegar'. The colonel's eyes lit up 'Fine!
You're just the man we've been looking for to dig the latrines.' I can't really

decide about Jean or Janet. Let's wait till I'm home before we decide. I think RG is quite definite – I hope they don't both come at once.

How are things at home? Is your Ma having stilboestrol? I've still not heard from my Ma.

All my love dearest. I think of you always whatever happens.

RB

[*29 August – 3 September 1944*
The Division swept from the Seine to Brussels, meeting jubilant crowds all along the way. Meanwhile the Canadians moved up the Channel coast and the Americans moved rapidly through Central France.
The Guards Armoured Division met pockets of resistance but casualties were relatively light. On the last day, they were ordered to bypass the enemy and covered 65 miles, meeting an overwhelming reception in Brussels.]

CHAPTER V

Breakout from Normandy, flight across northern France,
liberation of Brussels, encounter with German doctors in
military hospital in Brussels, battle for Nijmegen bridge
(a 'Bridge too Far')

95)

287225 Lieut R Barer
128 Field Ambulance
BLA

? 1st September

Dearest Gwen,
No time to write. Everything going splendidly. The final phase I think and
then Oxford!

All my love

RB

[*The rapid eastward advance had begun.*]

96)

287225 Capt R Barer
128 Field Ambulance
BLA

Saturday 2nd September

Dear M.I.L.,
I hear from Gwen that you've been misbehaving again so I'll just drop you a
line to cheer you up. The news really is cheering isn't it and the real situation
is even more cheering than the BBC? It doesn't look as though we'll be

away much longer. Our welcome has been tremendous and the French have been terrific. It's a scream to see them standing at the roadside cheering themselves hoarse and waving jugs of cider around. The children are having a terrific time. Whenever we stop a horde of them clamber on the vehicles yelling '*cigarette pour Papa; chocolat, bons-bons*'. It's quite common to see little urchins of 4 or 5 standing at the roadside calmly smoking their '*cigarette pour Papa*'.

Well I do hope you'll be up and about soon. Give my regards to Mr B.

Your loving S.I.L.

Robert

97)   287225 Capt R Barer
                                               128 Field Ambulance
                                               BLA

                                               ? 2nd September

Dearest Gwen,

My hands are so tired from waving and warding off kisses (at least some kisses) that I can hardly write. The most amazing things have been happening in the last few days and I think the next few days will be even more amazing. There's no doubt that the Germans are just about finished. The disorganisation and chaos is fantastic. The FFI are having the time of their lives. At one place we passed through they had herded over 300 prisoners into a local cinema. I spoke to some of them – many were men in their 40's – veterans of the last war. They seemed glad to be out of it.

Just got a pile of your letters at last. Afraid I can't understand my mother's remarks either – she occasionally leaves words out unintentionally and makes things sound funny.

Re: the accumulator, the size merely determines the capacity, not the voltage i.e. the bigger the cell the longer it will last (this is usually written on the label as so many amp-hours). The voltage is determined by the number of cells in series.

Re: the address, it doesn't really matter if you put GAD or not, but it's not usual to put the Div in units more forward than brigade level.

A horrible thought just struck me! Did you tell my Ma when RG was coming? She doesn't by any chance think that's why you're in hospital?!!

Well dear, I've always warned you, don't be alarmed by delay in letters. It's remarkably good that we get any at all under present conditions.

All my love

RB

PS Am writing to your Ma.

98)
                                      287225 Capt R Barer
                                        128 Field Ambulance
                                        BLA

                                        Wednesday 6th September

Dearest Gwen,

At last I can write you again. I'm terribly sorry about the gap but I will be able to explain the reason for it later. I've just had the most remarkable 3 days of my life. I shall never forget them. I certainly never expected to do anything like it. It has been quite bizarre. I hope to be able to tell you about it in a few days. All I can tell you now is that I have a beautiful medical book with autographs which I shall treasure as a souvenir and that you and I are going to do a lot of visiting of continental Universities after the war!

At long last I've got 2 of your letters written Aug 30th and 31st. It's amazing that we get any at all under present conditions, so don't worry even if there's a fortnight's delay. Very often it's impossible to send a letter.

Well dear, that's all for now. Don't worry, it will soon be over.

All my love darling

RB

99)

287225 Capt R Barer
128 Field Ambulance
BLA

Friday 8th September

Dearest Gwen,

Just got 4 of your letters, including two about Weddell. Well, it certainly does look good, doesn't it? I'll write to him right away. It looks as though my people will have to look round Oxford for a house. I do hope the wretched Germans give up soon. I don't see what hope they have. The slaughter is simply appalling and we're getting more German wounded than British.

Well, I suppose you heard about the GAD in Brussels. I can now tell you roughly what a remarkable adventure I had there. I was in the first column to enter and it fell to me to take over a German hospital there. I'll tell you more about it later, but the staff was composed of the greatest surgeons in Germany and several eminent Physiologists, working on shock. For three days I was the only British MO in Brussels and had to look after the interests of all our wounded. When I left they presented me with a beautiful book containing the results of their work and researches signed by the chief Surgeon and the head Physiologist. More details about this later. As you can imagine, I found the racial side highly entertaining, but I left with no doubt at all as to the attitude of German intellectuals on that question!

Well, so you've heard Brussels went mad. I've never seen anything like it. I could start a cosmetics shop with the amount I scraped off my face! I think half the men in the division want to go and live there after the war! I got mobbed on one occasion and had to have my photo taken surrounded by bouquets. I hope it gets home.

Well dear, Germany itself is now in danger. I hope they see sense and try to save what's left – not much, judging by the doctor's accounts of our bombing.

Love

RB

Souvenir cards from the liberation of Brussels

100)   287225 Capt R Barer
                                                 128 Field Ambulance
                                                 BLA

                                                 Monday 11th September

Dearest Gwen,

Another batch of your letters has arrived at last. I'm terribly sorry to hear about your Ma. Do you think I ought to write to your Pa? Gough (GP) seems to have acted very foolishly, but perhaps it is all for the best after all. I'm glad Max is doing his bit – he's like that. He'll never dream of answering a letter, but will go to no end of trouble in other directions – he's not written to me yet!

I think it's quite safe to hang on a month or two longer before you get antenatal supervision. It would be awkward to have to change if we went to Oxford. The prospects look pretty good don't they? I've already applied to Weddell.

Re: Mail. I'm afraid it's no use sending me postcards. The trouble is not so much finding the time to write as that we move so fast that we outstrip all postal services and have to wait a few days until mail can be collected. So remember if you don't get my letters that things are going well militarily. I don't know what Colyer meant about being back with us. He's never been with this field ambulance at all. I think you must have got it wrong.

Our welcome continues to be delirious. The people just can't do enough for us. The latest is that we've been so loaded up with beautiful tomatoes that we simply can't turn round without sitting on one! At one place one lady insisted on having all the officers in to meals, and she certainly was a superb cook!

Afraid I had no time to hunt for books in Brussels as I was so busy running the German hospital.

All my love dearest Gwen

RB

[*My mother was going downhill rapidly. My brother-in-law Max took my Father to see our Doctor – a Dr Gough, who simply said, 'Well she's got advanced cancer and there's nothing we can do' – Max brought my poor Father to see me, lying in bed. He was in a terrible state – it was heart-breaking and I could do nothing to comfort him.*]

101)

287225 Capt R Barer
128 Field Ambulance
BLA

Thursday 14th September

Dearest Gwen,
Just got another batch of your letters, the most recent written on Sunday 9th, so the post isn't too bad.

Caught a glimpse of Brian Warren on the road. He looks very fit and seems to have put on weight. Haven't seen Colyer recently. Afraid the chances of getting any French books are almost nil now. I found out where to go in Brussels but was so busy – never went to bed before 4 a.m. – that I never got a chance to go there.

By the way dear, I wonder if you'd mind dropping a note to Edith Bülbring at Oxford, telling her that Professor Duisberg is safe and well and sends her his regards. You can explain how I met him. He was in charge of the shock team. I think you'll understand.

Oh dear, I wish I could do something about your Mother. Afraid it looks as if I shall be too late. Hope Max is helping.

All my love dearest,

RB

102)

287225 Capt R Barer
128 Field Ambulance
BLA

[*To my Mother, dying of cancer*]   Thursday 14th September

Dear Mother,
So they've put you in Stanboroughs with Gwenda? Well that will be nice, to

133

be able to see each other, won't it? You'll get better attention there too, and will be up and about in no time now.

Hope you've got a wireless in your room and can listen to the news. It's been very good lately hasn't it? I had a marvellous time in Brussels where I took over a big German military hospital, complete with the staff of famous surgeons.

Well, we shall soon be in Germany now and after that we shan't waste any time coming home!

Your loving son-in-law

Robert

[*4-14 September*
The 11th Armoured Division had secured the port of Antwerp but only Dieppe among the Channel Ports was as yet in operation and almost all supplies had to come from Normandy. The lines of communication were now over 300 miles long. This, combined with a remarkable rallying effort by the Germans, slowed down the advance drastically. The Guards Armoured Division moved up to the Escaut canal, taking the bridge at De Groot Barrier in a surprise attack; fighting during these days was hard and there were some 600 casualties.]

103)
                                        287225 Capt R Barer
                                        128 Field Ambulance
                                        BLA

                                        Saturday 16th September

Dearest Gwen,
Just got a couple of your letters written 12th and 13th. Post is quite good but don't be surprised if at any time you get more gaps. Had a bit of luck the other day. Had to go back to Brussels for a couple of hours and spent some time looking round the bookshops. There are a large number of very good new and second hand bookshops there but unfortunately owing to wartime difficulties there wasn't much good second hand stuff. There has been a good complete edition of Claude Bernard's *Introduction to the Study of*

Medicine but it's very scarce and they wanted 15/- for it. It'll be much cheaper after the war. They also had all the collected works of Pasteur, but again expensive. I didn't buy anything in the end but there will be quite a lot of French stuff worth reading after the war. With regard to nutrition in Belgium, I must admit that at first sight it looked much better than I expected. However if you talk to children of apparently 13 or 14, they tell you that they are actually 16. It is they who have suffered most; they are grossly stunted in growth. This state of affairs is very widespread and not easily spotted, so they appear to be quite normal children of 13. Dieting hasn't hit the adults quite so much but everyone says they have lost weight. The incidence of TB has increased enormously.

The restaurants create a false impression. For about 15/- one could get a reasonable meal. Fortunately restaurants have now been put out of bounds for soldiers. I got invited to one man's home in Brussels and saw how they really fed. They had vegetable soup, followed by boiled potato and carrots with a little bacon fat – no meat. For all that it was so deliciously cooked that I wouldn't have swapped it for a steak! I told them to come over and teach you how to cook!

Things like white bread, milk and butter are a fabulous price – only the well to do can afford them. Remember this when you read some ill-informed drivel by some correspondent who only eats in restaurants – at his newspaper's expense!

There is malnutrition but it's not obvious. On the whole it's true to say it's less than I expected and once supplies arrive things should be all right. It's quite obvious we're not going to need those elaborate teams or relief workers – the people can look after themselves, given the food. Incidentally the German doctors said the food was better in Belgium than in Germany.

Afraid I can't give you details of my movements or unit at present. Continue to write to the same address. Anyhow I certainly seem to have got all the plums so far and more are on the way! It's been even more interesting than I expected but all the same I shan't be sorry when it's over.

All my love dearest

RB

104)
287225 Capt R Barer
128 Field Ambulance
BLA

Thursday 21st September

Dearest Gwen,

At long last I can write a few lines, but when it will get to you I don't know. I think you can guess the reason for the delay, though I suppose it's no use asking you not to worry. Nevertheless I'm very fit and having a simply marvellous time – perhaps the most interesting yet. At the moment I'm attached to the other FA, in the division, but you can continue to write to the above address.

My little adventure in Brussels seems to have brought me in a lot of interesting work. They seem to think I can speak any language!

Afraid I've got no mail for over a week so don't know how things are at home. <u>Please</u> write to my Ma, I've no time.

All my love dearest, in haste

RB

105)
287225 Capt R Barer
128 Field Ambulance
BLA

Friday 22nd September

Dearest Gwen,

There may be another chance of mail today – hope it gets through all right, but don't worry if there are more gaps. Afraid there's not much I can tell you at the moment except that I'm having a first class time. It's certainly exciting to be able to take part in some of the most remarkable military feats in history – exactly how remarkable you will no doubt learn later on. The division has certainly lived up to expectations – and much more. It's fun being with the other FA. They're a good crowd and it's excellent experience. I think I must have had the widest experience of any MO in the division. At the moment I'm doing rather more administrative than medical work – it's much more interesting in many ways and I'm moving in high circles.

I saw in the *Lancet* that it's intended to run Oxford in order to produce teachers, investigators and consultants, so any job there would be very interesting. We certainly are very lucky and I hope it comes off.

One of the MOs in this unit has been awarded the MC for getting casualties back from a battalion which had been cut off. Two drivers got the MM. I had to go up to Brian Warren's RAP the other day. He was in great form. Let me know how your mother is. I've written to her and your Pa.

All my love dearest

RB

[*21 September – 6 October*
The Guards Armoured Division were involved in 'Market Garden' – the rapid thrust to take the three Rhine bridges and enter Germany itself. The Guards failed to reach Arnhem bridge ('A bridge too far') and the 1st Airborne Division which had landed there. Twice, the Guards' main supply route to the south had been cut off. Nevertheless, the efforts of the Household Cavalry had enabled the survivors of the airborne troops to be evacuated. A large part of Holland had been freed and the Nijmegen bridge proved valuable in later Rhineland battles.]

106)

287225 Capt R Barer
128 Field Ambulance
BLA

Saturday 23rd September

Dearest Gwen,
Just got a pile of your letters through at last. Hope some of mine are trickling through.

I'm glad you've told me the truth. I won't worry as I know you're in good hands and are being sensible about it. If Morland thinks you should give up your job until after RG, you must take his advice. I know it's a great pity but perhaps in the circumstances it's a convenient way of leaving Miles – you needn't feel you've let him down. There are lots of ways you can fill in your time while resting. You can make a start on some of our books – it'll be really useful at Oxford to know where to find things. You can also read some good novels, Dickens etc. A bit of physiology or experimental anatomy revision would also be useful.

Monty has once more affirmed that the war will be over this year. If possible, in the circumstances I shall apply for compassionate leave as soon as this business is over. I'm afraid it's impossible at the moment.

The chief of the Brussels hospital was Prof. Wachsmuth, chief consultant surgeon to the German army. He succeeded Sauerbach in the job. The physiologist in charge of the shock team was Prof. Duisberg.

All my love dearest

RB

107)

287225 Capt R Barer
128 Field Ambulance
BLA

Saturday 30th September

Dearest Gwen,
Still no letters but am expecting some later today.

Had a surprise yesterday. I was standing around outside the CCS when a jeep drove up and a voice yelled my name. It was none other than Ken Green. He's been over here for about a month but hasn't been in action yet. He seems to have lost contact with most of his old pals. By the way Ben Bowen is married to the Seaton girl isn't he? He told me that Peter Deller got a subphrenic abscess as a result of his wound and now had a few adhesions.

Got letters from your Pa and Ma. It's very difficult knowing how to write under the circumstances.

We've been living on captured German rations for the last few days. Some of it is very good. The Germans have left masses of stuff behind. In one place I saw a complete trainload of hospital equipment – beds, lockers, an operating theatre lamp complete with power supply, thousands of bottles, bedpans, blankets etc.

By the way did I tell you I was offered a Leitz microscope in Brussels? It was probably worth £150 but it's a court martial offence to take such things.

All my love dearest. Longing to hold you
RB

[*6 October – 12 November*
The Division was moved south of Nijmegen and was refitted. Further
large-scale operations could not be undertaken until the port of Antwerp
was in working order. The Irish and Welsh Guards did spells defending the
road and rail bridges at Nijmegen, under heavy shelling.]

108) *OPENED BY CENSOR*   287225 Capt R Barer RAMC
                                                         8FDS
                                                         GAD
                                                         BLA

                                                         Friday 6th October

Dearest Gwen,
Just got 3 of your letters, written 23, 27 and 28 September. They're arriving
regularly now but don't be surprised if there's another gap soon.
    You'll be glad to hear that I managed to see Ridley. I found him after a lot
of trouble and then we went off to an Officers' club in a nearby town. There
we met Shipman who's also in an AA unit. It was quite bizarre sitting and
having tea and pastries in a luxurious lounge (still decorated with swastikas
and murals depicting German victories) with the noise of bombs and shells
going on outside. Ridley is very fit but rather bored. He has almost nothing
to do in the way of dealing with casualties. His one bit of excitement came
some time ago when a Tiger tank ran right over his slit trench! Like you he's
had several letters from Ross (Eric) but no reply to any letter he's sent.
Shipman too has had very little to do. There's no doubt that I've come off
best in every way so far. S said he met Charles Harris, who was an RMO
back in Normandy. By the way S's wife had a miscarriage – don't you do
anything silly like that.
    That's all for now, dear. Don't <u>send</u> me <u>anything</u> without asking first.
There's nothing I need at present – I can always get things over here.
    Don't worry if letters are delayed.

    All my love dearest one

    RB

GUARDS ARMOURED DIVISION

PROWESS ON WESTERN FRONT

From Our Special Correspondent, NIJMEGEN SALIENT, Oct 7

The Guards Armoured Division has proved itself one of the most formidable fighting formations ever to leave England. Goebbels has labelled the **Division** "Montgomery's murderers" and "Churchill's butchers," but the Guards consider that such abuse from such a source is high tribute to their fighting capacity.

I saw a good deal of the Guards Armoured Division in the months when the allies were preparing to break out from the Normandy bridgehead. Those were particularly difficult months for armoured formations. The country was unfriendly to tanks, and the infantry had to bear the chief brunt of the operations. But the Guards were unhappy about it. They knew the Guards traditions as infantry and old-fashioned cavalry were superb, but they felt that they still had spurs to win as armoured fighters. More than one Guards Armoured Division officer or man asked me in those trying days when they were itching for a chance really to test their quality : "What are other people saying about us ? Do they think we are putting up a good show?" They need not ask those questions now. Their record in the bridgehead was good; since the closing of the Falaise gap and the beginning of the Second Army's northward thrust across the Seine through Belgium into Holland it has been magnificent.

490 MILES IN 25 DAYS

The Guards were ordered on August 27 to move forward from the Falaise region across the Seine and push on as fast as possible. They met with some stiff fighting and minor skirmishing on the way, but by September 20 they were in the Nijmegen area – 490 miles in 25 days. On the night of August 30/31 they advanced 89 miles from the Seine to the Somme. It was the longest advance that any division of any nation has ever made in military history. Four days later the Guards broke their own records. They advanced 93 miles from Douai to Brussels on September 3 – and though enemy opposition on that day was not resolute anywhere, the advance was certainly not unopposed. They had to halt at several points to clean up determined enemy pockets which tried to hinder them.

It was a great moment for the commander, Major-General Alan Adair, when the Guards reached Arras. It was at Arras in the last war that he won the Military Cross while serving as a junior officer with the Grenadiers: and it was a great moment for the Irish Guards when they were chosen to capture Douai. There the Germans in 1940 cut up the Irish Guards in a furious engagement. Now the tables were turned.

The Guards were ecstatically welcomed when they entered Brussels on the night of September 3. In fact the fervour of the welcome actually delayed the troops in completing their occupation of the city. General Adair called up his men by wireless. "Hello, have you reached your objective yet ?" "No," came back the reply. "What is the trouble?" the General asked, "Are you meeting opposition?" "Yes, the population," answered the harassed unit commander. A little later he came through to the general by wireless: "Hello," he said, "Thank God its raining. We are moving forward to our objective now."

The Guards courageous part in the capture of the vital Nijmegen bridge in cooperation with American airborne troops is a matter of history. A curious story about one of their armoured-car squadrons from the Household Cavalry at about the same time is less widely known. The armoured-cars were patrolling when they saw a small ship with four barges in tow. The armoured-cars manoeuvred into position, opened fire, and sank three barges and damaged the ship. They signalled the news to divisional headquarters which replied: "Congratulations. Brilliant naval action. Splice the main brace."

(From The Times, Monday, October 9 1944)

Report by The Times *Special Correspondent*

'NAVAL ENGAGEMENT'

'Congratulations. Brilliant naval action. Splice the main brace.' Such was the message flashed by Divisional Headquarters to a squadron of the Brigade of Guards after an armoured car patrol of the Household Cavalry had sunk at Nijmegen Bridge three of a string of four enemy barges. *(vide The Times, October 9th, 1944.)*

It has been confirmed that the armoured cars were DAIMLER.

THE DAIMLER COMPANY LIMITED · LONDON AND COVENTRY

13

Mount Pleasant, W.C.1. and published by them weekly, with one additional et. London, E.C.4.—WEDNESDAY, December 27, 1944.

Naval Engagement

109)   287225 Capt R Barer RAMC
                                        c/o 19 Guards Light Field Ambulance
                                        Guards Armoured Division
                                        BLA

                                        Monday 9th October

Dearest Gwen,

Just got your letter of last Thursday. I'm afraid your next letter will bring the
sad news. There's nothing much I can say darling – I only wish I could be
there to help you. At least I'm glad she was sufficiently conscious to realise
and could speak to you – It must have been some slight comfort to your
Father. Don't know what to write to your Father – anything I say will
probably only add to his grief. It is a shame that it happened so soon –
another few months might have made a big difference. What plans have you
for yourself and Dad? Afraid I can't make any very helpful suggestions at
present. I do want you to rest dear, but I think your Pa should have
something to occupy his mind lest he should brood.

   All my love dearest – I do hope everything works out all right.

   RB

110)   287225 Capt R Barer RAMC
                                        19 Guards Light Field Ambulance
                                        Guards Armoured Division
                                        BLA

                                        Thursday 12 October

Dearest Gwen,

Post is definitely improving now – got your letter written on Sunday today.

   I'm not so sure about your idea of asking my people to stay at Watford. It
would mean a big upheaval for them – all their stuff is at Oxford now and it
would be difficult to shift. They're very well dug in at Oxford and it's useful
to have some contact there. There are other reasons too which would make
such an arrangement rather difficult. At the same time I think you should try
and hang on to your house as houses may be very difficult to get after the
war. Is there any chance of your Pa getting anything to fill in his time? – you
mustn't let him brood. I think a short holiday might do him good. Is there

anyone he'd like to stay with? By the way I hope you reassured him that we had no intention of 'turning him out'!

I'm sure my ma won't mind your asking her if she'd like those clothes. She'll probably say she has all she wants already – it's very difficult to get her to accept anything but she certainly won't feel insulted.

Afraid there's no real news at present, darling. What do you think of the enclosed advert? How would you like a 'first class consummation' right now?

ADVERT ENCLOSED:

GREAT DANCING 'ELYSEE'
15 Place Pontanas (1st storey)

FIRST CLASS CONSUMMATIONS

G BAY'S Dance ensemble
animation

I've had a dreadful couple of nights dealing with rats. First one ran across my outstretched arm, then one ran right across my bed and finally, just as I was dozing off one landed slap on my neck! I've now got to the stage of dreaming about them.

I've been trying out the waistcoat today, in a windy jeep and it's absolutely wind-proof.

All my love dearest

RB

PS Sorry to be always turning your ideas down. It's just possible my people might like it, but on the whole all things considered, I doubt it. There's no harm in asking but don't be hurt if they refuse and don't press them.

[*My Mother died on 6 October. I was allowed out of hospital to stay with my Father 1 week but could not attend the funeral. Miss Ramsay and relatives helped him.*]

111)
                                    287225 Capt R Barer RAMC
                                    19 Guards Light Field Ambulance
                                    Guards Armoured Division
                                    BLA

                                    Saturday 14th October

Dearest Gwen,

Just got your letter written on Monday 9th. Hope your Father is settling down by now. Afraid I haven't been able to think of any plans for him. I hope he won't be in any hurry to sell the house. After all Oxford isn't a 100% certain by any means and if I have to get a job in London the housing problem may be very serious.

I'm afraid you've got hold of the wrong end of the stick about me – too much idle speculation. There is no special 'job' – at least it's not part of the ordinary RAMC organisation. The result is I've had some interesting work in the way of taking over buildings suitable for oncoming medical units. Sometimes I stay behind with the wounded and hand over to the people coming up. Sometimes I go ahead and spy out the facilities. It's very interesting as no two situations are the same. Once these things are settled I go back to the Field Ambulance and work as an MO. As you can imagine the work is most interesting during a rapid advance, when everything's in a state of flux. Holland seems to be well provided with buildings suitable for hospitals etc. One place I saw was a huge Jesuit seminary (there are dozens of these – most beautiful and modern – I don't know where they get the money!) which the Germans used as a 'baby farm' for the children of their Nordic heroes. There were hundreds of prams in the place – I wish I could have taken one.

I've just moved into a sort of barn attached to a farmhouse. It's most embarrassing as there's a WC in one corner of the place with no sort of screen. The female members of the family just come in and do their stuff and carry on a conversation without being at all perturbed!

I share the place with rabbits, guineapigs, hens and a calf! Anyhow it's a change from the rats and it's nice to have a roof over one's head.

All my love dearest

RB

PS Latest excuse (after Brussels) 'Oh but it can't be VD, Dr – she's clean, she said so!'

112)

287225 Capt R Barer RAMC
19 Gds Lt Fd Amb
GAD
BLA

Sunday 15th October

Dearest Gwen,

Glad you got some flowers from me, but of course I didn't have time to ask you as letters take so long.

With regard to the money my Ma sent; <u>please don't</u> send me any more things – you just don't realise how difficult it is to carry them around and anyhow I can get things here for literally 1/10 the cost, twice the quality and no coupons. It would be far better to put the money into savings – incidentally you can buy another £40 worth of certificates for me – it would be nice to fill up our savings accounts quickly and then we would always have a useful reserve to fall back on.

I do hope everything went well at the service. It must have been very difficult for your poor Pa without you, but as you say, it would be foolish to take risks. How are the staphs? – don't hesitate to take some NAB or penicillin if necessary.

There <u>is</u> something you might be able to get me perhaps dear. That is a small (pocket) German dictionary and a German phrase book containing <u>useful</u> phrases – not merely 'Where is the pen of my aunt?' I must make a real effort to improve my German – I find I can understand nearly all that is said to me in German and a good deal in Dutch, but speaking myself is more difficult.

Don't despair dearest, the war may still be over this year.

All my love

RB

113)   287225 Capt R Barer RAMC
                                         19 Gds Lt Fd Amb
                                         GAD
                                         BLA

                                         Friday 20th October

Dearest Gwen,
Just a line to let you know that I've been having a couple of days in
Antwerp. It's been very nice, though a bit hectic. I had a good look round
the bookshops and picked up a couple of things – nothing very startling
though. The best is probably Ehrlich's collected papers on immunity, 1904,
in German. The rest are in French – a little book on metamorphosis by
Quatrefages – a celebrated naturalist who studied silk-worm disease before
Pasteur and who is often mentioned by Huxley etc.; a book on animal
intelligence by Flourens of cerebellum fame – it's useful as it sets out in
detail the opinions of earlier thinkers – Aristotle, Reaumur etc. Finally a
book on the brain by Luys – a useful summary of ideas on neurology about
1880 – very scientifically written.

I've also got some toys for Simon [*Janet's son*] which I'll send on to you.
Afraid I've not found anything worth buying for you dear – the prices are
terrific – there are lots of nice wooden things quite cheap but too bulky to
send.

All my love dearest – more details later

RB

114)   287225 Capt R Barer RAMC
                                         19 Gds Lt Fd Amb
                                         GAD
                                         BLA

                                         Sunday 22nd October

Dearest Gwen,
At last I have some time to carry on where I left off yesterday, with a
description of the books.
(1) *Le Cerveau & ses Fonctions* by J. Luys 1878 – physician at the

Salpetriere (there's a tract or nucleus of Luys – but I forget what it does – is it something to do with pain?) This seems quite an interesting book on neurology – rather philosophical with a good deal of psychology – such things as pain, memory, the genesis and evolution of visual and auditory impressions are dealt with in addition to the ordinary anatomy and physiology of the CNS. Luys seems to have been a pioneer in photomicrography and in brain histology – he wrote several books on neurology which might be worth getting. He certainly seems to think deeply about the subject and even includes a chapter on physical chemical activity in the brain. He says that Brown-Sequard revived decapitated dogs by injecting defibrinated blood and that on calling the dog's name it showed signs of recognition! It doesn't sound very likely, in view of the difficulty they had at UC in getting the thing to work.

(2) *De L'Instinct & de L'Intelligence des Animaux* by P. Flourens, 1870. Flourens too seems to have written a lot of good stuff, including a commentary on the Origin of the Species and a history of the discovery of the circulation of the blood, said to be very complete.

This book will need rebinding (but don't do it yet). Perhaps its main value is that he quotes in detail and comments on, the views of famous people – Descartes, Buffon, Cuvier, Aristotle, Plutarch, Leibnitz, Locke etc. He also has a lot about the separation of species pre-Darwinian.

(3) *Metamorphose de l'Homme & des Animaux* by A. de Quatrefages, Professor at the museum of Natural History, 1862. This contains a photo of the author which must be one of the earliest photos ever taken. There's nothing special about the contents. He mentions Carpenter and John Lubbock (I think they mention him in their books). He wrote a couple of books on silkworm diseases – I think he was involved with Pasteur.

(4) *Gesammelte Arbeiten zur Immunitatsforschung* by Ehrlich 1904. This is a biggish book and I don't know if I can send it as parcels must not exceed 5 lbs. It contains most of Ehrlich's important papers on Immunity, and includes papers by some of his pupils. It contains papers on haemolysis, bactericidal sera, the mechanism of amboceptors (with the famous diagrams), studies on dysentery bacillus by Shia, a reprint of a lecture by Ehrlich on protective substances in the blood, his great paper on the relationship between Chemical Constitution and Pharmacological action and a paper on the components of Diphtheria toxin (with the Lo and L+ business). All the famous names in Immunology crop up – Bordet, Roux, Madsen, Niesser etc. I'm afraid we'll have to improve our German somewhat before we can understand it all, but it's nice to have. There are 776 pages. This little lot cost me the grand total of 75 francs – about 8/6, which is hardly expensive considering the prices of other things.

I shall leave the answering of your letters till tomorrow – it's funny you suggested my getting some toys for Simon as I've already got them. Hope they arrive safely. What did Colyer say about me? I'd very much like to know.

All my love dearest one

RB

115)

287225 Capt R Barer RAMC
19 Gds Lt Fd Amb
GAD
BLA

Monday 23rd October

Dearest Gwen,

Will now try and answer a few points from your enormous pile of letters, but first I must tell you, that owing to a very sad event I am doing a locum (which may possibly become permanent) as RMO to the unit I was with at Scarborough. However, continue to write to me at the Field Ambulance for the time being.

I have now sent on Simon's presents to you and the books by Flourens and Quatrefages. Unfortunately I couldn't send the other two books as duty-free parcels may not exceed 5 lbs weight. I shall have to send them separately later. It was a pity I didn't think about getting material, but I may be going again later on and will try, though I expect it'll be rather expensive.

I agree about you Pa's insurance, it seems quite pointless now and he might as well have the capital. I know that despite anything we say he'll want to pay and it would be just as well if he had the cash handy so that his pride won't be hurt. Sorry if my little note wasn't appreciated but I thought it best to say as little as possible. [*Note to my Father about my Mother's death.*]

I'm enclosing a reprint from *The Times*. It's pretty accurate, though it gives rather the wrong impression about Normandy, where we did some of the dirtiest and most unpleasant fighting of the war with no apparent glory. Nor are some of our most remarkable military achievements mentioned. Incidentally I can now tell you that I was not unconnected with the airborne business – it might have been even more interesting if the Arnhem do had gone differently.

By the way you mentioned that some of my letters were opened by the censor. Did he cross anything out at all?

It's funny about Janet's big toe, for as a matter of fact I've been suffering from anaesthesia of half my big toe for the last 2-3 weeks. It doesn't seem to be spreading at all so I don't think I've got carcinoma of the prostate yet!

I think I've got another bout of scabies coming on, as I've been treating a lot of Civvies.

Well dear, that's all for now, all my love.

RB

PS The past tense of 'win' is spelt WON, not ONE. You're nearly as bad as my Ma who spelt 'eye' as YEY, in her last letter!

[*The MO to the 94th LAA Regiment, Capt Seavers, was killed at Graves – a shell splinter entered his abdomen. He was operated on but nothing could be done to save him – so RB succeeded him.*]

116)

287225 Capt R Barer RAMC
19 Gds Lt Fd Amb
GAD
BLA

Tuesday 24th October

Dearest Gwen,

Got your letter of Thurs. 19th today. I don't know what Colyer meant by a job with an ASU – unless he meant the field ambulance – or perhaps he was thinking of the time when I was connected with the CCS – they sent an ASU up before the main body arrived.

Had a very good time in Antwerp. Of course whenever I go anywhere something has to happen and this time a truck full of 30 men decided to turn over on the way. I thought I was in for a busy time but fortunately no-one was seriously hurt. One man lost his false teeth and wasn't sure if he'd swallowed them. Antwerp is a very gay city despite occasional visitations. There's an area in the centre of the city where every building is either a cafe, cabaret, night club, cinema or theatre. In one of them one gets a woman with one's drink. You're supposed to buy her a drink and she gets a chit which she hands in at the end of the evening, getting so much for each drink she's persuaded you to buy. I'm afraid they didn't do very well out of me. At one cabaret they had the ugliest lot of chorus girls I've ever seen – I don't know where they got them! I gather that the high spot was a place where a buxom lady with varicose veins came and danced naked round your table while you drank!

No, I'm afraid I enjoyed looking round the book shops better than all this. I discovered to my annoyance when I got back that some of the best old Dutch Masters are to be seen at Antwerp. I could have done with more time there. I visited the famous Diamond Bourse and got quite a welcome when I told them about people at Hatton Garden. Many of the Brokers are Jews and they told me that there used to be upwards of 20,000 Jews there but only 1000 were left now – they had been in hiding to escape deportation to Poland [*meaning of 'deportation to Poland' was not known at this date*].

All my love dearest

RB

PS Have received UCH mag.

117)

287225 Capt R Barer RAMC
19 Gds Lt Fd Amb
GAD
BLA

Wednesday 25th October

Dearest Gwen,

Just got your two letters of Oct. 20. I'm being looked after like a long lost brother by my batman here, which is some compensation for having to exchange the luxury of my barn for the comforts of a slit-trench. However, the Spartan life is much better for my health.

The officers here are still very upset about my predecessor – he was very popular. I always had a soft spot for him too as he introduced me to army work. It's almost impossible to realise he's gone.

The chap who taught me to ride (?) a motor bike came to see me yesterday and told me all about my accident. He said that I came round a corner at a modest (!) speed, skidded off some gravel and mounted a sort of pavement. Everything might have been all right except that a few yards further on there was a sort of break in the kerb with a lot of bricks lying around. I hit these and proceeded to soar feet first some 9 feet into the air, landing slap on my head! It must have been a very fine sight indeed.

What did you think of the UCH mag? It wasn't bad but I thought that letter on Edward's article on Dehydration was about as priggish as the article itself. Whatever is the modern medical student up to?

I'm reading bits of Luy's book and it's really rather good. He claims he was the first to emphasise that the optic thalamus was a sensory centre and that the corpus striatum was concerned with voluntary movement. By the way Claude Bernard wrote a book called *Histoire des Theories de la Vie* which I should like to get.

There was a priceless letter in last week's *Sunday Express* from Sir John Anderson on 'the weight of the soul' in which he proved scientifically that the soul has no weight. Wish I could find it. I wonder what AV would think of his parliamentary colleague?

All my love dearest

RB

118)

287225 Capt R Barer RAMC
19 Gds Lt Fd Amb
GAD
BLA

Thursday 26th October

Dearest Gwen,

I'm enclosing John Anderson's letter (re weight of soul!). Isn't it priceless? I wonder if he's ever measured the weight of his soul ray?

I thought you had those German books at home. I already have Hugo's *German Conversation Simplified*, so don't send that. I got your parcel yesterday, dear; 2 pairs of socks & 1 pair of mittens. The mittens are a bit tight, but will alter that. All the same dear let me remind you not to send anything without asking me first. The waistcoat is very handy as someone has pinched the windscreen off my jeep! It simply isn't safe to leave a jeep about. There's been an epidemic of cases of stolen jeeps, stolen rotor arms, distributor heads and now a windscreen! However I hope to get another soon.

Keep smiling, dear – despite everything I still think the war will be over this year.

All my love

RB

119)   287225 Capt R Barer RAMC
                                         19 Gds Lt Fd Amb
                                         GAD
                                         BLA

                                         Friday 27th October

Dearest Gwen,

No letters today – expect a double dose tomorrow. Got a short note from your Pa yesterday.

I'm getting well settled in at my new unit. My kit is being decently looked after for the first time – I've got a couple of very good metal ammunition boxes for it, and I've got a lot of new stuff – socks, gloves, a good leather jerkin etc. I've just got an improvised fire rigged up in my RAP, so it's not too bad. It's certainly a change being one's own Master. Most of my time at present is taken with visiting the batteries which of course are widely scattered at strategic points, so I see quite a bit of fun.

I went to a very good film last night – Noel Coward's *This Happy Breed.* It's well worth seeing – it depicts the life of an average lower middle class family from 1919-1939. Do you ever get allowed out to a film dear?

All my love dearest

RB

120)

287225 Capt R Barer RAMC
94 Lt AA Regt RA
BLA

Saturday 28th October

Dearest Gwen,

I think you had better write to the above address until further notice. I got your letter of 22 October yesterday evening. Glad you're being allowed up. You said you were enclosing something about women FRS's but I couldn't find it. I think the only women who might deserve it are Ida Mann, the eye expert & Kathleen Lonsdale, who works on x-rays.

Glad you're reading *Growth and Form*. I think D'Arcy Thomson is a great scholar – not merely superficial. I think you should ignore people who make remarks like 'not being able to understand Science till you know Maths'. That sort of thing is merely snobbish and is usually said by people who don't really understand Maths themselves. It depends what you want to know. After all I don't think Huxley, Darwin, Claude Bernard and many others knew much Maths, but I wish I could have their understanding of science. The reverse criticism is equally true – very few great mathematicians and physicists have the faintest idea about biology. The trouble is it's fashionable to say you understand Einstein and Planck – though of course very few people really do.

Afraid you may have to wait a long time for photos from Brussels, but have just had another taken here, wearing your waistcoat.

All my love dearest

RB

121)

287225 Capt R Barer RAMC
94 Light AA Regt RA
BLA

Sunday 29th October

Dearest Gwen,

No letters again today – expect it will be delayed both ways. Let me know as soon as you get the parcel. I've just been listening to the German-controlled Radio Arnhem. It's very funny. They have 2 women announcers who speak perfect English and sound very glamorous. They try to make you think you're listening to the BBC. They use the 6 pips as a time signal and refer to the 'Home Service' or 'Expeditionary Forces Programme'. Their news is cunning – they give the full truth about the Japanese Naval defeat for example. They try to make the European war seem like a stalemate with heavy losses on both sides – all tending to create the feeling that the war's a waste of time and not worth fighting. The 2 glamorous females will launch out on a long discussion as to whether they could remain faithful to their boyfriends at the front etc., etc. I doubt very much if the station is actually at Arnhem – they probably chose the name because of it's unpleasant associations. Can you suggest any special treatment for a man with a chronic constitutional eczema behind the knees? – rather like a Besnier's prurigo. It tends to get inflamed and dries up with painful fissures. He had x-rays in England. At present he's on tar ointment. What other things are worth trying?

Afraid I've not been able to find out what the diagnosis of that odd eye case was. I hope to see Colyer this week and he may be able to tell me.

All my love dearest

RB

122)   287225 Capt R Barer RAMC
                                                   94 Light AA Regt RA
                                                   BLA

                                                   Wednesday 1st November

Dearest Gwen,
Got your letter written on 26th October. When does Winter start officially? There's one thing, we shan't miss our fireworks display on November 5th. I wouldn't take too much notice of Churchill's statement about the duration of the war – he has to appear pessimistic in order not to raise false hopes and in any case he has to provide some reason for prolonging the life of parliament for another year. I don't think Monty has altered his opinions.

The officers here are a very intelligent lot. The CO is a lawyer, as well as a regular soldier and was at Oxford. We have two other Oxford graduates in the mess, one in Classics, the other in Economics. Two others took degrees in modern languages, the second in command was a school teacher and his brother has just been made a fellow of Trinity Cambridge in physics. Send Foyle's book if you like – any sort of phrase book would be useful and if you can send it as a letter it'll come by air.

No news I'm afraid.

All my love dearest

RB

123)

287225 Capt R Barer RAMC
94 Light AA Regt RA
BLA

Thursday 2nd November

Dearest Gwen,

Got your letter of 27th October. I agree that it would probably be rather dull for you at the seaside and on the whole Highgate seems the best solution provided there's no trouble from buzz bombs; unless of course you have some friends elsewhere. I think you'd probably be happier at Janet's though. You might learn a few tips and you could have a look at those bookshops in Highgate! I dreamt I was in a whole street of bookshops in London yesterday! I had a very interesting time the other day as I went round a radiolocation installation and had it all explained in detail. The chap in charge was a physicist at Newcastle. He told me there was an awful scandal about the Newcastle medical school about 1937 and there was a Royal Commission. It was virtually being run by a small clique who got all their own friends and relatives the best jobs and scholarships.

All my love darling

RB

124)
287225 Capt R Barer RAMC
94 Light AA Regt RA
BLA

Friday 3rd November

Dearest Gwen,
No letter today I'm afraid. Am hoping to see Colyer today and will show him his wife's card. I don't know where he got the idea of leave in 3-4 months time – I hope it'll be over long before that.

I had a very interesting time last night. I went round to the house of a Dutch doctor [*Dr Govaerts who became a close friend*]. He had a very nice house and both he and his wife spoke excellent English. He is very up to date and used to be a pupil of Einthoven. He had a copy of Tom's book [*Thomas Lewis, cardiologist*]. He knew of AV [*A.V. Hill, Physiologist and Nobel Laureate – father of our friend Janet*] and showed me a photo of a Physiological Congress in Leyden showing AV, J.B.S. Haldane, Dale, Einthoven and himself. He has a very fine library of books in French, English and German. The Dutch tend to regard the Americans as the leading school and adopt their methods. It was practically impossible to study medicine under the Germans – students had to take a sort of oath of allegiance to them. He told me about the Dutch University towns and said that Amsterdam was the best place to get old books, so I'll have to try and go there. The RC–Protestant question tends to be a little difficult too and they have a special RC and Protestant University!

All my love dearest

RB

125)
287225 Capt R Barer RAMC
94 Light AA Regt RA
BLA

Sunday 5th November

Dearest Gwen,
Got a pile of your letters today, written 28, 29, 30 & November 1st. Just in case any of my letters have gone astray I'll just repeat (a) you should see

Uncle as soon as possible [*popular obstetrician at UCH – real name Norman White*], (b) I think Janet's is the best place to stay. With regard to the money problem, of course the upkeep of 73 Woodland Drive, Watford will be much less now if it's empty, but I agree you should pay for the woman weekly.

I'll start writing to Highgate right away. I sent the books and toys to you at Stanborough's – hope it doesn't go astray.

Glad you're getting some clothes for yourself – don't worry about expense. The only trouble is coupons. I do wish you hadn't wasted coupons on those socks – they're quite unnecessary as the ordinary army socks are infinitely superior to anything you can buy or even knit. The same applies to almost any clothes and I'm very well fitted out indeed – as many pullovers and underclothes as I'd need in the Arctic so <u>don't</u> send me anymore. By the way, talking of clothes, when you get to Jan's do see that our things, especially my uniform are not mothy.

Isn't Fred's salary fantastic [*an American soldier we knew*]? I don't know what our friends would have to say on the subject. I saw an article in the *Daily Herald* about the horrible harsh life the RAF are suffering – they actually live under canvas the poor dears – I wonder what they think we're on – a bloody picnic! I think it would be a good idea if everyone in uniform were made to live for 3 days in a flooded slit-trench under mortar fire – it would give them some idea of what this was about. Some of the selfishness that goes on is simply incredible. People living in luxury will grudge the fighting soldier even a few hours relaxation – I wish I could write more but the censor would probably object.

Well my dear, all my love, it'll soon be over.

RB

126)
                                        287225 Capt R Barer RAMC
                                        94 Light AA Regt RA
                                        BLA

                                        Tuesday 7th November

Dearest Gwen,

Got a very belated letter yesterday – the one written October 23rd with Weddell's letters enclosed, also the bit about women FRSs. I see dear little Edith Summerskill actually had the nerve to get up and ask why there weren't any women VCs. I think she should join my slit-trench brigade. Considering the number of men dying in the act of quite extraordinary feats of bravery who never get any decoration at all (remember the VC is the only decoration which can be awarded posthumously) I think her remarks show gross lack of balance – especially when the relative number of men and women in positions of danger are taken into account. I could tell you some quite amazing stories of courage which went unrewarded and so could everyone else out here. You've no idea how furious stupid things like that make us. There was an uproar in the mess yesterday when someone read that the MP for Brighton was going to ask why men in the RAF were not issued with pyjamas, and they actually had to sleep between blankets without sheets! I wonder how many of us would have liked to take our clothes off, let alone get into pyjamas! (At the moment bathing suits would be more appropriate.) Talking of bathing I'll tell you one day how but for a chance I might have had to swim the Rhine, I'll also tell you about a very remarkable man who did swim it and with whom I was associated.

Got a PC from John and a note from your Pa today. Had guessed David's address [*David Hill, AV's son*]. Will try to see him if I get a chance.

All my love dearest,

RB

PS Do you ever see the marvellous 'Giles' cartoons in the *Sunday Express*? He's captured the spirit of things perfectly.

127)

[*Addressed to 81 Highgate West Hill*]

287225 Capt R Barer RAMC
94 Light AA Regt RA
BLA

Saturday 11th November

Dearest Gwen,
Am enclosing photo which has just arrived. You will see I'm wearing your waistcoat – under the battle dress blouse – it wasn't big enough to wear over it – which despite your remarks is the usual way, so I look rather peculiar. However, anyone who dresses conventionally in this Division is rather frowned on so it doesn't matter and actually I've received several envious glances from Guards officers for thinking of some new eccentricity.

Glad you're at Jan's at last. Have you seen Uncle yet? So glad you've seen Max again. Isn't he a wretch not to tell anyone about his accident [*injured by a buzz bomb in Tottenham Court Road and in hospital for 6 weeks!*]. Still he seems all right now. How are the buzz bombs at the moment? Pity he saw those things of his but I don't suppose he'll take them.

All my love dearest

RB

PS Have been promised 6 copies of photo so don't get any more made

PPS Don't be surprised if mail is delayed – weather awful.

[*12 November – 16 December*
The Canadian Army, having finished its operations in south-west Holland, took over the whole front from Nijmegen to the sea and the Guards Armoured Division was moved south to the area centred on Sittard. Patrolling duties were performed in the cold, uncomfortable conditions and there were steady casualties.]

128)   287225 Capt R Barer RAMC
                                       94 Light AA Regt RA
                                       BLA

                                       Monday 13th November

Dearest Gwen,
So sorry if letters have been delayed – I've not had any from you for a couple of days either.

With regard to defence bonds, I believe the trouble with them is that you have to give 6 months notice before withdrawing. However someone just told me that you can get an extra 500 National Savings certs. at a lower rate of interest. Could you enquire about that? They are by far the most convenient form of savings. I got your *Englisch in ein paar Tagen* all right – I thought it had been mutilated in the post. Why did you cut it up? Hope your other book arrives soon – it should be very useful now. Had an amusing incident in one Dutch town. I was looking for a place in the dark and asked a civvy the way.

Nijmegen 1944

I spoke in German, got the directions and turned the car round. As I did so I noticed a little crowd had gathered and there was an angry mumbling. They thought I was German, which was quite a compliment to my efforts! I was lucky they did not shoot me first and ask questions afterwards!

All my love dearest

RB

129)   287225 Capt R Barer RAMC
                                             94 Light AA Regt RA
                                             BLA

                                             Tuesday 14th November

Dearest Gwen,

Just a very short note, as I have to catch the post. I got 2 letters and parcel containing dictionary and *All you want in Germany*. It looks quite useful. I discovered I've been making an awful mistake in my German. The word for 'to bandage' is '*verbinden*'. Unfortunately it also means 'to copulate' which once led to embarrassing results.
    Sorry no time.

All my love dearest

RB

130)   287225 Capt R Barer RAMC
                                             94 Light AA Regt RA
                                             BLA

                                             Thursday 16th November

Dearest Gwen,

Got your letter of November 11th but still no book. It seems impossible to realise that Jan has been married 5 years already . . .
    Met a very interesting and charming Dutch doctor [*Dr Govaerts again*].

His wife is the daughter of Prof. Keesom, Professor of Physics at Leiden University, a great expert on helium and low temperature physics. He's giving me an introduction and I hope to go and see him when Leyden is free. Their apparatus is marvellous. Unfortunately he thinks the Germans are removing some of it. This chap spent 8 months in a hostage camp and while he was there, 10 hostages were shot. While we were talking in walked a priest who had been at the same camp and was afterwards transferred to concentration camp in Germany. This priest had been one of the leaders of a society for hiding Dutch Jews. There used to be 240,000 of them in Holland but only about 10,000 of them are believed to be left. My host had himself kept a Jewish doctor secretly in his house for 6 months. Things got too hot and he tried to escape to Portugal. He got as far as Spain but was then handed over by the Franco Government to the Germans, who shot him. I'm afraid it's very difficult to find any arguments in the face of people who have suffered at the hands of the Germans. It's obvious that the French, Belgians, and Dutch will have an intense hatred of everything German for years to come. It's simply appalling to think that a few hooligans could have led a great nation to such a state.

You really are naughty dear to keep raising the question of my job. Don't forget that I worked for a CCS for a few days and I know what they do. It's only the surgical specialists there who have anything good to do. The others do far less than in a Field Ambulance and they don't get any of the fun. Honestly dear my present work is very interesting in every way and altogether I have had a far more interesting time than I ever expected and I think the best is yet to come. As you say 'To him that hath shall be given' and I've certainly been given plenty – it really is a wonderful experience and one of the few things I should not mind repeating if I had my time over again. Please be sensible dear and don't worry. I don't take unnecessary risks and at the moment I'm by no means uncomfortable.

All my love dearest

RB

131)

287225 Capt R Barer RAMC
94 Light AA Regt RA
BLA

Friday 17th November

Dearest Gwen,

Got your letter of Sunday today. No <u>don't</u> send my trench coat as I don't need it.

Went to dinner with local Doctor and Carmelite monk. Both have been in concentration camps and they told me some dreadful stories. The Germans treated the Russians infinitely worse than anyone else. On one occasion a Russian accidentally broke a German soldier's plate so they just hanged 10 of them on the spot! It's almost unbelievable.

The doctor is a very rich man and regaled me with expensive wines. He insisted on giving me an old German book – a commentary on the bible written in 1783.

I didn't really want it but he insisted. He studied at Leyden and told me all about it. I must go there as it seems very interesting, rather like Oxford.

All my love dearest

RB

132)

287225 Capt R Barer RAMC
94 Light AA Regt RA
BLA

Sunday 19th November

Dear Gert,

Hullo ducks, how are you! Hoping this finds you as it leaves me in the best of health in the Pink. I think you are the sweetest girl in all the world. The girls out here are smashing especially the blondes. Har Har! No offence, ducks. You know me. I wouldn't do anything like that. You're the sweetest girl in all the world and I love you with all my heart and soul. Hoping this

reaches you in the best of spirits as it leaves me.
   Your loving and devoted husband

RB

XXXXXXXXXXXXXXSWALKXXXXXXXXXXX
XXXXXXXXhollandXXXXXXXXXXX
ITALYXXXXXXXXXXXXXXXXXXXXXXXXXX
XXXXXXXXXXXXXXXXXXXXXXSAGXXXXXXXXXXXX

Hope the censor opens this one!

133)   287225 Capt R Barer RAMC
                                  94 Light AA Regt RA
                                  BLA

                                  Wednesday 22nd November

Dearest Gwen,
   Just a note to let you know I'm all right and having a good time. Sorry for the delay in letters – afraid it was inevitable.
   You'll be pleased to hear I spent a very pleasant couple of hours with David. Have bought Simon a very nice little clockwork car which has a little gadget which prevents it running off the end of the table. Also a really marvellous (and expensive!) car which has 4 gears and reverse, brake and accelerator like a real car. I don't think I'll send it yet as I don't want to lose it and anyhow he's too young for it at present. However it was so marvellous I couldn't resist buying it!

   All my love dearest

   RB

134)   287225 Capt R Barer RAMC
                                        94 Light AA Regt RA
                                        BLA
                                        Friday 24th November

Dearest Gwen,

Only 1 letter waiting for me when I got back! Afraid this will have to be a short letter as I have to catch the post. I had quite a good time and bought a few things but no silk or wool. There isn't any. Eventually I bought a blue satin jacket and bonnet quite nice but rather expensive 55/-. Hope it gets home safely. Afraid that you'll have to produce a boy now to match the colour! Of course a few minutes later I found a much better shop with magnificent white quilted bed wraps. I should imagine they would be about £4 or £5. Do you think they would be worth getting if I have another chance? Bought a few books, will tell you about them tomorrow. David was looking very well and very comfortably installed in a magnificent block of flats. He even complained that the central heating wasn't working properly yet! I invited him to come and try mine! We had a long chat about things. He seems rather bored with his work – it's all too vague and uncontrolled and he said he was longing to get back to his muscle work at Cambridge. He hadn't heard of the EM (electron microscope), but got quite interested when I told him its possibilities. You'll be pleased to hear that he also agreed with me about my job and said he didn't think much of the chaps who had chosen Lulworth – so at least someone is on my side even if my wife isn't. You women are all the same though. All the officers in the mess keep getting urgent 'orders' from wives to change their job preferably for one in England. The Colonel's wife is a scream. She wrote 'Is there going to be another offensive before this Winter? Please answer. I <u>must</u> know!' At least you haven't quite come up to that standard yet.

Actually dear, it's quite clear I've had a far more interesting time than David. I admit that at times it gets unpleasant but it never seems so bad when one looks back on it. I even felt a little guilty that I was enjoying myself so much and poor David was undergoing all that drudgery. Still I suppose all that will change next time I hear a mortar!

All my love dearest – long letter tomorrow

RB

135)   287225 Capt R Barer RAMC
                                              94 Light AA Regt RA
                                              BLA

                                              Saturday 25th November

Dearest Gwen,

No letter again today – I suppose the weather is too bad. I'm sending off the pictures, baby dress and car for Simon in one parcel. I do hope it arrives safely. I'm keeping the other car for the time being, as he won't be old enough for it for several years. Afraid I didn't buy anything for you or for your Pa as there wasn't anything suitable and it was all fantastically expensive. I bought a few books, the most interesting being *A Listing of Natural Science from 1799 to 1830* written by Cuvier in 1838. It's really rather like an annual review of Physiology but covers all science including Physics, Chemistry, Biology and Medicine. It deals with the years 1809-1829 year by year – listing all the main discoveries. It was quite an interesting period, particularly in Chemistry, with the work of Lavoisier, Dumas, Davy, Gay-Lussac, Berzelius etc. Many new elements were discovered then. His references to Biology and Medicine include Jacobson, Magendie, Flourens, Dupuytren, Lisfranc, Larrey, Lamarck etc. I should think it must be quite a valuable reference book for that period and there must be many things there which have been forgotten. Magendie in particular seems to have done an awful lot of work, including a lot of stuff on the mechanism of vomiting. There are 2 volumes, totalling 500 pages in first class condition. A book on animal parasitism by Von Beneden 1875, a standard work and a book on the role of osmosis in Biology by Leclerc du Sablon 1920.

I tried to contact the doctors I met in Brussels but eventually found that they had been evacuated, probably to England, so it's possible that Bulbring may be able to get in touch with Prof. D via the Red Cross in England.

I had quite a good time in Brussels. I stayed at a club run by the GAD and had a very fine room and double bed to myself. The food was very good too. There is a simply luxurious officers' club where one can have meals very cheaply if one can get in – it seems to be very popular with officers stationed there! David took me there and stood me a lunch and wine, but the mean old devil was too lazy to send Simon any toys for Xmas – he said he thought Simon would probably get enough anyhow! The displays in some of the shops are simply marvellous – like England in peace time and Simon would have loved them. One shop had a live St Nicholas in the window, waving to all the kids.

Well all my love, dearest, hope your letters come soon.

RB

136)

287225 Capt R Barer RAMC
94 Light AA Regt RA
BLA

Sunday 26th November

Dearest Gwen,

Got 2 of your letters yesterday written 19th and 20th. Thanks for diagram – the distribution fits C4* exactly. I posted a parcel containing RG's cloak, car for Simon and 4 pictures. I couldn't send the other 4 as it was over weight. We can only send 5 lbs. Glad to hear other parcel has arrived at Watford. I hope it hasn't been tampered with. I got some nice toys for the local doctor's children in Brussels – he has 7. I got a couple of dolls for the girls – one of them has eyes which move.

Have just seen a perfectly fatuous article in the BMJ by a man describing himself as Captain RAMC. He suggests that an estimate of volume of blood lost should always be made and Hb done before and after transfusion! I should have liked to see him do it the night I had to transfuse 4 men in a stable with badly wounded people arriving every moment! I'd like to know if he's ever left England!

We're hoping to have clinical meetings out here and they're asking for MOs to give papers. If you can lay your hands on either my essay on viruses or UCH mag with the article on EM, could you please send them?

All my love dearest Gwen and <u>please</u> don't worry. I'm perfectly safe and well.

RB

This must refer to an injury. C4 is cervical vertebra 4. I must have sent a diagram showing the distribution of injury to the nerves of the spinal cord at this level.

137)

287225 Capt R Barer RAMC
94 Light AA Regt RA
BLA

Monday 27th November

Dearest Gwen,
Just got 3 of your letters 21, 22 & 23 November. So glad Simon liked the

toys; hope he'll like the car which should arrive in about 4 weeks. By the way you just mention the cart but not the horse – I presume that arrived? Does Simon build little animals for himself or does he need help? Sorry you're having difficulty getting material but it's no better here. You needn't think it's any less embarrassing for me either as all the shop assistants are young women and they all asked me how old the child was and whether it was a girl or boy!

I'm terribly glad about the pram – it sounds fine and not at all dear for the times. Why not get someone to put a new coat of paint on and smarten it up generally. You'll have to reach a <u>very</u> high standard to please my Ma!

Don't you remember John's paper in BMJ about 6 weeks ago describing work on soda lime? I asked you if you'd seen it.

I'm picking out snippets from Cuvier's book and will tell you about them soon. Magendie seems to have done a lot of first class work – rather like Claude Bernard but not so brilliant. His experiments on the mechanism of vomiting were very well conceived. He also did a lot of work on absorption of substances into the circulation, and of course on neurology. Apparently he was the first to state that the CSF [*Cerebrospinal fluid, the fluid surrounding the brain*] was a normal thing and not the product of disease.

I'm very pleased with Cuvier. I'm sure it contains lots of forgotten facts.

All my love dearest one

RB

138)

287225 Capt R Barer RAMC
94 Light AA Regt RA
BLA

Tuesday 28th November

Dearest Gwen,

No letter today but German phrase book arrived. It seems quite useful but a little old-fashioned.

Afraid there's not much news I can tell you at present. The weather's a little better – it can hardly have got much worse! One of my orderlies has just had a write-up in his local paper describing his bravery under attack while we were defending a certain bridge. He's certainly a very good chap and I hope he gets a medal.

Cuvier is full of interesting stuff, French Physiology seems to have been much better in those days. Dupuytren in 1810 cut the vagi and noticed the effects on heart and lungs, but didn't seem to pursue the matter. Legallois in 1811 observed the effects of destruction of parts of the spinal cord on the heart and concluded that the heart was influenced by the sympathetic system.

A man named de Montigne seems to have done some interesting work on gastric digestion in 1811. He appears to have been able to empty his stomach at will and examined the juice. He noticed its acidity but said it wasn't necessary for digestion as when he took enough magnesia to neutralise it his digestion was not affected. The juice became acid again in a short while.

Magendie really did some first class work. I'll describe some of his stuff on vomiting. He noticed that some emetics worked very rapidly after intravenous injection and therefore it wasn't a local cause in the stomach. He opened the abdomen and noticed that during vomiting the stomach was inert but there was a violent contraction of the abdominal wall and diaphragm. If the stomach was pulled outside the abdomen, retching continued but there was no actual vomiting as the stomach was not compressed. Vomiting occurred only when the stomach was replaced in the abdomen. He also noticed that pulling on the oesophagus via the stomach would excite vomiting without an emetic. He then excised the abdominal muscles and found that did not much affect the force of vomiting, but cutting the phrenic nerve greatly diminished the force. He then completely extirpated the stomach and replaced it by a hollow bag containing coloured water which he connected to the oesophagus. He then closed the abdomen and gave an emetic. 'Vomiting' occurred.

He also did some work on nitrogen metabolism. He fed dogs on a nitrogen-free diet (sugar, oil, butter, distilled water). The N_2 contents of the secretions diminished, the muscles wasted, and there was severe corneal ulceration – often ending in perforation (has this ever been reported?). He noted the great decrease in urea and uric acid and suggested that a low N_2 diet (i.e. vegetables) might be useful in urinary calculus.

His work on the nerve roots and CSF (foramen of Magendie) are also described. Altogether he appears to have been a very great physiologist and doesn't seem to have achieved full recognition. Flourens too did an enormous amount of work on neurology.

Well dear, hope a letter comes tomorrow. All my love darling.

RB

139)   287225 Capt R Barer RAMC
                                              94 Light AA Regt RA
                                              BLA

                                              Thursday 30th November

Dearest Gwen,

No letter today so I'm afraid there's nothing much to write about. Have been given a present of two vests and a pair of socks for RG by local Dr's wife. Will send them off soon. Hope my other parcel arrives OK. By the way be careful when you play with the little car which doesn't run off table. When you first wind it up its speed is so great that it may just go over the edge but after that it's all right. Am enclosing literature about car with gear changing.

Can you tell me what to do for (1) Chilblains (2) early alopecia areata?

Have an 8 months pregnancy on my hands at the moment – hope we move on soon or I may have to deliver her! I'm afraid the nutritional problem for expectant Mothers is very grave as they get very little nourishment – no eggs, milk, very little meat. At least I don't think you'll have that problem.

All my love dearest one, am longing to hold you once more.

RB

140)   287225 Capt R Barer RAMC
                                              94 Light AA Regt RA
                                              BLA

                                              Tuesday 5th December

Dearest Gwen,

Got 2 of your letters of 29 & 30 and also Dutch book. You've probably heard it announced that we're all to get leave in the New Year. I was thinking of asking mine to be postponed till about April 5th but perhaps it might be better having it earlier if possible as anyhow the exact EDD [*expected date of delivery*] is rather variable for a primip [*primipara, woman in first pregnancy*] (that's you!). What do you think about it?

There's only one thing I'm going to ask you dear. If and when I do come on leave <u>please</u> don't mention the old subject of the job as we'll only ruin the whole of our leave together arguing. Please believe me dear, my present job is fine and is not really as bad as you think – at least I'll be able to reassure you about that when I see you and I'll be able to explain things to you which I could not say in a letter. If you must know dear I had the chance of a very fine job with one of the Guards battalions but I didn't press for it as I knew how you'd feel, so you see I do take notice of what you say, even at the expense of my conscience.

About the toe, which seems to worry you a good deal – it's absolutely trivial and is gradually improving. I think it's probably a numbness due to local pressure.

I also saw another UCH chap, named Tasker – you may remember him.

I bought a nice pipe for your Pa and a pretty toy clown for Nick [*Janet's 2nd son*]. Will send them soon. You must get Simon to try and build those animals by himself – they should be simple enough. Surprised about S beating N – I wonder if he's jealous? He used to be so considerate. Don't see why you can't stay at Jan's – after all they haven't got Stella now and anyhow I expect they like it. At all events <u>don't</u> go to Mrs D. Uncle seems to be quite keen about hospital and I agree with him, but I'd like you to have a private room if poss.

All my love dearest

RB

141)   287225 Capt R Barer RAMC
                                                        94 Light AA Regt RA
                                                        BLA

                                                        Wednesday 6th December

Dearest Gwen,

Got 2 letters dated December 1st. I like the material you sent very much indeed. Am sending you some copies of the photo taken at Nijmegen. Also one photo of my chief medical orderly. His name is Marcus (a Jew) and he comes from Leeds. He's rather a good violinist and used to play in the Huddersfield Symphony Orchestra. He won some big prize when he was 13. I'm sending a copy of photo to my parents directly so don't you send one.

I'm living in comparative luxury at the moment. I even have a bed – or at least a mattress to lie on.

Saw a ridiculous example of medical bureaucracy the other day. A Dutch doctor showed me a lot of drugs that had been sent from England. About half were useful – M&B and Ferrous Sulphate etc. but there were dozens of ampoules of Leptazol and lots of useless things like pilocarpine for injection! I wonder how much shipping space they wasted on that? There are vast quantities of cardiazol and similar stimulants over here – I've had thousands of pounds worth through my own hands – but it'll never be used. I think someone is probably trying to get rid of dumps or surplus stores in England. I'm rather afraid that's the sort of thing that might happen under a state medical service. What do you think of events in Greece? I'd like to know just why they decided to suppress the left wing partisans rather than the right wing ones! We seem to go in for foisting unpopular governments. Mr Eden might have been less sarcastic to Bevan (Nie) if he could see 'Pierlot assassin!' chalked up all over Brussels and if he could have heard P's name hissed at an ordinary music hall.

All my love dearest

RB

[*Two rival Greek governments in exile, one controlled by the communists and the other by the King, were brought together in a coalition under Georgios Papandreou. Accompanied by a small British force, his government returned to Athens as the Germans withdrew from Greece in October 1944. It disintegrated a few weeks later when the communist members refused to disband the guerrillas. Civil war broke out on 3 December which the British military suppressed with great difficulty. The communists accepted defeat in February 1945.*]

142)
287225 Capt R Barer RAMC
94 Light AA Regt RA
BLA

Thursday 7th December

Dearest Gwen,
No letters yesterday but one today. Also a surprise which I expect you had

something to do with – namely a copy of *Punch* and of *Nature*. The latter certainly makes a welcome change from the daily routine but believe it or not I am so busy that I scarcely get a chance to read it. I'm nearly always out visiting guns and have to cover enormous distances. The trouble is that no sooner have I finished a tour of one group when another one moves in and I have to start all over again; it gets pretty hectic as I try to get done before dark as very odd things are liable to happen round here after dark. Visited Colyer's RAP today but he was out. Left him some captured staph vaccine as we're getting a lot of boils. I must say that despite my scepticism it seems to do some good. Incidentally a lot of people are trying to persuade me that boils will disappear magically if treated by vitamins (B & C). I refuse to believe this but can you let me know what the evidence is? I know that vitamin C requirements are increased in people with infections but I refuse to believe the converse.

All my love dearest

RB

143)

287225 Capt R Barer RAMC
94 Light AA Regt RA
BLA

Saturday 9th December

Dearest Gwen,

Afraid there's not much news at the moment. I'm busy delousing a lot of people – all the women seem to have lice in their hair. I hope we don't get any typhus. Have sent off some Division Xmas cards. Sent one to Weddell, Prof. Miles and one to St Andrews. Will send one to Janet and John. Will try and keep one as a souvenir. Have you heard any more about getting in to UCH yet? I'm sure they'll fix something up for you.

All my love dearest

RB

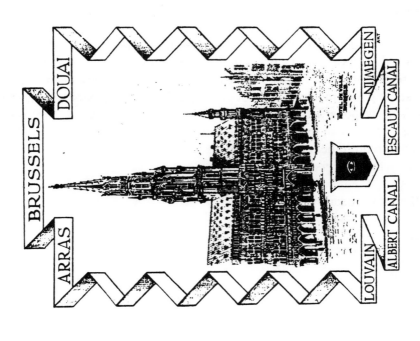

Christmas card 1944

WITH BEST
WISHES FOR
CHRISTMAS AND
THE NEW YEAR

144)

287225 Capt R Barer RAMC
94 Light AA Regt RA
BLA

Sunday 10th December

Dearest Gwen,

Got a whole pile of your letters today, 6 in fact! Glad Max turned up at last –
he's an awful scream really – but terribly irritating at times. Did you drop
him any hints about things for RG? Anyhow I'm glad he asked you to stay
with him over Xmas if you can't stay at Janet's. I was going to suggest it
myself but didn't know if he had any room – you'll probably find he hasn't
and will have to sleep in the scullery. If my Ma does come you'll have to be
careful about taking her to Highgate . . . By the way, if there's a Russian
film on (Russian talking) they might like to see it.

That flat of Mrs Hill's sounds a very good idea if you could let 73 [*my
father's house in Watford*] (don't sell it). The only thing is I'd be scared stiff
of AV but it sounds an excellent temporary solution for you and your Pa,
especially if Mrs H can get him a job. Anyhow there are plenty of things to
do in London and you'd be near Jan.

Was interested to hear what AV thought of G-L [*Graham Little, MP for
London University*] but you must be careful what you write otherwise he'll
be up for libel. Don't send me the *Lancet* as I've very little time to read it
and anyhow I'm not really interested in half the tripe these medical journals
contain. You include a very nice heading – Eva's address in one of your
letters, but never gave it!

All my love dearest, think I should see you some time in February.

RB

145)

287225 Capt R Barer RAMC
94 Light AA Regt RA
BLA

Tuesday 12th December

Dearest Gwen,

No letter today. Am enclosing a reprint from a newspaper which I'd like you to keep as a souvenir. It's quite a good account though it rather belittles the number of planes shot down, which is really fantastically large for this sort of regiment (indeed any sort of AA).

I've just sent off 3 parcels. The duty-free parcel contains baby clothes, pipe for your Pa, doll for Nick, book and the bowl of the cherrywood pipe. The stem of the pipe is in another parcel with some books and pictures. The 2 Cuviers are in another parcel. Do hope they all get home safely.

Have written to Max dropping hint about baby clothes. Also sent Xmas card to your Pa in Lancs. (Is he staying there for Xmas?)

All my love dearest

RB

PS Think it may be January?

[*In the event he didn't get leave until after the European war was over (May 1945).*]

DROVE GUNS FOUR HUNDRED MILES IN SIX DAYS

A number of DONCASTER and BARNSLEY men are in a regiment of YORKSHIRE ack-ack gunners which took part in a Guards Armoured Division's spectacular advance, the fastest the world has seen, from NORMANDY to Brussels and on to Nijmegen, where the Lower Rhine flows from Germany into Holland.

This time last year the regiment was completing its training for the Second Front with the division on the Yorkshire Wolds.

Now, writes a military observer, they are Second Army veterans. They are proud of the world fame which the Guards Armoured Division has won. It's not their fault that their own contribution to the Guards' victories has not been larger.

Thirty six aircraft certainly destroyed, 22 probable kills and a larger number damaged isn't a high total on the face of it, but it is an impressive proportion of the small numbers of German planes that have ventured within range of the Yorkshiremen's guns.

GRIM FIGHTING

The regiment's first job was the protection of artillery concentrations in the grim fighting around Caen in late June and July. Of the few Nazi planes that darted out of the enemy line in 'scalded cat' sorties, 20 fell

176

to the Yorkshire lads.

Those victories most certainly contributed to the gradual disappearance of Luftwaffe planes from the Normandy skies. The disappearance was complete in August, during which month the gunners saw no more enemy planes than their folks saw at home in Yorkshire. It looked as though the Luftwaffe had been firmly broken.

But better things were in store. Late in August General Adair received the orders for which he and his division had been longing since D-day. The Guards were to break out across the Seine and plunge on into Belgium and beyond.

The amazing advance which followed, culminating in the liberation of Brussels at the end of a day's advance of close on 100 miles, on the fifth anniversary of the declaration of war is history now.

The Yorkshire gunners drove the guns over 400 miles in six days, one troop pausing long enough near Arras to engage a force of 17 Germans holding out in a wood. They killed 5, wounded 4, and took the remaining 8 prisoners.

BRUSSELS WELCOME

In Brussels they received an unforgettable welcome from a people mad with joy.

There was no pause at Brussels for the Guards smashed on to liberate Louvain and force the first crossing of the Albert canal at Booningen. Here the troops suffered casualties in heavy enemy shelling. On into Holland in a dash to link up with the three Allied airborne landings.

It was at the great Maas bridge at Grave that they got their one chance to do the job they had been especially trained for.

Diving out of morning mist a formation of enemy fighters attempted to shoot up massed columns of the division that were temporarily blocked near the bridge. The guns in the column went into split second action.

Two aircraft crashed immediately, and the others made off in a hurry. Farther north, American paratroopers cheered as another troop's guns killed a couple of the half dozen enemy strafers that had attacked regularly each morning since the airborne forced had landed. They never attacked again.

When the Grenadier Guards had taken the great Rhine bridge at Nijmegen by storm, German fighter bombers made persistent efforts to wreck it. A troop which had made a name for itself by escaping intact from a force of enemy infantry and tanks which had almost surrounded them in confused fighting in Normandy went into action on the bridge itself, and knocked two out of the skies.

When the fighting in the area grew less intense there was still an occasional shoot to be had. One evening when a certain gun had been brought into regimental workshops for repairs a Junkers 88 bomber droned over the British Lines.

With a shout of command the sergeant sent his men who were eating their supper nearby, to the gun. Five lines of crimson tracers climbed through the sky. The Engines faltered, and stopped and the bomber crashed beside a canal.

Reproduced from the *Yorkshire Evening News*
Nov 30 1944

146)

287225 Capt R Barer RAMC
94 Light AA Regt RA
BLA

Thursday 14th December

Dearest Gwen,
No letter from you today. Afraid the mail may get a little messed up owing to Xmas.

I may be going to Brussels in about 2 weeks so let me know in good time if there's anything you want – I shall probably bring it back with me if I come on leave. Do you think £5 would be too dear for a white shawl?

I'm really terribly busy just now – I hardly have time to sit down. In addition to looking after my men I've got a flourishing civvy practice which causes me much anxiety. I've got one case almost certainly Diphtheria [*there was a severe diphtheria epidemic – they had no vaccine*], a woman with diabetes, sugar ++ but no insulin and a ?? appendix, so I lie awake waiting to be called all night! There's one little girl of 5 who had an operation for a meningocoel and who's never learned to walk – I'm sure she's not paralysed. The parents just keep her sitting in a high chair. I'm hoping for dramatic results here.

All my love dearest

RB

[*16 December 1944 – 16 January 1945*
On 16 December the Germans launched the surprise Ardennes offensive to the south of the Guards position. This was a bold attempt to break through to Antwerp and separate the British from the Americans. The Guards Armoured Division were redeployed in holding positions around the Belgian town of Namur on the Meuse. After a rapid initial advance in which the Americans bore the brunt of the attack, the Germans were halted in early January not far short of the Meuse, and by the 16th they had been driven back. Losses in the Division were light.]

147)

287225 Capt R Barer RAMC
94 Light AA Regt RA
BLA

Sunday 24th December

Dearest Gwen,

Got 3 letters at last but all quite old 12th, 13th and 15th. Am still waiting for a pile, but I doubt if they'll come before Xmas now. It looks as if we're going to have rather an unsettled Xmas but that won't worry us. Judging by the amount of liquor it will be pretty merry for some people. Glad your x-ray was OK but you don't tell me what Morland said as regards what exercise you could take etc. Do tell me that.

I don't see why David C should be hurt about my not mentioning RG – it's just never came up as a topic for conversation – we have other things to do besides talk about our families, which is all you feeble women seem to do!

Glad you bought Prof. Miles a present – hope it was 2 record tokens.

Have you definitely fixed things at UCH yet?

Afraid things are as you say in Greece. The truth is we are altogether too anxious to bolster up these puppet monarchies whether the people want them or not.

All my love dearest.

RB

148)

287225 Capt R Barer RAMC
94 Light AA Regt RA
BLA

Monday 25th December Xmas 1944

Dearest Gwen,

Am writing this at the end of a hectic day, though quite enjoyable despite various disturbances. I got several letters today, including a copy of UCH mag with my article and Glynn and Himsworth's reprints. Don't send me any more stuff like that please dear as the days for that are now over and I doubt if I shall have time to read much. Incidentally dear please don't send bulky things in patched up envelopes – they were nearly torn to pieces and it's a miracle your letter never fell out. Afraid I don't think much of JS' remarks on boils. What does she mean by 'stepping up the diet'? – increased calories, vitamins or what? Anyhow this simply can't apply to soldiers who get a very adequate diet + extra vitamins. As for treating boils as an infectious disease, does she think we purposely smear staphs all over the place? Anyhow it's scarcely original!

I don't think people in England have much idea of what we're up against here.

There was a time when people had only to cut themselves to go septic and then they'd get boils and septic manifestations for several months – it might start with a septic finger, then a leg, then axilla, scalp, neck, buttock or anywhere else – apparently a blood stream infection. It isn't a question of cleanliness as that has usually been very good but I think there must be some peculiar predisposing factor perhaps connected with the diet or water. I must say that this Bayer staph vaccine does appear to do some good – I've a dozen men on it and they all say they're much better for it. Large doses of vitamins seem to have no effect.

I do not want any mittens dear as I've been issued with several pairs of gloves.

Glad Max has been helpful again. I did drop him a hint when I wrote to him.

I'm glad they're calling up some of those limpets at UCH. I expect they'll all be graded specialists! If any of them came out here to face the horrors of war in Brussels or similar places I expect I shall be sending my cases back to see them. The more I see of people in hospitals over here the less I like them.

Well, all my love dearest. I'm sure our next Xmas will he spent together.

RB

149)
287225 Capt R Barer RAMC
94 Light AA Regt RA
BLA

Thursday 28th December

Dearest Gwen,

No letters for a couple of days. Afraid I haven't been able to write either. I don't suppose any of my parcels have arrived yet? I've had the copy of *Nature* with John's letter in it. It's quite interesting.

I've been billeted with a nice old Belgian Doctor with 8 daughters (all the right age!). He insisted in calling me '*confrere*' and shaking hands every time we met. They had a nice piano and violin so we had some good concerts. His son has now taken over his practice. They were both trained at Louvain. All the courses there are duplicated in French and Flemish, which must be very uneconomical. The size of the families in Belgium and Holland is a real eye-opener. Families of 8-12 are the rule. It's difficult to understand why their families are so much bigger than ours – their economic standard is no higher. It's the same even in the intellectual classes, so one is forced to the sad conclusion that the British are more concerned with amusement than families. I must say nevertheless that their families seem rather too big. This doctor's son is aged 30, has been married 4 years and already has 4 children. I should think they'll end up with at least 10. His wife is one of those enormous women – a typical 'Flanders mare' to whom child bearing is easier than defaecating. The Belgians and Dutch know we have small families and rather despise us for it. I'm afraid they tend to put the blame on English women. Most women over here would regard it as a matter of personal shame to have less than 6 children. I suppose Catholicism had something to do with it. The south Dutch are intensely religious and all catholic. The Netherlands are far from being Protestant. Over 40% are Catholics – nearly all of these live in the south. Holland proper is just composed of 2 provinces in the north and the dialect is different. There is considerable friction between Protestant and Catholic – rather like Ireland. They even have separate radio stations and Universities. The amount of religious symbolism in the catholic houses is simply fantastic. The walls are covered with images and crucifixes. Neon light crosses are common in the drawing room. At one place there was a crucifix with a little music box attached. The church is very powerful and rich. Most of our hospital and CCS buildings have been Jesuit seminaries and colleges.

Well dear, hope your letters arrive soon – all my love
RB

150)

287225 Capt R Barer RAMC
94 Light AA Regt RA
BLA

4th January 1945 (from the
'Eye' club Brussels)

Dearest Gwen,

Haven't seen any more of your letters yet but hope there will be some waiting for me when I get back. Have had quite a nice time here. Took David out to lunch. Found him kicking his heels at about 11.30 and he seemed relieved to have something to talk about. We had a nice long talk about things in general. He too didn't like the prospect of having to go to Burma. I bought a very little lace table centre for Mrs Hill. It's nothing much but it's genuine Brussels lace, entirely hand-made and cost over a £1; and anyhow the shop-girl was so nice.

Have bought 1 book so far – in English, looks good, will tell you about it later.

All my love dearest
RB

CHAPTER VI

Bitter winter on German border, Dutch friends, visits to Antwerp, more books

151)

287225 Capt R Barer RAMC
94 Light AA Regt RA
BLA

Monday 8th January

Dearest Gwen

No letter today, but weather is bad again. Am going to send you another parcel soon. It will contain Mrs Hill's table centre, a lace 'Dickie' which I want you to send to my Ma and a little lace blouse for you – don't suppose it'll fit you at present, but you won't always be enormous. I also got a few lace trimmings. I don't know if they're the sort of things you want but let me know and I'll see if I can get any more. I couldn't get them anywhere but eventually saw them in the 'Caledonian Road' of Brussels. There were also a lot of old book stalls but I couldn't find anything I wanted. The book I did buy is called *Habit and Intelligence* by Joseph John Murphy, 1879. I seem to remember Huxley mentioning him. Could you look him up? It looks quite interesting and contains a summary and analysis of Darwin's theory. It deals with such things as the origin of life, the origin of man, instinct and intelligence and an immense amount of stuff on variation and natural selection. He quotes Huxley, Darwin and Carpenter a lot. It's quite a big book (580 pages) and in excellent condition.

By the way it is true that muscles have no lymphatics, isn't it? Just read an official pamphlet which talks about them.

All my love dearest

RB

152)

287225 Capt R Barer RAMC
94 Light AA Regt RA
BLA

Wednesday, 10th January 1945

Dearest Gwen,

Just got 2 of your letters 3rd and 4th January, including Prof and Mrs Miles' letters. He needn't have commiserated so much about the weather as it's rather fun in some ways. There was an amazing scene the other day when the adjutant could contain himself no longer and went out into the blizzard to test the latrine. When he got there he found that the wooden cover had frozen stiff on the seat and he couldn't lift it at all. Eventually he had to take the whole seat outside and kick away at it until the lid came off! I must say this weather makes one tend towards constipation but it's surprisingly pleasant once one has plucked up courage.

I think on the whole we'd better retain our separate subs. I think the reduced rate applies up to 3 years from qualification so we wouldn't save much by a joint sub.

I'm glad Mrs H has found something for your Pa to do. It seems just the thing and will keep his mind a little occupied. It's probably the sort of job he'd like too. Haven't heard any more about leave yet. We have a ballot for it as vacancies fall but I'm afraid it may take some time.

We now have a canary in the RAP. It's supposed to be a good singer but seems to spend most of its time eating. However I don't think its quite recovered from its journey in the jeep from Brussels.

Am returning your pattern, it looks quite nice (*material for lining cot*). Will have a look round for bed covering but it's very expensive.

All my love darling

RB

[*Mrs Hill, A.V. Hill's wife and Janet's mother, gave my father and me a flat at the top of their house in Highgate.*]

153)
287225 Capt R Barer RAMC
94 Light AA Regt RA
BLA

Thursday, 11th January 1945 [*to FRB*]

Dear Dad,

Thanks for your letter. Glad you like the pipes; hope they're good to smoke. Have you tried the long one yet? I had a Dutch clay pipe for you also but I'm afraid it got broken on my travels. Hope you're settling down in your new home by now. It really is very kind of the Hills.

We don't have too bad a time really, though I don't suppose I shall ever persuade Gwen of that. At all events the really unpleasant times are soon forgotten and it's all very nice to look back on. We've certainly had a marvellous Cook's tour and even if I never do any more medicine I shall at least be able to say I've practised in France, Belgium, Holland and Germany.

I'm with a very good crowd now. They're mostly Yorkshiremen with a smattering of Londoners.

Kindest regards and a very happy New Year.

Hoping to see you soon

Robert

154)
287225 Capt R Barer RAMC
94 Light AA Regt RA
BLA

Thursday 11th January

Dearest Gwen

Got 2 letters, or rather 1 letter in 2 halves written 6th January. Have also sent off parcel containing various lace articles – bib for my Ma, envelope for Mrs Hill and blouse for you. Also odd trimmings.

Afraid you're right about the petrol. Don't think Max could get it. Anyhow, as you say, it would be better for you not to travel.

It's a pity you never told me to get you a bed jacket before I went to Brussels. However I expect I will be able to get one somehow. Sorry the clothes were too small for my Ma. I think it would be nice to get something for RG with the money. Your Mother would have liked that I'm sure.

I've not seen Colyer lately but one of the officers saw him today. I think I prefer my jeep to an armoured car – they're very awkward to get out of in a hurry and don't offer great protection and you can't beat a slit trench.

However, if you insist I'll raise the matter with the General. Perhaps he'll let me have a tank!

Can you look up the action of sulphur on the skin for me?

All my love dearest

RB

155)   287225 Capt R Barer RAMC
                                                94 Light AA Regt RA
                                                BLA

                                                Saturday 13th January

Dearest Gwen,

No letter again today. I'm afraid the weather has been remarkably cold but fortunately there's been no wind, so it's bearable. I don't think I've ever experienced such low temperatures before – one's hands go numb within a few seconds of exposure, I've had to be right out in the open for the last few days but it's quite pleasant as long as I'm walking about. I'm wearing 3 pairs of socks, and 2 pairs of gloves but it doesn't make much difference. It's amazing the way the gunners manage to fire in such conditions. In fact it's very surprising to see how much one can endure if one has to. I used to think that winter warfare on the Russian front must be absolute hell but one could easily get used to it given adequate clothing. The point is that in civvy street one never wore enough clothing for fear of looking ridiculous but out here one wears several pullovers and 2 or even 3 overcoats – I must look almost spherical! I'm having a very interesting time at the moment and am learning a lot about gunnery.

By the way, I wonder if it would be possible to find out where Profs Wachsmuth and Duesberg are at the moment? Possibly AV might suggest how to set about it. If at all feasible I'd like to visit them when I come on leave.

All my love dearest
RB

156)
                                            287225 Capt R Barer RAMC
                                            94 Light AA Regt RA
                                            BLA

                                            Sunday 14th January

Dearest Gwen,

Yet another day without a letter. There's bound to be one tomorrow. Have you had that railway voucher yet? And have you applied for an antenatal allowance?

I wonder if you can find among my belongings some books on elementary algebra, mechanics and trigonometry? I know there's one called *Matriculation Mechanics* and I think I have similar ones on other subjects. Anyhow could you send me what you can find as I've promised to coach someone. A book with problems and answers is needed. Don't buy any.

Have you given Nick the clown yet? I shall be annoyed if you keep it, you greedy thing. I can get lots of other things for RG. Have you had any more symptoms from your cystitis? Don't you think you ought to have another culture done?

All my love dearest

RB

157)
                                            287225 Capt R Barer RAMC
                                            94 Light AA Regt RA
                                            BLA

                                            Monday 22nd January

Dearest Gwen

One more letter today written 17th. Glad to hear you've received some of my back letters. Afraid a lot of them will be out of order (have you got the one containing the antenatal form back yet?).

Have just had an interesting half hour solving a problem in our division newspaper. See if you can do it (I expect AV could do it in his head!).

Four men are to share a number of carrots equally between them. They are sleeping in a house and the carrots are in the cellar with a Donkey. They don't trust each other however and during the night 1 man goes down and splits the carrots into 4 equal heaps (numerically) and finds 1 over which he gives to the donkey. He takes his pile and goes to bed. Later another man goes down splits the remaining carrots into 4, finds 1 over, gives it to the donkey and takes his pile. The 3rd and 4th men do the same, giving 1 to the donkey each time. In the morning they all meet and divide the remainder equally and again there's one left over which they give to the donkey. How many carrots were there originally? There's no catch, you have <u>all</u> the data required. There is an infinite number of answers, the smallest one being 1021. It's quite easy really.

Afraid I've no news at the moment.

All my love dearest

RB

[*16 January-8 February – After the German Christmas offensive in the Ardennes the Guards remained in the Namur area. This was a good time for the men; billets were comfortable and their hosts were generous.*]

158)

287225 Capt R Barer RAMC
94 Light AA Regt RA
BLA

Wednesday 24th January

Dearest Gwen
Got your letter of last Thursday.

Walked into George Clark while taking a patient to hospital [*contemporary student and friend at UCH*]. It's a scream. He's now a skin specialist to a big hospital! I shall know where not to send my cases in future. He had a very hectic time in his former job and is really rather lucky to be alive. However, he's pretty safe now. He told me that John Lawton – the tall dark chemistry demonstrator has been killed. The news looks very bright, doesn't it? Perhaps I won't need to come on 7 days leave after all.

All my love dearest

RB

159)

287225 Capt R Barer RAMC
94 Light AA Regt RA
BLA

Tuesday 30th January

Dearest Gwen,

1 letter today written last Wednesday. There's no need for you to get excited about Burma. I think DC got unduly alarmed about his change of job and rather jumped to conclusions. All the same I'm afraid it's obvious that he's liable to be sent to Burma some time as he's only been in the army such a short time. As far as I'm concerned there's been nothing said, except that I'm staying with this unit and am unlikely to be sent on a draft. Incidentally there would be much more chance of being sent out east if I was with the FDS or even a field ambulance. (I'm sorry you read anything cryptic into my conversation with David. We were only discussing the problem generally with nothing specific in mind. Afraid I can't tell you why I left the FDS in a letter, but I'm very glad I did as the type of work would scarcely appeal to me. Anyhow I hope I've set your mind at rest.)

I don't think you can send telegrams out here except for a specially urgent reason. [*I probably asked if I could send the news of the birth by telegram.*]

If you do intend to put anything in the papers, I think the *Telegraph* and BMJ will do, not *The Times* – we're not really as important as all that.

Sorry to hear about your Pa. I think you had better pander to his wishes e.g. regarding medicine for colds. You could probably include some sedative which would do him good in his present frame of mind. It must be very difficult for you.

(Afraid I don't understand your difficulty with the curtain problem [*for carry cot*]. Obviously, provided the curtain begins to slope up at the same place and ends at the same place the angle α will be the same however many folds are put in the sloping part [*diagram*]. In practice if the final result is as dotted [*another diagram*], the original curtain, unfolded can be shown with the value of y.)

All my love dearest

RB

160)

287225 Capt R Barer RAMC
94 Light AA Regt RA
BLA

Tuesday 30th January

Dearest Gwen,

No letter today but have received the 3 books. They should be quite useful. The chap I am coaching is one of the Sergeants in our workshop.

Have just had a simply awful day in a blizzard. Had to drive with jeep windscreen open, as it frosts over completely within about 30 seconds. Then my glasses frosted over! Finally landed among a lot of snow drifts and had to be lifted out! However am none the worse for it now although my coat was just one solid mass of ice.

All my love dearest, am going to Brussels in a couple of days so letters may be delayed.

RB

161)

287225 Capt R Barer RAMC
94 Light AA Regt RA
BLA

Thursday 1st February

Dearest Gwen,

No mail again today. Afraid I've drawn unlucky in the leave ballot and am near the bottom end – however judging by the rate things are moving in Russia the war will probably be over long before I'm due for leave. Even if they don't get Berlin right away they've dealt a pretty crippling blow. Had an MO's conference the other day. Brian Warren asked after you. DC is still at FDS and knows nothing about Burma.

I see Rimington is taking Harington's place at UCH (what a pity Wiley isn't there. He'd have terrific discussions on porphorin metabolism). Anyhow he's a first class man and it's probably a good choice. Wonder if he's a good teacher?

Off to Brussels tomorrow.

All my love dearest
RB

162)   287225 Capt R Barer RAMC
                                  94 Light AA Regt RA
                                  BLA

                                  Saturday 3rd February (from
                                  'Eye' club Brussels)

Dearest Gwen,

Have been having a quiet time in Brussels and haven't fallen from grace yet
though it's damned hard I must say. The sight of women after a month or
two in the wilds is just too much for most people. I sometimes wish I
weren't born so respectable.

I went to the Saddler's Wells Ballet last night. It was a very good show.
The orchestra was conducted by Constant Lambert. I think '*Les Syphilides*'
would be the most appropriate ballet for this place but it wasn't on. They
showed *Promenade, Les Patineurs* and *Miracle of the Gorbels*. The latter
is a most remarkable 'problem' piece which you must see if you get the
chance. Have sent off a couple of things for RG. Not very good I'm afraid
but will get better ones later.

They don't appear to wear bedjackets over here – and nor will you either
if I feel anything like I do at present when I get back.

All my love dearest, hope there'll be a pile of letters waiting for me when
I get back.

RB

163)   287225 Capt R Barer RAMC
                                  94 Light AA Regt RA
                                  BLA

                                  Tuesday 6th February

Dearest Gwen,

No letter yet so will deal with a few more points from your pile.

First of all the problem. You've got the method right more or less up to
the last line. However your arithmetic is a little wrong. I've indicated the
corrections in pencil.

:   *solution with my mistakes* . . .

However you seem to have got further than most people in the GAD!

About your Pa, I do wish you wouldn't quarrel. I know it's very difficult dear but I'm sure he doesn't mean it. I agree with you that it's most certainly arteriosclerosis; as a matter of fact, I noticed the symptoms coming on some time ago. You <u>must</u> learn to remain absolutely silent in the face of provocation. It does no good to have rows and it's <u>absolutely useless</u> to try and change his ways. Let him criticise your cooking if he wants to – it won't get him anywhere. Do <u>please</u> try.

As regards Convocation I don't think I'll do anything about it just yet. It's rather a waste of £1 at present.

I'd very much like to see Schrodinger's book when you've read it. Has AV said anything about it?

I don't think you need have any fears for RG's safety in UCH. After all he wouldn't get any better care and attention anywhere and anyhow as you say they've never had any catastrophes yet.

What a pity Sister Billings isn't on your ward!

As regards tracing Profs W and D, I should think the Red Cross would be most helpful. I'm sure Bülbring wouldn't know.

I'd very much like to meet W again. He's a most remarkable personality. He was once nearly arrested by the Gestapo for helping Belgian hostages.

Well dear, I don't think it'll be very long now so try and hang on for another few weeks.

All my love dearest. Don't worry if mail is delayed.

RB

[*8 February – 9 March*
In Operation Veritable, the Canadians and British were to clear the area between the Meuse and the Rhine, south-east of Nijmegen. The battle took place largely on German soil, weather conditions were appalling and there was serious flooding. The Germans destroyed dams on the Roer to the south, which postponed the American attack by ten days, delaying the link-up with the British. The Guards Armoured Division did not spearhead this time but were in the thick of the fighting and suffered nearly 500 casualties. The battle concluded with the Germans destroying the Rhine bridges in that sector.

Meanwhile the Americans took Cologne on 7 March and a few days later the whole west bank of the Rhine had been cleared as far as the Moselle at Koblenz.]

164)

287225 Capt R Barer RAMC
94 Light AA Regt RA
BLA

Wednesday 14th February

Dearest Gwen,

A whole host of your letters at last – from February 7-10.

You are a silly old darling really. You know very well I wouldn't have anything to do with anyone but you, though I must admit the desire at times becomes almost overwhelming [*I had said I wouldn't mind under the circumstance!*]. It's amazingly strong, particularly after we've been out in the wilds and we all suffer in the same way even the most respectable of us. I must say I never even visualised anything like it – one had to fight all the time. For example, a Belgian Nurse, whose grandfather I had treated gave me her address in Brussels and asked me to visit her there. I had to deliberately destroy her address to avoid being tempted. I'll tell you a very amusing story of my last leave in Brussels, which I shared with another highly respectable officer, when I come home, I don't think you need worry. I'm pretty strong-willed and I'd rather die than risk anything or hurt you. You know very well you're the only person in the world I could ever really love. It's just the awful desire for feminine companionship that's so overpowering at times. As regards the names I think we should leave them as we've decided. Robin Geoffrey or Jean Margaret – that should be enough unless they're twins!

Do you like Eric as a name? I think it would be quite nice to get the new pram cover – it's not very expensive really.

As regards Royal Northern you must suit yourself and get Uncle's advice. It's well worth paying a few extra pounds for a little extra comfort and safety. I should feel quite happy if you were at either place, though RN [*Royal Northern*] would be less embarrassing for you. Don't worry about expense at all and don't let leave considerations enter as I don't think there's the faintest hope for April.

Sorry to disappoint you about bedjackets. Afraid there simply weren't any and there are none round here!

Visited FDS today. Colyer quite OK. Alderson is going at last! – to a field ambulance.

All my love dearest one.

RB

165)   287225 Capt R Barer RAMC
                                                 94 Light AA Regt RA
                                                 BLA

                                                 Saturday 16th February

Dearest Gwen,

No letter today but the weather seems to be improving so perhaps things will run smoothly now.

Saw Colyer the other day. He's very well. A dreadful thing has happened to poor little XX. He got a telegram saying that his wife was in an institution and showed suicidal tendencies . . . I do hope it's only a neurosis but I fear the worst. She has been under the care of a Specialist(?) who has been charging them 3.5 gns per week! I do think people like that are despicable – at least that's one thing a state medical service may stop. X has gone off on compassionate leave. I can't imagine anything more dreadful to happen to anyone – death would be much kinder.

Have been reading some of Murphy's book. Have you found any reference to him yet? The book is quite interesting. He's a catholic and a vitalist but presents all the evidence quite fairly and quotes an immense number of interesting facts and it's quite good exercise to try and find flaws in his arguments. He deals with Darwin quite fully but does not agree with him in the end.

All my love darling – miss you very much indeed.

RB

166)   287225 Capt R Barer RAMC
                                                 94 Light AA Regt RA
                                                 BLA

                                                 Monday 19th February

Dearest Gwen,

Letters today 14th and 15th February.

Sorry about the christening robe, but you'll have to be tactful but <u>absolutely</u> firm on the point. Afraid dear it's quite ridiculous for you to hope I'll get leave for RG, unless the war is over by then. It's next to impossible to get leave even in cases of severe illness. Only today a man in the regiment got a war office telegram telling him his child was seriously ill but he could not be granted leave. 6 hours later he heard that the child had died. Leave is not even granted in the case of death of a wife or parent, unless there is no one else to settle up the estate. Have you fixed up anything definite about my people going to see you? My Ma told me she was looking forward to it. As regards food it would be best to keep off meat. They both like eggs and fish, cheese dishes etc. – my Pa likes anything soft as he's got no teeth. My Pa does <u>not</u> like green (or any vegetables) though my Ma does. I'm afraid I've no idea of what the food situation is like over there so I hope my suggestions aren't silly.

By the way Beric told me that Tom [*Lewis, cardiologist*] has been ill again – lung infarcts and is definitely retiring.

They want Pochin to take over but he isn't keen to work in an atmosphere polluted by x and x.

DW has been called up at last – presumably as a surgeon.

All my love dearest

RB

167)

287225 Capt R Barer RAMC
94 Light AA Regt RA
BLA

Wednesday 21st February

Dearest Gwen,

No letter now for 2 days, but Schrodinger arrived yesterday. It looks interesting. I'm glad that he thinks that the ordinary classical physics can't explain the origin of life. I'm sure it would be worthwhile trying to grow viruses in 'asymmetrical' media – with diffusion gradients and active surfaces – the sort of conditions that must occur in living cells. Schrodinger is a great expert on Quantum physics and has made fundamental contributions to the subject. It's a pity he deals so much with genetics and doesn't seem to mention viruses.

Afraid there's no news dear. Hope the mail improves.

All my love darling
RB

168)

287225 Capt R Barer RAMC
94 Light AA Regt RA
BLA

Thursday 22nd February

Dearest Gwen,

Three letters at last (one of them written 13 February – all out of place, others 16 and 17. I now understand what you meant about Joan Stokes – I thought you meant she might get Miles' job when he retires – but to get it now would be fantastic!)

Glad you like Weddell's letter [*prospects of a job in Oxford*]. Miles' departure will certainly be a blow for UCH. I think as you say that Hampstead might well be a possibility with both Miles and Harrington there [*for jobs*]. I don't know if they've got an EM there yet but I expect they will have. However I think I'd prefer Oxford on the whole if the facilities are OK. The whole life and atmosphere are so much pleasanter and besides there would be teaching to do. Hampstead (NIMR) is very good but seems rather cold and impersonal – all life ceases in the evening.

As regards Red Cross [*to locate doctors he met in Brussels*]. I think its quite likely that if you explained that you were a doctor wanting to visit a doctor it might be easier. They are supposed to be protected personnel and not prisoners of war. I expect they are working in some hospital. However you know their names and can say they were working at the Military hospital in Brussels. Anyhow try and find out where they are and if you can't visit them you might write sending my regards and hoping they are well looked after. Say I tried to visit them but found they had gone. You'd better explain who I am as they've probably not remembered my name. D would probably like to hear from Bülbring too. Glad you like the toys – afraid I've almost forgotten what they look like. Will try and get some more in the dim future when I might go to Brussels again – afraid David, Beric and Harky, especially Harky will have to demolish that cake [*three friends stationed in Brussels – I had sent a cake for R via one of them hoping he would get there*].

All my love dearest and a big hug

RB

169)
> 287225 Capt R Barer RAMC
> 94 Light AA Regt RA
> BLA
>
> Monday 26th February

Dearest Gwen,

So glad to hear you've got some of my letters at last. Yours have been quite regular, and you've no idea how lovely it is to get them in this wilderness. Am longing for the time when I can hold you again and we won't have to hang about waiting for the post.

You needn't worry about what I shall do if I get sent out East dear. I shall certainly do everything possible to get a suitable scientific job. It's much easier out there as there are so many things connected with the tropics. All the same I'm hoping it won't be necessary. It all depends on Oxford. Have just heard that I'm definitely <u>not</u> going on leave in March. I should think May or June is possible at the present rate. Colyer will probably go in April.

Thank you for renewing Nature dear. It makes quite a pleasant change. I suppose my people have come and gone by now. Hope everything went well.

All my love dearest, am longing for you more than ever.

RB

170)
> 287225 Capt R Barer RAMC
> 94 Light AA Regt RA
> BLA
>
> Wednesday 28th February

Dearest Gwen,

Got 2 letters of 23rd and 24th February. Oh dear! I'm afraid I've been laughing all day about your weeping episode at lunch [*with his Mum and Dad and Max*]. Whatever made you do it? Anyhow did you find the glove? As regards the circumcision problem you know perfectly well I agree with you. It's exactly comparable to christening and of course we shall have neither. I shall write to my Ma and explain things. I'm quite sure she doesn't set any store by these things and nor does my Pa really. I think that what is at the back of his mind is the fear that the child will be brought up in ignorance of his ancestry and traditions and I'm sure you don't want this to happen either. What I shall say, and I think you will agree, is that this child will not be brought up in any special religious atmosphere, he will have all the facts presented to him impartially. I should like him to learn Hebrew and to know something of Hebrew laws and traditions. The same applies of course to Christian principles. I think this would to some extent reassure my Father, though, as you say, both sides will have to be a little hurt. Still we knew that was bound to happen all the time, didn't we? I don't think it will be too bad and things have gone very smoothly so far.

Anyhow dear, we must always remember we have married each other and not our families and that the upbringing of our children is our own affair. We must do everything possible to avoid hurting anyone, but we must never deviate from our own opinions. I'm sure they will see our point of view.

Quite apart from the religious aspects I think it would be a good thing and I'd like it done as soon as possible. I'll have to leave it to you to fix it, perhaps they could do it at the RN.

Incidentally I'm glad you've decided on the RN, it will be much nicer for you.

Very amused to hear about Max and membership! [*MRCP exam.*] Afraid he's been saying that for the last 15 years but always ends up by saying he doesn't know enough. I can sympathise with him as I feel just the same about exams. Hope there won't be any more. However, perhaps I'm wrong at last and he really will take it – you must force him to. Darling I really think you're wrong about telegrams – I think it only applies to Middle East. Anyhow there is none from here to England. Finally, don't take any notice whatsoever of what Fred Allen or anyone else may say. Your sources of information have invariably been wildly wrong. These people know nothing of what really happens, so ignore them.

All my love dearest and don't lose any more gloves!

RB

171)

287225 Capt R Barer RAMC
94 Light AA Regt RA
BLA

Saturday 3rd March

Dearest Gwen,

Two letters today both written 27 February. Glad you had Eileen to supper. You must try to see more of old associates. Interested to hear the latest news from UCH. Hope PL's husband finds her a little more responsive than A did!

I'm glad Pochin is returning. They need someone at UCH to carry on the old tradition. I expect Squire will come back after the war, too. What did Beric say in his letter to you? I hope he told you I was in a nice comfortable spot at the time – I wouldn't mind being there now as it's bitterly cold and windy. However, will soon be across the Rhine I hope – and then we'll have to prepare for the victory parade.

All my love dearest

RB

PS Regarding W and D I can't remember their initials – the book is at the bottom of my trunk but they were both Professors. W was chief of the *Chirurgisches Sonderlazarett'* at O.K.H. Brussels (actually the 'Institut Bordet') and D was in charge of the shock team there.

172)

287225 Capt R Barer RAMC
94 Light AA Regt RA
BLA

Sunday 4th March

Dearest Gwen,

One year today! But what a difference from the lovely sunny Saturday morning when you finally got me under your thumb. The weather is ghastly – I don't know how the infantry stick it. Still it's worth the discomfort to feel that we're on the eve of big events judging by the excellent progress being made.

Glad you saw John Gray. His job sounds quite interesting but I think I'd prefer to have solid ground under me. Beric told me Angus was a Major. Don't worry dear, I shan't get left out and I promise you I'll try. Anyhow there's always the chance of Oxford materialising.

By the way I think Rosie's [*Max Rosenheim, our mentor at UCH – later Lord Rosenheim*] brother has been killed. He was a Major in the infantry over here. I saw it in the *Telegraph.*

All my love dearest and here's to many more and happier anniversaries.
RB

[*Undated note delivered by hand*]
Next year, and for the next forty years, I shall bring them myself.
Robert

[*I believe this came with flowers on our first wedding anniversary, 4 March 1945.*]

173)   287225 Capt R Barer RAMC
                                                           94 Light AA Regt RA
                                                           BLA

                                                           Monday 5th March

Dearest Gwen,
Long letter today to relieve the monotony.

Sorry the wireless is misbehaving. I should think there's a reliable wireless shop at the Archway – it would be worth getting it done.

I don't think you need shed any tears over Poland. I think there's a lot to be said for all frontiers to be settled by an agreement between the 3 powers. So called democratic principles can be overdone and the presence of all the interested parties merely leads to bickering and nothing gets done – witness the League. There is a far better chance of a permanent settlement if that settlement is maintained by a few great powers. All these small nations are a threat to future peace and Poland is one of the worst. I agree that if there had been a representative Polish government they should have been invited. But no-one could possibly say that either the Lublin or the London people were in any way representative. I'm afraid the Poles have only themselves to blame for their complete lack of political realism and I'm pessimistic enough to believe that they'll <u>never</u> get a reasonable government. In actual fact I think they will gain from the present arrangement. They do away with the corridor and gain a wider sea coast. Most of the area they lose is waste land – the Pripet Marshes. I think they're doing better than they deserve.

Glad you had a nice evening with John Gray. I shall write to Crewe when I think the time is ripe – not very long now I hope.

All my love dearest

RB

[*A reference to the Yalta conference 4-11 February 1945 at which Roosevelt and Churchill sacrificed the legitimacy of the Polish Government in exile to one backed by Stalin. Free elections were promised on Poland's 'liberation' but were never held. On 2 August at the Potsdam Conference, Poland was shifted west to the Oder-Neisse line, taking over 39,596 square miles from Germany. On 16 August, the Polish-Soviet treaty confirmed the eastern frontier along the Curzon line: 69,290 square miles were lost to the Soviet Union.*

R's unsympathetic attitude may have been a reaction to the anti-semitism that was rife in Poland at the time.]

174)   287225 Capt R Barer RAMC
                                         94 Light AA Regt RA
                                         BLA

                                         Thursday 8th March

Dearest Gwen,

Got your letters of 4th March today. Glad you liked the flowers and am <u>specially</u> glad you couldn't find anything to send me as I'm already carrying far too much junk [*flowers must have been with note 'Next year and for the next forty years'*].

You need not worry any more about the ritual business [*concerning new baby*]. I have now received a reply to the letter I wrote to my Ma on the subject and it's very satisfactory. I'm sure I'm right about what was really worrying my Father and my Ma says he is very pleased. I have given a definite promise (and I'm sure you will agree) that RG will not grow up in ignorance of his traditions. Like your people, they've taken it very well.

As regards the problem of your aunts etc. [*who wanted to lend christening robes etc.*]. I think it's best not to mention the subject if possible. There's no point upsetting them, as you say.

Interested to hear what Harry [*Professor Harry Himsworth, UCH*] is doing but I rather think he's on a wild goose chase. People's imagination tends to run a little wild at times and a lot of the tales I've been told about similar things I have found to be wildly untrue. However, we can only wait and see, but I shall be very surprised if he has to use his casein hydrolysate. My faith in people's veracity has been so badly shaken that I'm rather sceptical about all these wonderful stories.

By the way, the officer in charge of the unit workshop, Captain Allsop, is going on leave. He lives in South London and offered to phone you. It's very good of him though I don't know what he can tell you, but don't embarrass him and waste his leave by inviting him up to Highgate. I've told him not to go in case you did, as it wouldn't be fair.

All my love dearest

RB

[*After the Rhineland battle the Division returned to the Nijmegen area to rest until late March.*]

175)
287225 Capt R Barer RAMC
94 Light AA Regt RA
BLA

Saturday 10th March

Dearest Gwen,

Letter of 5th arrived today. Regarding newspapers, they are very variable. We usually get them within 2-3 days, sometimes longer. We usually manage to get the *Telegraph* so that would be best. Actually a letter would probably be even quicker. As regards my sending telegrams, we can only send them in case of urgency [*there were plans to inform him of the birth of our child*].

I saw in the newspaper that a pathologist, T.H. Belt had been found dead in his car. Apparently he was in trouble over the Dangerous Drugs Act. It rather looks like the chap who was to come to the sector. I met Ken Green today. He is now in a field ambulance.

The Colonel told us a dreadful story about Sir Henry Wood today. He really is very funny. At a certain orchestral production he got rather fed up with the cellist (female) and at last turned to her in disgust and said 'young woman, you have between your legs something which might be a source of pleasure to millions, and all you do is sit and scratch it!'

GW has got his compassionate posting. Things look rather bad for him, poor chap.

Well dear, afraid there's no news.

All my love dearest
RB

176)   287225 Capt R Barer RAMC
                                             94 Light AA Regt RA
                                             BLA

                                             Monday 12th March

Dearest Gwen,

Two letters today, one 6th with bank statement and another of 9th.

Glad you heard from David (H). There may be a chance of seeing him again, but not for 3-4 weeks I'm afraid so he'll have to eat the cake! As regards expenses, there's no need at all to worry. Remember that when RG comes I shall be getting about £45 per month tax free (24/6 per week for RG) so that by July we shall have had £180 in pay. Even assuming you have both the nurse at 3.5 gns and a home help at £2 each for 1 month (making £22) and assuming RG's arrival costs us £50 (including a present to Uncle which should cost at least £10) that will leave £108 to last 4 months – i.e. £27 per month which is more than you actually spend. At present we have £84 in the bank so that we only have to find £20 to pay the insurance. Anyhow, as you say, we can always make use of the 30 days grace they allow and wait for July's pay. Actually when is the payment due? At the beginning or the end of July? I don't think there'll be any need either to withdraw savings or to borrow any money from your Pa, though it's very good of him to offer. My own expenses are very small. I took £11 with me when I went to Brussels last but I still have £8 left so I probably shan't draw any more for a couple of months. Certainly there's nothing to spend it on in Germany!

So you see, dear, there's no reason for stinting yourself and I think it would be a good idea to have both the nurse and a home help. We can always meet any extra unexpected expenses by our savings.

Incidentally you must start asking people what Uncle would like as a present.

Have you heard any more about Belt?

All my love dearest

RB

177)   287225 Capt R Barer RAMC
                                         94 Light AA Regt RA
                                         BLA

                                         Tuesday 13th March

Dearest Gwen,

No letter today, but copy of *Punch* arrived. I've just finished reading St Matthew. It's very interesting and I think a lot could be said for not making children read it at an early age, when they're liable to accept everything at face value.

There are a number of awkward points which are not stressed in the official teaching. For example, chapter 10, verses 34-37 are at variance with the usual idea of Christ as a lover of peace.

'Think not that I come to send peace on earth. I come not to send peace but a sword. For I am come to set a man at variance against his Father and the daughter against her Mother and the daughter-in-law against her Mother-in-law. And a man's foes shall be they of his own household' etc. Again it's usually taught that Christianity differs from the Mosaic law in being a universal religion, not confined to one race. However Chapter 15, verses 22-28 take some explaining. A Canaanite woman asked Christ to heal her daughter, 'But he answered not a word,' she persisted and the disciples asked him to do something, 'but he answered and said I am not sent but unto the lost sheep of the house of Israel' . . . and later 'It is not meet to take the children's bread and cast it to the dogs.' I suppose the theologians answer would be that he was testing her faith but in Chapter 6, verses 31-32 he makes a rude remark about gentiles. I'd like your opinion on these points. Were they glossed over by your scripture teachers? I think people tend to explain away everything to suit their own convenience. Not, of course that such things detract from the value of the greater mass of Christ's teachings.

All my love dearest
RB

178)

287225 Capt R Barer RAMC
94 Light AA Regt RA
BLA

Monday 19th March

Dearest Gwen,

Letter of 15th came today. Afraid you still ask a lot of questions I can't answer. (However, as regards driving, I sometimes drive myself, sometimes my batman drives – it depends on circumstances. As regards a car, it's obviously a silly question as you don't know anything about the supply situation and I can't tell you that. Anyhow I'm not entitled to one, but if it's any consolation to you, there's just a chance I may get one in a few weeks. As regards RDS I sincerely hope there's no chance of that!)

You ask if the Colonel is a nice chap. He is, very nice indeed. He's a regular soldier aged about 45 and is a qualified barrister as well. He's had a lot of experience in India and Palestine. He's very well educated and a brilliant speaker. His strong point is military law and if ever I'm court-martialled I shall get him to defend me! The adjutant has a unique collection of abject crawling letters of apology sent by numerous people to the Colonel in reply to one of his stinging letters. He's brilliant at picking out one salient feature and then hammering it home till his opponent hasn't a leg to stand on. His hobby is finance – he collects old books on economics. He believes that banks exist merely to provide him with overdrafts. His argument is that he has to pay the bank 2.5% for his overdraft but he can make 3.5% on the loan on the Stock exchange so he gains 1%.

He once wrote an amazing letter to Cox's bank because they had written to his wife complaining of his overdraft. He attacked them for their lack of moral courage in writing to his wife while he was overseas and threatened to remove his overdraft to another bank! Sure enough, a crawling letter of apology came back!

I think one of his best stories is about how he scared off the War Office. He ran a big camp in Northern Ireland once (he has many tales about the ATS there). One day he received a stiff letter from the War Office saying that they had been informed by the Censor that the men were complaining in their letters of the bad conditions at the camp. In particular there was only one hurricane lamp to each Nissen hut and they couldn't see to read or write. He wrote a very meek reply enclosing a copy of the Barrack Schedule (written by the War Office itself!) pointing out that he was only allowed 1 lamp and had been repeatedly refused any more by the War Office! They soon revised the schedule. One of his best clashes has been with a certain

205

MP over here. I wish he'd taken the matter further. That particular man has no right to be in Parliament judging by his behaviour. However I'll tell you about that later.

All my love dearest

RB

S P E C I A L   O R D E R   O F   T H E   D A Y

by

Lt-COL J. C. WINDSOR - LEWIS DSO.,MC.

COMMANDING WELSH GUARDS BATTLE GROUP.

B. L. A.   11 MAR 45.

         Operation "VERITABLE" which was the name given to 1st Canadian Army's advance to the RHINE, is now virtually concluded, and concluded very successfully, for it has resulted in many Germans being routed and killed. The Canadian Army, including its vast proportion of British Divisions, now stands lined up alongside our American Allies, all set for the "last round" of this memorable contest.

         Forming a portion of 30 Corps, under the vigorous and bold leadership of General HORROCKS, the Guards Division has fully maintained its high fighting reputation. 32 Gds Bde were the first to be summoned into action, and the Welsh Guards Battle Group have added further lustre to their name by their participation in the last three weeks fighting. It was unfortunate that we were never destined to operate as a group, each Bn fighting separate actions, with the Sqns of 2nd Bn giving support on different occasions to all the Infantry battalions in the Bde.

         The 1st Bn set the ball rolling by a successful action on Feb 14th in the woods SOUTH of HOMMERSUM, followed a few days later by a swift and practically unopposed entry into the bomb-shattered, but key village of HASSUM.

         Then came that neat victory at BONNINGHARDT on Mar 6th, when, in a bold and determined advance the Bn cleared the enemy-held woods WEST of BONNINGHARDT, and subsequently the long straggling village itself, a fine performance - as captured enemy documents, in addition to the topographical layout, made it obvious that the enemy intended to defend this sector stubbornly. This certainly proved to be the case.

         Of the Armoured Bn., No 2 Sqn were the first into the fray, supporting the Coldstream and Irish Guards in the attack on HOMMERSUM on Feb 14th. Later, they put up an excellent show, though unfortunately not without loss to themselves, when supporting 2nd Bn Scots Guards in their attack over the canal on March 8th, while the next day, Mar 9th, saw this same Sqn shooting a Bn of 52nd Div on to their objective in the same area.

         In a bitter action on Feb 16th, No 1 Sqn gave useful support to Coldstream Guards who captured MULL under appalling conditions of mud, which caused most of the Sqn's Tanks to become bogged.

         No 3 Sqn assisted Scots Guards on March 6th in clearing a part of the BONNINGHARDT woods, and later on that day came under command of our 1st Bn for the attack on the village.

         The Lt Sqn whose debut in 2nd Bn was hailed with such enthusiasm, for no finer body of men ever rode in Tanks, made an auspicious entry into the lists, supporting 1st Bn in their successful operations at BONNINGHARDT. It was an action that called for swift thinking and quick manoeuvre, and the new Sqn emerged with high honours, although semi-crippled by loss of Tanks.

                                            2/..........

2.

A special mention must be awarded to L.A.D. and Technical staffs of both Bns, through whose prodigious efforts our vehicles are still standing up to all the heavy work that is demanded of them.

Operation "VERITABLE" has proved that the efficiency and dash of both Bns have been maintained at the same high level as that attained during the training in England, and in the battles fought in Normandy, Belgium and Holland.

There is no finer Infantry Bn in this sphere of operations than the 1st Bn Welsh Guards, and it is the earnest desire of their brothers in the 2nd Bn, that they will still be retained in the group on the EASTERN banks of the RHINE.

Tank casualties have been rather more heavy than usual, but recent losses in personnel have, thank God, not been excessive, but we deplore the passing of those gallant officers, N.C.Os and men who have sacrificed their lives for this Regiment, for their country, and in support of the most righteous cause for which man has ever shouldered arms

Once again, as at CAEN last July, British and Canadian troops have attracted and grappled with strong German forces rushed to meet them, so that our American Allies have been able to stage yet another spectacular break-through. Operation "VERITABLE" has served a useful purpose, as it has enabled the U.S. Armies to reach the RHINE so quickly, and at so many points.

Germany is now rocking on her knees under the prodigious blows rained upon her by land and air, from Allied weapons.

This is no time to let up. We have laboured and striven hard to achieve results since we landed in EUROPE - but our greatest effort must now be mobilised, for it will cause tottering Germany to crash before the overwhelming might of the three great Allies - Ourselves - America - and Russia. We are living on the crest of history, indeed we are creating history. GOOD LUCK TO US ALL!

J.C.(Castle)

Lt-Col,
Comd WELSH GUARDS BATTLE GROUP.

CHAPTER VII

Crossing the Rhine, plight of German civilians, desperate resistance of German paratroopers, capture of Sandbostel concentration/POW camp, unbearable sights

179)

287225 Capt R Barer RAMC
94 Light AA Regt RA
BLA

Friday 23rd March

Dearest Gwen,

Just a quick note to let you know everything is OK. Am returning wireless estimate. On the whole I think it's worth getting done. The charge for components is very reasonable. The main item is £3 for the work itself. I think they're probably a reliable firm and the set would be almost as good as new. It would certainly last another 2-3 years and I think wireless sets will be rather dear after the war. It has a good speaker and amplifier for a radiogram attachment. The quality is excellent. It sounds extravagant looked at from a short term point of view, but it isn't really. I expect in 2 or 3 years time we shall want a television set if they're cheap.

Well dear, afraid I can't give you any news, but keep your ears glued to the news – RG may yet be born in peace.

All my love dearest – how I wish I could be near you now.

RB

[25 March
The divisional artillery took part in the huge bombardment which preceded the assault on the Rhine. This was in the Rees area to the south-west of Nijmegen and was part of a combined American-Canadian-British operation over a wide front. After that the 21st Army Group of which the Division formed a part, was to make for the river Elbe and take the ports of Bremen and Hamburg.

The remaining weeks of the war allowed no spectacular advances for the Guards Armoured Division; instead the battles were hard and slow, often fought at squadron/company level against paratroopers, who only retreated when they had to, leaving behind a trail of mines and demolished bridges.]

180)
                    287225 Capt R Barer RAMC
                    94 Light AA Regt RA
                    BLA

                    Sunday 25th March

Dearest Gwen,

Sorry I've not been able to write much. All sorts of things have been happening – people having their legs blown off by mines, planes crashing, men overcome by the effects of smoke screens and of course the great bombardment. I wish I could describe it to you. We probably played the most spectacular part and dropped a mere 20,000 shells over the Rhine in 2 hours! The CO and I went to see the effect when it was all over. We certainly gave the assault a good send off. The Rhine was remarkably peaceful and it was a beautiful day. We sat by the water and it might have been the Serpentine. Well dear, I think the next few days will see the final stages well on the way. Don't worry if mail is delayed, communications will soon become OK again.

    All my love dearest

    RB

181)
                    287225 Capt R Barer RAMC
                    94 Light AA Regt RA
                    BLA

                    Tuesday 27th March

Dearest Gwen,

Two letters today an old one of 18th and one of 22nd.

Glad you've heard from Red Cross [*about German doctors, Wachsmuth & Duisberg*] but it doesn't sound so good. However you might like to write to W, find out how he is and if he wants anything – books etc., he might know about D.

Have you written to the Directorate of POW (Curzon St House, Curzon St W1) about visiting? I'd rather you wrote as the censor might think I've some ulterior motive if I wrote from over here.

Glad Allsop cheered you up, though I wish his remarks about the pictures were true! He's gone round telling everyone that you said I was not really a doctor!

Hope your domestic troubles are settled by now. I doubt if David will see much of me in the next few weeks – he'd better eat the cake.

Will keep the Red Cross letter so here's the address in case you haven't got it.

> Prof Werner Wachsmuth A428915
> POW Camp No 7
> Great Britain

All my love dearest

RB

182)

> 287225 Capt R Barer RAMC
> 94 Light AA Regt RA
> BLA

> Saturday 30th March

Dearest Gwen,

Letter of 26th came today, also parcel from my Ma – would you thank her for me in case I don't get a chance. No need to worry about odd post marks – it was only a temporary thing we did over the big shoot.

Well, dear, afraid I've nothing much to say. Don't pay for the wireless in advance but see that it's working properly first.

All my love dearest
RB

[*This letter was scribbled.*]

[*28 March to 4 April*
On 28 March the Guards Armoured Division moved forward. The Grenadiers crossed the Rhine, on a pontoon bridge, and passed through the mined town of Rees. After several days of severe fighting, the Division reached the river Ems to the north-east and forced a crossing on 3 April (the day RG was born).]

183)   287225 Capt R Barer RAMC
                                         94 Light AA Regt RA
                                         BLA

                                         Monday 2nd April

Dearest Gwen
Arrival of letter about Sarah came today [*our friend Janet's new baby*]. Am glad it was OK.

About canvas bath, can't suggest anything – they sometimes stop leaking after being used a lot. If not you could try linseed oil or else rest it on towelling to catch the leak [*no baby baths were available – in the end we used a zinc wash tub with a towel in it!*].

As regards W, I think your suggestion might be quite good. If it is possible to send him medical papers he might like something on the use of penicillin in surgery – he rather thought it might be just a passing fashion, of no real value. I don't know if he reads English well – he knows French and German of course.

Have seen a lot of liberated Holland – no sign of gross starvation so far – much about the same as the rest of Holland. Possibly the big towns may be worse off.

All my love dearest

RB

[*Our baby was expected on 5 April, arrived in fact on 3 April. R learnt of this by means of an announcement in the* Daily Telegraph *and, simultaneously, on the back of a letter from me, 'It's RG'!*]

184)
287225 Capt R Barer RAMC
94 Light AA Regt RA
BLA

Tuesday 3rd April

Dearest Gwen,

Letter of 31st came today. I agree with what you want to put in *Telegraph* and including the names. Hope to see the announcement soon! Afraid I can't give you any news. As usual the newspapers are completely irresponsible and inaccurate. The 6th Guards Armoured <u>Brigade</u> did <u>not</u> enter Brussels after a 60 mile advance (anyhow it was 93 miles). They don't even bother to check up what they wrote last September. However despite their irritating drivel things are going very well, though it's by no means a walk-over. This number of *Nature* contains a review of Schrodinger by Haldane. He says it's interesting and thought-provoking but quotes many recent experiments which do not fit in with Delbruck's theory. What does AV say about it? [*A.V. Hill, Nobel Prize Winner in Physiology, and our friend Janet's father; I was currently living in a flat at the top of his house.*]

All my love dearest
RB

185)
287225 Capt R Barer RAMC
94 Light AA Regt RA
BLA

Thursday 5th April

Dearest Gwen,

The great EDD (expected date of delivery!) has arrived but I've no news. Nothing in *Telegraph* of April 3rd anyhow. Afraid it looks as if he'll just miss having his birthday on V day though not by much. Do wish I could be with you just now. I suppose Colyer will be visiting you soon. Hope he brings the books safely. I suppose you heard the bit about us on the wireless yesterday. You will probably guess where we're going.

All my love dearest. Hope the good news comes soon.

RB

PS Enclose German propaganda leaflet. One of them looks like you!

Look here:

This is the man who stands between you and me

Poor Jerry!

You don't have this: the slacker for whom we fight and to whom we leave our girls

German propaganda leaflet

WENN MEINE TANTE RÄDER HÄTTE

. . . . wäre sie schon längst an der Westfront eingesetzt.

Denn alles, was Räder hat und was sich fortbewegen kann, muss heran, um den unaufhaltsamen Strom amerikanischen Kriegsmaterials zu dämmen.

Daher die russischen Kanonen, die tschechischen Panzer, die französischen Maschinengewehre, daher auch die tartarischen Legionäre, die georgischen Hilfstruppen, der slawische Tross.

Mit diesem Mischmasch kann man doch nicht Krieg führen!

Da gibts eben nur eins:

SCHLUSS MACHEN!

M.W 110

Allied propaganda leaflet

5-14 April
The Guards Armoured Division fought their way to near the river Weser.
On the 14th they were ordered to pull out of the advance. Since crossing
he Rhine, they had covered over a hundred miles against stiff resistance
and suffered over 700 casualties, including 128 men killed. Meanwhile,
some of the other formations on the south had been able to make rapid
progress.]

Headed paper: DER BURGERMEISTER DER STADT NORDHORN

186)

287225 Capt R Barer RAMC
94 Light AA Regt RA
BLA

Friday 6th April

Dearest Gwen,
Two letters today of 2nd of April but no big news. You'll see I'm writing
this on paper kindly donated by the burgermaster of Nordhorn. As you have
heard on the BBC we took this place several days ago.
   Am interested to hear what AV thinks about Schrodinger. Haldane goes
into it rather more deeply. He question's S's belief that genes cannot be
treated statistically and points out that organic catalysts can sometimes
transform more than 100,000 molecules per sec. If genes behave like that
then even a single gene requires statistical treatment. H also thinks the
Delbruck theory requires modification. Says that the single event which
causes mutation must be an ionisation or similar process. Recent work has
shown however that many lethal mutations in Drosophila are due to
chromosome breakage followed by restitution and in another case at least
17 ionisation's are needed to produce a chromosome break. S explains the
fact that wild type genes mutate more rapidly than less stable genes when
the temperature is raised on quantum grounds. However recent work shows
the mutation rate of a very unstable gene fell off at high temperatures. H
accuses S of turning a somersault in his account of mind. I must say I found
that particular chapter rather extraordinary. However H says the book is
provocative and wants S to write a much larger one. I'm afraid I can't share
AV's enthusiasm. I think Haldane himself could give a much better account
of life than most people – it's a pity he doesn't do so instead of messing
about with politics. As regards AV's argument about life always being

present, I suppose it all depends on what he means by life, as Joad would say. Complex intermolecular forces and organisation can always exist, but I think most people would only associate life with proteins which can only exist under rather narrow conditions. Perhaps AV could tell you how proteins originated? I should be satisfied if I could answer that before I die!

All my love dearest

RB

187)   287225 Capt R Barer RAMC
                                         94 Light AA Regt RA
                                         BLA

                                         Saturday 7th April

Dearest Gwen,

Have just got the great news – your letters and *Telegraph* arrived together. Am so glad everything went all right. Was a little disturbed about the episiotomy. Was there any special reason or does Uncle do them as a routine? I don't know what you mean by only 6 lbs 13 ozs – after all that's only 1 oz under 7 lbs! You mustn't try to hurry back home. Try and stay at RN [*Royal Northern Hospital*] as long as you can – at least 2 weeks.

Have you decided what to give Uncle yet? Incidentally you were well within the IT [*Income Tax*] time limit so we can afford a nice present!

While I remember can you send me a copy of the Birth Certificate as soon as possible so that I can inform the army.

Well dearest, there's no need to tell you how glad I am. Am longing to come home and see you both.

All my love dearest

RB

188)   287225 Capt R Barer RAMC
                                               94 Light AA Regt RA
                                               BLA

                                               Monday 9th April

Dearest Gwen,

Glad to get your letter of 5th. You've left out one point – the colour of his eyes. Have you told Max yet? Have just realised there are 16 oz in a pound, not 14, so I'm afraid you'll have a laugh at my expense. I bet Glyn and Harry had a good laugh at your ringing up. Does Cowell know? – he'd probably be embarrassed!

Afraid I've no news again. Things have been very sticky here, but the end isn't far off. Eric Bacon provided me with an interesting case of sulphonamide sensitivity today. He was treated for impetigo a few years ago with sulphapyridine. He cut his finger the other day and I dusted a <u>tiny</u> bit of sulphanilamide-proflavine powder on it. The next morning his face had come out in a weeping eczema. The speed and tiny sensitising dose were remarkable.

All my love dearest

RB

189)   287225 Capt R Barer RAMC
                                               94 Light AA Regt RA
                                               BLA

                                               Tuesday 10th April

Dearest Gwen,

Got your letter of 6th today. Glad to hear everything's going OK. When you get him registered make sure you get a copy of the birth certificate and send it to me. Quite pleased he was born in Islington. It makes him a good cockney and it's a place with a history. My school was in Islington. Hope our next will be born in Oxford.

The weather has been glorious here for the last couple of days. Hope you're getting the same. Have you a balcony? Have had an interesting time finding stores of German medical supplies. They seem to have stuff from all over Europe, including Russia, Greece, Latvia and Poland.

Well, all my love dearest – take an occasional look at the map – it's very encouraging.

RB

[To Mr Briggs]
190)

> 287225 Capt R Barer RAMC
> 94 Light AA Regt RA
> BLA
>
> Wednesday 11th April

Dear Dad,

Well, how does it feel to be a grandpa? I'm afraid it's been a difficult time for you though. I only wish I could have been there to take some of the burden off your shoulders. All seems to have gone well with Gwenda anyhow. It's a pity those wretched Germans couldn't give in a little earlier so that he could have been born in peace. It's been tough going out here and we've had to fight every inch of the way against crack paratroops. However it's certain they can't last much longer – so many of their big cities and communication centres have gone. They're quite mad to resist like this as they'll have very few homes left. Most of the towns I've seen are just a mass of rubble.

Well – here's hoping to see you soon – I don't think my leave will be very long now.

Yours

Robert

191)

287225 Capt R Barer RAMC
94 Light AA Regt RA
BLA

Sunday 15th April

Dearest Gwen,

Got 2 letters – 11th and 12th April and also a letter from Max. He only said that RG was OK and did not have Erythroblastosis Foetalis! He said he was as ugly as one would expect from his ancestry. Am sending vaccination certificate and will let you have birth certificate later. Get him suitably vaccinated and inoculated when the time comes.

I don't know what to suggest regarding Uncle's present. Has he no special hobbies or likes? Get what you like for the HS.

Glad to hear DC didn't forget the books. Pity he didn't bring you them. Will ask my Ma about Janet's necklace and ring. Am sure my Pa can do it and the cost would be negligible.

All my love dearest

RB

192)

287225 Capt R Barer RAMC
94 Light AA Regt RA
BLA

Wednesday 25th April

Dearest Gwen,

Got your letter of 22nd today. Afraid I'm still busy but am hoping to get my leave date today. Had a very exciting day yesterday – got 4 British officers out of one hospital. Fortunately they'd all been well treated, but they were certainly glad to see us! Met Brian Warren today. He told me that when he was having lunch at UCH at the staff table, Harry [*Professor Harry Himsworth*] was holding forth on his experiences in Holland. He described how he had actually gone down a road marked 'verges not checked' (i.e. for mines). Brian was quite sure it was an old notice left by us 6 months previously and roared with laughter. Harry would be more useful if he went round some of the German concentration camps. He would certainly find real starvation there.

Well dearest, that's all for now – all my love

RB

[*16 April – 6 May*

The Division resumed its advance northwards on 17 April and were not far from Hamburg when the War ended. Fighting was hard until the last. Around 26 April, contact was made with Sandbostel POW/Concentration Camp near Zeven. During the period 29 April – 5 May, the Grenadiers took Sandbostel and the inmates cheered them from the roofs of their huts as they crossed the nearby river Oste. Once in, they had to prevent the prisoners from breaking out and spreading typhus all over the country.

This was the Grenadiers last operation of the War. Hitler had committed suicide on 30 April and hostilities with Germany ended officially at midnight on 8 May. The official toll of the Division which contained some 13,500 men was: killed, 956; wounded, 3,956; missing, 545; Total 5,447 of all ranks.]

193)   287225 Capt R Barer RAMC
                                               94 Light AA Regt RA
                                               BLA

                                               Saturday 28th April

Dearest Gwen,

At last I've a few minutes to spare before the biggest job of all. Afraid I've just not been able to write for the last couple of days. Had a great thrill yesterday – managed to find the Quartermaster of one of our Field Ambulances who got captured 10 days ago. There were great celebrations. Interested to read John Bates' letter. At least he's frank! Oh dear! I nearly forgot the most important news of all. I'm coming on leave on May 17th – which probably means I'll leave here on the 14th. It looks as if the war will certainly be over by then too, judging by Himmler's declaration.

All my love dearest
RB

PS Have you got W's book yet?

194)   287225 Capt R Barer RAMC
                                                94 Light AA Regt RA
                                                BLA

                                                Wednesday 2nd May

Dearest Gwen,

Two letters today but obviously some are missing. Glad my people have
been down.

Afraid my big job has been even more horrible than I could ever have
imagined. There is only one solution so far as the SS are concerned. Expect
you'll read all about it in the papers. (Poor Marie – afraid there's no hope at
all).

Enclosed may amuse you.

All my love dearest

RB

[*ENCLOSED*]

Subject: PW camps   G A D / 1 9 2 / 2 /
MD

RMO
94 LAA Regt RA
The following is a copy of a letter received from DDMS<12 Corps:
    'Please convey to Capt Barer my thanks and congratulations on the
prompt and useful report he has forwarded on the PW camp at Wester
timke'

....

BLA   p (TW Davidson)
30 April 1945   COLONEL ADMS
jr   Guards Armoured Division

[*There are interesting newspaper cuttings with this letter, about PW camps, Sandbostel, Berlin*]

195)

287225 Capt R Barer RAMC
94 Light AA Regt RA
BLA

Thursday 3rd May

Dearest Gwen,

A few minutes to spare for another letter. Looks as if the war is really ending at last. I've left that terrible place at last – the cutting may tell you something about it. I wonder why the newspapers have to be so dramatic? No words could possibly convey the horror of the place, yet some idiot has to tell a ridiculous lie about the Germans meaning to murder the 500 political prisoners. Actually the SS had left days ago and the shells were not aimed at the prisoners anyhow. My respect for the press is now almost nil. I've seen so many deliberate lies about things I've seen myself.

I shall never forget Sandbostel. It was much smaller than Belsen but the individual suffering was the same. I laughed at some of the things the papers said about Belsen but now I would believe anything – absolutely anything. The SS are just not human they <u>must</u> be exterminated. It would be far better to kill a few thousand innocent ones than allow a single man of them to escape. Fortunately I got the names of 2 of the SS chiefs at Sandbostel. I could think of no worse punishment for anyone than to be made to live in such a camp. I think I should go mad within a week. I forced the German commandant of the ordinary POW camp to go round the political camp with me. At the end he said 'I must confess that at this moment I am ashamed to be a German'. I don't really think they knew what went on in these places. However, they are not the only ones to blame. I think one of the enclosed cuttings put our share of blame quite well. It makes me boil with rage to think that I should have been treated as a criminal for what I did in 1938-39 [*he assisted in helping Germans (probably Jews) who had escaped and reached London on cargo ships, to stow away on ships to the Far East. He used to climb into the docks at night. He broke some ribs one day when he fell climbing a wall – he had got a man onto a boat for Shanghai, but did not rate his chances of survival high without papers. This activity was, of course, illegal*]. Even now I suppose people in England will not believe these things. They'll say the pictures are faked. No picture on earth could possibly convey one millionth of the real horror. One felt no pity for these people – only loathing and disgust. It would have been

Opportune

An introduction to the White Paper explained that, in view of baseless German propaganda about British atrocities in the Boer War, His Majesty's Government now considered it "opportune" to publish some of the reports it had received from Germany of the treatment accorded to German nationals. "In 1933," the introduction continued, "members of the opposition parties were arrested wholesale and consigned to concentration camps where they were subjected to the most barbarous treatment. Flogging and torture were the order of the day ..."

The White Paper added that "so long as there was the slightest prospect of reaching any settlement with the German Government it would have been wrong to do anything to embitter relations between the two countries. Even after the outbreak of war His Majesty's Government felt reluctant to take action which might have the effect of inspiring hatred."

It required Dr. Goebbels' tales about the Boer War—rather than the rape of Poland—to sting Mr. Chamberlain's Government to this candour.

If it had been possible to reach "any settlement with the German Government" the White Paper would not have been published, and the British Government would officially have averted its eyes from Buchenwald. Several other Governments were in a similarly Pharisaic mood. In other words the laws of humanity were already in abeyance, the police system was paralysed, the League of Nations was betrayed.

We are trying at this moment in San Francisco to make another League of Nations. One of the prime necessities is that the new League shall have a machinery, power and principles which will throttle at its first appearance, anywhere in the world, the kind of tyranny which Hitler and Mussolini first exercised in their own cities, then came near to imposing on the whole human race.

BRITISH GUARDS' SACRIFICE

SANDBOSTEL HORROR

SANDBOSTEL CONCENTRATION
CAMP, GERMANY, Tuesday.

The Germans fought frantically to hold this hell on earth. Last night they fired mortars and airbursts meant to fall not more than 100 yards from the flags we had hoisted over the main gate at 5 p.m.

They meant to murder the 7,500 political prisoners herded into Sandbostel Concentration Camp, which approaches Belsen in the ultimate of frightfulness, and in which 2,600 men have died since April 5. Grenadier Guardsmen died to save and free these prisoners.

There are two Sandbostels, the big camp with 14,000 prisoners of war and the smaller camp with a typhus notice nailed to the entrance. The first official report counted 107 typhus cases, but 8,000 vaccines are being given.

There were 320 British, Canadian and American prisoners of war in the larger camp when we liberated it. There were also 290 Belgians, 2,200 French, 2,500 Poles, 234 Italians, 11 Rumanians, 5,000 Russians, 500 Czechs, and 1,700 Jugoslavs.

British generals came to Sandbostel yesterday. The most senior said: "You must tell the world about this and make the people believe."

best if I'd poured petrol on the place and burned everything. I can still feel the stench in my nostrils. I'm quite sure that if every German were made to see these camps there would never be another war. You may be horrified at the pictures of German women being made to bury the dead but it is the best thing that could happen. They will never forget it. I am sure there has never been anything like it in the history of the world. The Middle Ages and Inquisition were probably humane by comparison.

Well dear, I'm sorry this has been such a horrible letter but I had to get it off my chest and I think it's as well you should know. I know how hard it is to believe all the stories one hears but I can assure you no story could be anything like so fantastic as the truth.

All my love dearest

RB

Sandbostel Prison Camp

British Seamen Freed

When the Guards Armoured Division liberated 3,000 British seamen from a war prisoners camp near Bremen the Royal Ensign and the "Red Duster" were hoisted amid cheers.

CHAPTER VIII

*The end, guns silenced, German reactions to Sandbostel,
first home leave and sight of new-born son, appointed to
Oxford job.*

196)

287225 Capt R Barer RAMC
94 Light AA Regt RA
BLA

DAY BEFORE SURRENDER!

Dearest Gwen,

Just heard the news about the surrender tomorrow, so I shall be coming home in peace after all! At least it won't be so bad going back. Have written to Weddell asking for interview about May 20th [*for job in Oxford*].

Afraid, dear, I shall have to ask some details about Income Tax as the forms have just arrived. I'm ashamed to say I've lost details. Can you let me have by return?

(1) Name of firm

(2) Date of Policy

(3) Amount of premium, also the amount of your income for the year ending April 5th 1945 (I think you worked about 2 months).

Even the mad Germans seem glad the war is over. God knows why they fought us. It would have been so much simpler for them to fight the SS.

All my love dearest

RB

197)

287225 Capt R Barer RAMC
94 Light AA Regt RA
BLA

Saturday 5th May

Dearest Gwen,

Have managed to collect several days' mail at last and have about 4 of your letters including the photo of the ugly little brute. I'm afraid he has inherited your nose. Well dear, I think you'll agree that the European war is virtually over – completely as far as we are concerned. Our guns fired a last salvo at 8 a.m. Now I suppose we shall have to fight another war, on the political front. God knows how we're going to save any of Germany from the results of her criminal folly. In many ways they've got off very lightly despite the destruction of many of their towns and the huge loss of life. The people obviously have not the slightest idea of what the Nazis and SS have really done. Until last week I always felt very strongly that they could not be held responsible in any way. Now, however, I feel differently. I'm quite willing to believe they didn't really know what was going on but in this particular case ignorance must be regarded as a crime. Every nation has the responsibility of knowing what goes on in prisons and similar places and the Germans have shirked their responsibility. I can forgive them almost everything except that. I've not suddenly become a German-hater – people still accuse me of being pro-German but there are some things that must not be forgotten or glossed over. I don't think I shall ever be able to look at a group of healthy people again without wanting to vomit over a certain other memory. Especially as I go about this beautiful old German town which surrendered without a fight and is quite undamaged, and see the crowds of well-fed and happy women and children, I realise that they must not be allowed to continue to go about in ignorance of what has been done. No one in the world has a right to be happy, least of all the Germans, while such things are being uncovered. We have seen the greatest degradation of the human race of all time and everyone of us has been defiled. It will take centuries for us to become purified. The camp commandant said he was ashamed of being a German, but I'm ashamed of being a human – no animal would ever do anything like it. The tragedy of it is that it should have happened in Germany – which has given so much to the world.

Please forgive me, dear, for bothering you like this but I can think about nothing else at the moment. Hope I'm better by the 17th.

All my love dearest
RB

198)
287225 Capt R Barer RAMC
94 Light AA Regt RA
BLA

Thursday 10th May

Dearest Gwen,

Only 3 more days till I start on my leave journey! Am still immensely busy –
you've no idea of the problems we have, but it's all great fun really. It's
quite fantastic to think that all these thousands of paratroops and sailors I
have to deal with were ready to slit my throat only a few days ago. Now they
are all salutes and 'Ja-wohl's'. I think it's a mistake to send any British
helpers to concentration camps and similar places. The entire thing should
be done by the Germans themselves. I've spoken to many German doctors
of what I saw but they can't believe it. It's hardly surprising as no normal
person could even begin to think of such things. I'm hoping to arrange for a
party of doctors from the area to visit one of the camps. They'll get a terrible
shock but it'll do an immense amount of good.

By the way I had to go into Hamburg the other day and I met the
Professor of Physiology, Dr Mond. He knows Meyerhof very well and

Mauthausen Prison Camp

229

worked in Fenn's lab in America. He's done some interesting stuff on permeability and was just reading a paper by Danielli [*Academic at University College*]. About half of Hamburg has been completely destroyed but the 'west-end' is not too bad, the University has also not suffered much.

Well all my love dear – only one week till we see each other.

Love

RB

PS I've already written to Weddell about an interview. I shall have to go to Oxford so there's hardly any point my people coming to London unless they want to.

199)   287225 Capt R Barer RAMC
                                                 94 Light AA Regt RA
                                                 BLA

                                                 Saturday 12th May 1945

Dearest Gwen,

Well at last my work here is over and I'm starting on the journey home tomorrow morning at 11 a.m. I've just had a bath, my first for over a month. It's amazing but I've scarcely even had time to defaecate on this job. I don't think I could go on with it very much longer, though it's been much easier in the last few days as we haven't had the accompaniments of war. I think that I can tell you now that I've been in some pretty unhealthy spots in the last month – I've usually gone in with the leading tanks. At Sandbostel we went in with the infantry in assault boats. However that's all over now and it's just a pleasant memory.

I had the good fortune to be able to take a mixed party of German Naval, Army and Civil MOs round Sandbostel yesterday. They've done a good job there but the political prisoner's compound is by no means cleared and there are still the same unpleasant sights – rows of corpses, men defaecating on their dying comrades and so on. They've been able to get about 200 into a hospital after delousing and washing (done by German nurses and women specially imported). The hospital alone is bad enough. The Typhus is still increasing and there were over 200 cases (known). This was the 4th time I'd been round the political camp and each time I've seen some fresh horror.

It's terrible to think that even after this time we haven't been able to help them all.

I think it did the Germans an immense amount of good. Even the doubters were convinced. I seem to have escaped Typhus from my first visit so far. The incubation for yesterday's visit should end about the end of my leave!

Have just finished packing my bags. They weigh a ton! The weather is dreadfully hot and I shall probably die of heat stroke before I get home.

Well darling, only 4 more days – I don't know exactly when I shall get home so don't wait for me anywhere. It may be the 16th, 17th or 18th – probably the 17th. May not have a chance to write on the journey so don't worry.

All my love dearest

RB

[*We had a wonderful leave, enjoying our baby and each other at last (we had spent only 14 days of married life together before). R got the job in Oxford. Thus when he left the sting of parting was removed, though we still expected he would have to go out East for several years – there was no sign of an end to the Japanese war.*]

CHAPTER IX

Army of Occupation, German problems, Middle East problems, British election, prospect of going to Far East, Japanese surrender, Welsh Guards, sudden release, coming home.

200)

287225 Capt R Barer RAMC
94 Light AA Regt RA
BLA

Wednesday 30th May

Dearest Gwen

Am now back with my unit once more. Afraid I didn't get a chance to write to you on the journey as I was travelling most of the time. Had an hour or so in Folkestone but couldn't find any book shops open! I passed through Munster coming back. It really is a mess – about 90% destroyed – in some ways the worst I've seen. A lot of odd things are happening here but no-one knows anything definite yet. Things don't look too hopeful but something may turn up. The final number of Typhus cases at Sandbostel was 800 and cases are beginning to appear in the surrounding villages. Incidentally my German medical orderly went down with ? Typhus 2 days after I left!

Well darling, all my love and thank you for a lovely leave – am longing to hold you again, my arms feel so empty.

RB

[Letter from R's German medical orderly who went into Sandbostel with him.]

Hamburg, 26-2-46

Dear Captain Barer!

Yust returning from upper Bavaria, where I lived the last 5 months I found Your kind letter and let me say that I thank You very much that You did remember me after such a long time. I often tried to send you a letter but from the American Zone it was too difficult, nobody could do it for me.

Let me tell You what happened to me after Your going on leave last May. Three days after You had gone I went seriously ill by a heavy influenza, which I think I got at Sandbostel – Conzentration – Camp. Your driver Winter brought me over to the German Naval Hospital Cuxhaven where I had to stay in bed for about 5 weeks. After recovering I tried to find a similar job I had done before, but there was nothing left for me except a 14 days work in the Royal Navy's sick bay in Cuxhaven harbour. The doctor over there was the surgeon-lt. Who took over our nice Mercedes, he ist still driving it. – After that I was send to the POW camp and discharges on August 13th. Coming home my brother arrived a few days later and invited me to pay a visit to him in Berchtesgaden Bavaria where he now lives. I had such a nice time down there. That my visit took much longer than exspected. – I always tried to finish my studies in Hamburg or Munich but there is no chance for me unless I start again from the beginning because my papers from the University are lost. In the moment I really do not know what to do, if I could again work for You I would begin in this minute.

I often think of the nice time I had with You and where the other men of our section now may be. Couldn't You sometimes come to Hamburg I would be very much obliged to see You again, may be we could sometimes make our trip through the land to look after the Electron-microscop. Would it perhaps be possible for You to send me any certification that I have been working in Your division as interpreter because that would help me to find any work in the Mil. Gov. or so until I go back to the University.

I hope to have good news from You the next time and to see You as soon as possible.

With kindest regards
ever Yours
Sijmed, Otto

201)   287225 Capt R Barer RAMC
                                         94 Light AA Regt RA
                                         BLA

                                         Saturday 2nd June

Dearest Gwen

Got letter from you and one from Weddell – I presume you opened it. Glad you find Hinshelwood's article interesting. He's a very great Physical Chemist and would certainly be a very useful man to contact – I'm certain to have to consult him sooner or later. We must certainly explore the possibility of your getting a job with him. [*Yes I did get a job with him in 1946 – a Nobel Prize Winner for Chemistry on kinetic theory of gases – in middle life he started to apply his theory to bacterial cells!*] Have you any ideas on his article? If we got the EM going we might be able to demonstrate his 'enzyme network' in bacteria.

I've been thinking about what I might do at Oxford. An intensive study of muscle structure from a new angle might be useful to start with, especially as Le Gros [*Professor Le Gros Clark, Professor of Human Anatomy*] has been doing a bit on muscle regeneration. It might be useful to study embryology, growth regeneration and degeneration of various types of muscle, especially the very primitive types as seen in invertebrates. It might be possible to find a method of recognising regenerated fibres, e.g. by a staining reaction. At the same time it would be a good idea to start a collection of pathological specimens of muscle diseases – atrophies, tumours etc. and see how they differ from the normal and to what extent, if any, regeneration occurs. I'm sure people haven't studied this side sufficiently. These odd muscle degenerations seem to be very specific in their choice of muscles and are usually symmetrical, which suggests some local anatomical factor. Possibly it's a question of type of blood supply.

At the same time it might be worth seeing how far the properties of muscle correspond with their myosin. It might be possible to bring myosin gels in contact with certain types of membrane and produce an 'artificial muscle'. The contractile power of muscle must depend ultimately on the contractile power of the myosin molecule. If pure myosin doesn't work one might try various crude muscle extracts.

I'm sure that some invertebrate muscles are very little more than myosin gels and various pigments and electrolytes and enzymes. It might be a first step towards creating life to try out myosin gels and mixtures of crude muscle extract to produce a muscle!

Have you any ideas on the subject? You might look up the subject of muscular dystrophies.

I'm writing to Weddell and asking him to be on the look-out for suitable grants or Fellowships I might get – I'd like to get one settled as soon as possible. You might keep your eyes open for anything too – particularly any grants the government might offer to people like me – Le Gros promised to let me know as soon as they came out but I don't want to miss anything.

By the way in case you're interested I'm now in the village of Walle, near Verden, about 20 miles from Bremen. We're living in great comfort – I have a nice big room to myself and there's a bath! All my love dearest – am almost longing to go to Burma so that I can have an embarkation leave with you!

RB

202)   287225 Capt R Barer RAMC
                                         94 Light AA Regt RA
                                         BLA

                                         Sunday 3rd June

Dearest Gwen,
No letter today and nothing much to write to you about, except that I love you very much. I've hardly done anything but sit and think of you since I came back. It's marvellous to feel that it's only a matter of time before we're together for good.

Saw Colyer yesterday. He's quite well. Forgot to tell you we had a photo of all the officers taken, so I hope you'll get that much desired picture of me after all.

All my love dearest

RB

PS Hope RG's behaving himself. He'll be over the 14 lb mark before 3 months if you're not careful!

203)

287225 Capt R Barer RAMC
94 Light AA Regt RA
BLA

Thursday 7th June

Dearest Gwen,

No letter today. Mail is rather poor. Hope you're making the best of the sunny weather. I suppose RG spends most of his time on the balcony.

Have found a pond with tadpoles and frogs here and am trying out the effect of sulphonamide on metamorphosis. The experiments are rather crude – just a tablet of sulphathiazole and one of sulphapyridine dissolved in 1 litre of pond water with half a dozen tadpoles, and the control jar. It's possible that sulphonamides may have an effect on calcification in frogs, or perhaps they might upset the many enzyme actions which must go on during metamorphosis. The only trouble is finding the right concentration. One tab per litre gives 50 mgm per 100 cc, which would be OK if the tadpole had it in it's blood stream.

Have been demonstrating frog's heart and nerve-muscle preparations to some of the men.

The photo is now ready and I look frightful – as one officer said – 'as if I'd been telescoped' – I appear to have no neck. Will send copies as soon as ready.

All my love dearest – always thinking of you.

RB

204)

287225 Capt R Barer RAMC
94 Light AA Regt RA
BLA

Tuesday 12th June

Dearest Gwen,

Got your letter of last Thursday, with Wachsmuth's letter enclosed. Afraid the mail is still very poor, as several of your letters appear to be missing. I'm glad W seems content and appears to have all he wants. I wonder how long they intend to keep him in England? I don't suppose he particularly wants to go back to Berlin.

Group photograph – Verden, May 1945
RB back row, extreme right

I'm afraid I had no chance at all of seeing the old DDMS before he went. I haven't met the new man yet. No-one has any idea of the relative chances of going or staying. I see that there's a chance that school teachers may be demobbed under Class B, but nothing was said about University teachers, I think myself that I should probably be sent out East in a couple of months or so. However I don't think I should wait so long before applying for Path training. I don't think I'll write to Crewe as I'm sure Path would be far more useful out East and the training would be so useful to me too.

Don't understand why RG's hair should be fair!

All my love dearest

RB

[*On 9 June the Guards Armoured Division was disbanded and reverted to infantry.*]

205)
        287225 Capt R Barer RAMC
        94 Light AA Regt RA
        BLA

        Thursday 28th June

Dearest Gwen,

Got 2 of your letters today. I agree that it would be worth while getting a car if I come on embarkation leave, but I've not heard anything yet. Colyer hasn't gone yet either.

Well I saw the R's today (Raders)* and they are all well. Ma R was upstairs in bed with a septic hand so I sat at her bedside. They looked very frightened when I demanded to see her. I handed her your photo and said in German 'Do you know this woman?' and she answered 'Ja' in a very quavering voice. I expect she thought you were a spy! However they were delighted when I told them, and kept cooing over RG's picture. All the children looked nice and plump – the youngest boy is 7 – I don't suppose he was conceived when you knew them. They kept talking about your dimples and showed me your photo. They haven't heard from their eldest boy (in Russia) since February. I told them something about the concentration camps and of course they said they hadn't known about them. I suppose it's true but I'm afraid I now feel like yelling 'well most Germans didn't <u>want to</u>

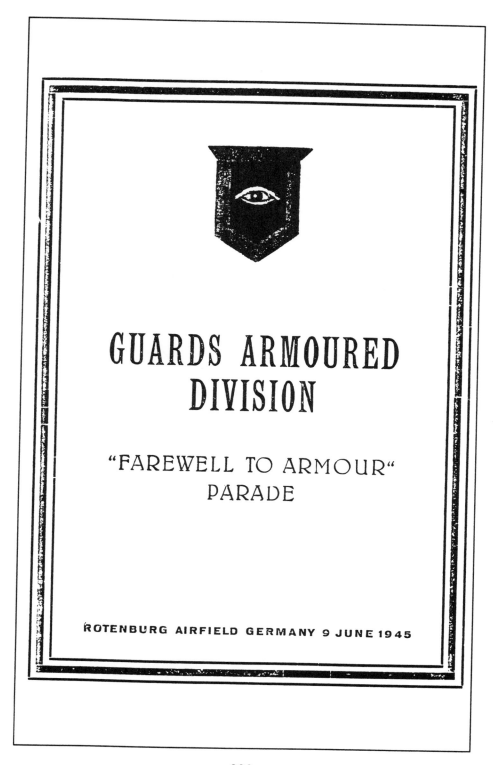

GUARDS ARMOURED
DIVISION

"FAREWELL TO ARMOUR"
PARADE

ROTENBURG AIRFIELD GERMANY 9 JUNE 1945

SPECIAL ORDER OF THE DAY BY BRIGADIER HC. PHIPPS, DSO, RA
COMMANDER ROYAL ARTILLERY, GUARD ARMOURED DIVISION

TO ALL RANKS, 94th. LIGHT ANTI-AIRCRAFT REGIMENT, ROYAL ARTILLERY.

Today is a sad day in the history of your Regiment when you part with your guns - the guns that have shot down more German aircraft than any other L.A.A. Regiment in the B.L.A - the guns that have protected every Regiment in the Divisional Artillery and every Regiment that has come under my Command during the time that we have been on the continent - and the guns that have protected Divisional Headquarters so well and truly for the last eleven months.

But your guns have departed in a haze of splendour that has never been surpassed and I am sure   you would like to hear from me that I have never heard so many expressions of amazement as I did yesterday from everyone including the Commander-in-Chief - the M.G.R.A. and everyone, that your guns which have been fought so well by you, could look as magnificent as they did.

So I should like to add my congratulations to you all, and I know we will have many more happy days together in your new role.

                                        H.C. Phipps, Brigadier, DSO
                                        C. R. A. Guards Armoured Division.

10 June 45.

know about them – they were unpleasant things which they blotted out from their consciousness. However they were very pleased to hear about you and sent greetings to your Pa. I told them about your Mother. Their house was very slightly damaged but is now repaired.

I'm glad the newspaper reporters like the leave hotels in Paris. After all some one must use them even if the soldiers can't. The entire allocation for the regiment for July is <u>one</u>! Still there's always the Brussels 'Eye' club!

All my love dearest

RB

PS You haven't answered me about the soap coupons. (Also why is David living at home?)

These were friends of mine (and my Mother's) from pre-war, who had sent us a telegram when war broke out saying that nothing would change our friendship. They had a factory near Cologne and had survived despite helping prisoners of war (Russian), going to a Jewish doctor and other anti-Nazi acts.

206)
287225 Capt R Barer RAMC
94 Light AA Regt RA
BLA

Saturday 30th June

Dearest Gwen

Not much to write about today. Am kept fairly busy with all sorts of odd jobs. Latest is checking up on Nazi doctors in district who are suspected of giving false certificates to get people off work.

As regards applying for path training. We are <u>not</u> allowed to write direct to heads of services – it all has to go through the ADMS and of course takes some time. However, if I don't get any satisfaction I shall write direct, so don't worry.

Did you see AV's letter in *Nature* about the refusal of the government to allow certain scientists to go to Russia? It was most bitter and sarcastic about the Government's attitude towards science in general . . . However, did you notice that two of the people concerned, Bernal and Blackett, were communists? Bernal was on holiday so the official excuse that he was too busy on war work was rather lame.

Oh dear, I shall be glad when all this . . . is over and I can go and bury myself in Oxford. At the moment I feel that I just want to hide away from all these dreadful intrigues and just work away at what I want without having to talk to more than a bare minimum of people.

All my love dearest

RB

207)   287225 Capt R Barer RAMC
                                        94 Light AA Regt RA
                                        BLA

                                        Monday 2nd July

Dearest Gwen,

Am enclosing the insurance bill. There was actually no need for me to sign it if you remember. I am <u>not</u> in the Temperance section. I think you should send them the cheque about July 20th. I've now received the election addresses for Watford and will vote by post. The conservative is Air Commodore Helmore. He is undoubtedly a good man and a very good scientist and inventor. The labour chap is someone called Major John Freeman. His election address contains the usual fiery remarks and promises one expects from Labour, but I expect I shall have to vote for him. I'm afraid the present Labour leadership is really pathetic and I don't think they stand an earthly chance of getting in. A coalition would have been much better.

As regards films, I believe they are obtainable in Brussels but at about 6/- a roll!

I thought I told you about the penicillin. Tabs remain active indefinitely but solution begins to go off after 48 hours – though probably quite useful for 3-4 days.

Will write to Uncle [*Obstetrician*].

All my love dearest

RB

208)
287225 Capt R Barer RAMC
94 Light AA Regt RA
BLA

Wednesday 4th July

Dearest Gwen,

No letter today. Weather seems to be improving at last. How is it at home? By the way dearest, you promised to tell me what Bob says about muscular dystrophies. You might look up Kinnier Wilson's *Neurology* too if you get a chance. If you should be in Lewis' you might try and get me a book out of the library. It's by R. Beutner but I forget what it's called. I think it's 'physical chemistry of the cell' and is about cell models. It's quite old – about 1932 but still useful.

It's an odd life here. Just a handful of soldiers keeping an eye on thousands of civilians. We don't have the slightest trouble – in fact the 'slaves' are far more trouble than the Germans. It's a trial not being able to talk to people but actually I have to talk to a good few in the course of my work. The shops are beginning to show things in their windows now, which is a first sign of trust.

Eric Bacon has been promoted to Major. I'm very glad as he's worked extremely hard.

All my love dearest

RB

209)
287225 Capt R Barer RAMC
94 Light AA Regt RA
BLA

Saturday 7th July

Dearest Gwen

Got 2 of your letters and W's letter. Wonder what was cut out? I agree G-L's [*Graham-Little, MP for London University*] latest effusion was not so good, I still don't feel like entrusting the future to the present labour leaders. [*He certainly changed his mind about Attlee later.*] I somehow feel they're bound to make a mess of <u>something</u>. It's a pity the Liberals have faded out so badly. I sent off my vote to Watford. It was for the Labour candidate. I don't think they've an earthly but I didn't want the Tories to have too big a majority.

I see Bragg has written a letter in *The Times* about the ban on scientists going to Russia. It's on the same lines as AV's (but much more dignified).

All my love dearest and many happy returns for your Birthday. Will send you something from Brussels.

RB

210)   287225 Capt R Barer RAMC
                                                    94 Light AA Regt RA
                                                    BLA

Dearest Gwen,

Sorry for the gap. I had to go to Brussels yesterday and didn't have time to write. As regards your questions about the Raders. Mrs is as fat as ever. I stayed there about 40 minutes. Their attitude towards us did not seem resentful and they felt to some extent that they had been liberated. They rather seemed to feel the air raids were overdone, but I pointed out they started them first and the V1 wasn't exactly humane. The camps came up as a result of her asking me about the non-fraternisation order. They seemed very distressed about that. I explained the reasons saying we wanted to bring home to <u>all</u> Germans exactly what had happened and this was our way of making them think about it. However, I doubt if it's having much effect as most Germans even if they believed the stories have absolutely no sense of responsibility but just blame the Nazis. It's too easy. She pleaded ignorance of course so I asked her whether she knew how the Jews had been treated in 1933. She said she had once been to some town or other in one district of which most of the Jews lived. There were frequently cries and sounds of shooting in this district and the Germans decided it was not 'nice'(!) to go for a Sunday afternoon's promenade there. I think this sums up their attitude very well. They blinded themselves to things which were not 'nice'. Now they're paying the price. Perhaps in future they'll be more careful to investigate instead of ignoring. Afraid our propaganda still isn't intensive enough. Hans was fighting in Russia and they haven't heard from him since February. They don't know if he's a prisoner.

Afraid I didn't get you anything in Brussels yesterday, dear. I wanted to get you something but it had doubled in price since my last visit, so you'll have to wait.

All my love dearest

RB

211)

287225 Capt R Barer RAMC
94 Light AA Regt RA
BLA

Sunday 15th July

Dearest Gwen

Two of your letters today. Sorry you're still worrying about milk (breast milk) – I'm sure it's just a vicious circle – you worry about it and then it goes off. Hope you don't spend too much time looking after Gulla [*friend of mine*]. However she'll probably be quite useful in helping you with RG.

Spent the afternoon cleaning up the Mike. It really is super – everything about it bears the mark of superb craftsmanship.

Afraid my path application will be somewhat delayed as after all this time they sent me a form to fill in – my ordinary written application wouldn't do! However don't worry as I've heard something which makes it almost certain that I shall get it. I've no idea where one does it – it may be over here, England or India.

At all events I shall certainly try to get my 28 days embarkation leave before I go.

Thank you for the notes on muscular Dystrophies. There was no need to copy it word for word! It looks quite interesting – most of the structural changes seem to have been looked at from the pure morbid anatomy viewpoint. I think there's probably quite a lot to be learned by using modern methods – polarised light etc.

Can you get more details about myosin and adenosine triphosphate. It sounds quite reasonable – possibly myosin will only absorb ATP at a certain phase of contraction – when the polar groups are an optimum distance apart.

I wonder why the muscle fibres themselves seem to enlarge in some of the myopathies? It presumably means that excess myosin is being laid down

– possibly an inactive form of myosin. The theories about the role of the sympathetic nerves would lend themselves well to animal experiments.

All my love dearest

RB

212)   287225 Capt R Barer RAMC
                                               94 Light AA Regt RA
                                               BLA

                                               Saturday 21st July

Dearest Gwen,
Two of your letters including Uncle's letter. It was a very matter of fact letter wasn't it? However, it put things quite clearly so that's decided. Don't worry about the parcels. Actually it's only about 3 weeks since I sent them and they take anything up to 5 weeks. It would be no use making any enquiries either as the APO accepts no responsibility. One can only register parcels below 4 lbs. Will get some films in Brussels next week.

Glad you found the grips useful. How many more do you want? Are there any other oddments like buttons, fasteners, needles, thimbles, pins etc. that you want? There's a large factory which make them here and I can buy some.

Sorry to hear about Jan. Hope she's better by now. I think it was probably tummy trouble – they don't always get much diarrhoea. I've got a similar case at the moment – ran a high temperature for a couple of days.

I see that no more women doctors have been called up since VE day. As about 1 in 7 doctors were women this means that the men will have to serve 1/7 extra time – about 2 months in every year. You can think about that when I'm in Burma and someone says there ought to be more women doctors! Dr Summerskill who was so keen on women getting VCs doesn't seem so vociferous when it comes to sending them to SEAC. Equal pay for equal work! – don't make me laugh!

Sorry the wireless has gone off again. You must see that they do the job properly this time and don't pay any more.

All my love dearest
RB

213)   287225 Capt R Barer RAMC
                                         94 Light AA Regt RA
                                         BLA

                                         Sunday 22nd July

Dearest Gwen,
Got your letter of 19th and photo of Ram's* secretary. I don't think I can do
anything about her friends. We can't write to Germans. Don't be too
optimistic about Class B releases and don't listen to false rumours. All the
information we get out here is far from encouraging in that respect. You've
only to read some of the letters at the back of the BMJ to see what people
think. There's a letter in this week's copy from a specialist who's been
overseas 4 years, release group 21, has only spent 7 weeks with his wife
since 1939 and has just been posted to Burma! It's just impudent piffle on
the part of CMWC to say that he'll be released with his age group. We
know damn well that we won't. The fact that no more women doctors are
being called up makes things even worse. I'm so furious about it that I've a
good mind to divorce you! I think it was a mistake ever to call up women at
all but after all the fuss they made about equal status and equal pay (I
suppose Summerskill would also say equal danger!) the new decision is
disgraceful. I know it's no use sending them to Burma but there's no reason
why they shouldn't be employed in military hospitals in England and the
continent and so release more men. There are still lots of ATS being looked
after by men. Everyone out here is absolutely livid about the whole business.
The average army MO feels like a lost soul at the moment – no one seems to
be on his side. We all know what's going to happen but we just can't stop it.
I see some people in the RMS have had the nerve to complain about how
hard they've had to work and that it ought to count as war service. Much as
I've enjoyed it out here I would have been glad at times to swap my flooded
slit trench for their arm chairs. It's the same old trouble – the civilian
mentality – the soldiers don't have such a bad time really! I told some of the
chaps about X's remark. It would have done him good to hear what they
said. His ears would still be burning.
    All my love dearest, even if you are a b female Dr!

    RB

* *Miss Ramsay, G's headmistress.*

214)   287225 Capt R Barer RAMC
                                                        94 Light AA Regt RA
                                                        BLA

                                                        Monday 23rd July

Dearest Gwen,

Got your letter of 20th. As you say post has improved enormously.

You'll be pleased to hear that I'm off tomorrow to 21 Army Group for an interview. They don't say what for, but presumably it's about my Path application. Everything's going to turn out fine.

The IT (Income Tax) was a terrific surprise. It's absolutely fantastic only having to pay £2.16.3 for a whole year! Anyhow it came just at the right time, when our ready cash was running low. We're fabulously rich! It'll pay for a nice holiday together. Glad you've been able to show Jones the trouble with the wireless. They've <u>got</u> to get it absolutely right.

Don't worry about dysentery. None of our troops have got it – except the usual summer diarrhoea. All our water is chlorinated – we use our own trucks, never tapwater.

Don't be disappointed if you don't get a letter tomorrow as I shall be travelling. However will do my best.

All my love dearest

RB

PS Can now tell you that I can add two extra letters after my name. It's not an exam but some people might think I'm a master of Surgery. Will send you a ribbon to sew on my tunic. It's all rather silly but should be quite useful at the interview. [*R was awarded the Military Cross. The citation reports, as his letters do not, that he treated wounded tank crews in extreme danger under shellfire and, 'Typhus was raging and his quick appreciation and report enabled the right medical requirements to reach the camp (Sandbostel) soon after . . . his complete disregard for personal safety in the face of enemy fire . . . to his organising ability many owe their lives'.*]

215)   287225 Capt R Barer RAMC
                                         94 Light AA Regt RA
                                         BLA

                                         Tuesday 24th July

Dearest Gwen,

Well you've got your wish at last. I've been accepted for training in Path. When I got to 21 AG HQ I was interviewed by none other than Fairbrother, the Bacteriologist. He was very pleasant and we talked a lot about bacteriology. He's quite interested in the electron Microscope and told me about the German ones they've found and are sending back to England. I told him about Oxford and he seemed quite interested. He said he thought Biophysics was the coming thing. He told me that I must expect to be sent out East when my training is over. They expected practically no class B releases. However that's only fair and what I expected. They are only allowed to have 4 path trainees but he's going to try and get a 5th place for me, in which case I should probably start in a couple of weeks. If not, I shall have to wait until one of the 4 has finished his training – probably 1-2 months. However, it's quite definite and he's arranged that I don't get posted out east until I do the training. The training will be done in a hospital out here – possibly in Brussels!

Well dear, I think that should satisfy you. I'm glad I shall have to go out East, as I should have felt a worm if I'd missed it. I'm sure it won't be for long and you won't have anything to worry about this time I hope. The times seem to be working out OK for J.M.* too – she'll probably be started about November!

All my love dearest

RB

PS Have you a photo of Gulla you can send me? Have been teasing Allsopp about her, but I think there may be a hope! He's going on leave about August 10th.

Name of prospective daughter (we never got one, but two more sons!)

216)   287225 Capt R Barer RAMC
                                              94 Light AA Regt RA
                                              BLA

                                              Wednesday 25th July

Dearest Gwen,

Only 1 letter when I got back today. Spent last night at Cologne with the 128th Field Ambulance. We had a nice evening talking over old times – very few of the original MOs are left now. The CO and 2nd in command of the 19th have gone to Burma. I also heard that Alderson has gone. I asked the CO of the 128th his views on breast feeding – he was a consulting obstetrician in Exeter. He believes in 3 hours feeding to begin with, changing later to 4. I told him what you thought about it – that it just meant you were on the job all day and he said that feeding a baby <u>was</u> a full-time job and that's all there is to it. I asked him about night feeds. He says he doesn't allow them in hospital or nursing home, but he's not sure at home – the Mother can't stand the baby howling all the time. He has a theory that we really ought to feed the baby when it's hungry – not at any definite time interval. It would certainly seem more natural. I don't suppose the savage people stick to any time interval.

The bank statement you sent looks OK. If we've been paid the £40 odd rebate on IT we shall have more than enough. Try and get a statement about the 7th of August. I think we shall be able to start filling up our savings certificates again. We shall be fantastically well off when I go to SEAC. I shall get extra specialist's pay and Far East rates of pay – probably about £100 per year extra.

All my love dearest

RB

217)   287225 Capt R Barer RAMC
                                              94 Light AA Regt Ra
                                              BLA

                                              Thursday 26th July

Dearest Gwen,

Have just been listening to the amazing election results. I seem to have been wildly wrong in my expectations! I just can't understand it and I don't suppose anyone can explain it. All I reasonably hoped for was some reduction in the Tory majority. Anyhow Labour now has a clear working majority so they've only themselves to blame if they fail. The *Daily Express* will look pretty foolish now after all the fuss they made about Laski [*Harold, LSE*].

Sorry you don't want me to sleep with anyone in Brussels. I'd got it all arranged too! However perhaps you'll grant me permission when I'm in SEAC (South East Asia Command, Burma).

Don't worry about the notes, dear. Beutner has arrived and I've got enough to keep me busy for a long time. I met an interesting man yesterday. I was asked to see a doctor who had some special apparatus no one could understand. I found it was someone called Hagemann, who claims to have introduced fluorescent microscopy into bacteriology in 1937. He works in what's left of the Hygienic Institute in Cologne. He showed me several slides of Trypanosomes, TB, viruses and they were very good. He said that the Nazis made his method compulsory for finding TB as it's 100% more effective. His apparatus was very interesting and he gave me several reprints. I wrote to Fairbrother about him as he knows several secret technical processes in the making of ultraviolet lamps and quartz lenses and condensers for his work. He co-operated with Zeiss and Reichert. He refused to become a Nazi party member so they wouldn't let him take a degree, but as his work was known internationally they made him go to foreign congresses!

Do try and control yourself about 'Major'. He can't help it.

How is Jan?

All my love dearest

RB

218)   287225 Capt R Barer RAMC
                                         94 Light AA Regt RA
                                         BLA

                                         Saturday 28th July

Dearest Gwen,

Am writing this from Brussels. The big Parade is over and everything went smoothly. Am just getting ready to go to the ball at the Hotel de Ville. It starts at 10 p.m. and goes on all night! I won't do any dancing but I mean to do pretty well at the cold buffet!

As I wasn't allowed to sleep with anyone last night I went to a performance of Shaw's *St Joan*. It was very well done. Won't be able to get any of your letters until Tuesday so I shan't have much to write about. James Booth is going to another FDS – probably for SEAC.

All my love dearest
your faithless husband
RB

219)   287225 Capt R Barer RAMC
                                                  94 Light AA Regt RA
                                                  BLA

                                                  Sunday 29th July

Dearest Gwen,
Am spending today recovering from the effects of the Ball last night. It was quite a grand affair. Prince Bernhard of the Netherlands and the Princes and Princesses of Luxembourg (Prince John is in our Division) were there. The Buffet was most luxurious – lots of marvellous cream cakes. Unfortunately it was very crowded and one just had to grab anything within reach so I found myself mixing cream cakes and sardines, which nearly made me sick, especially as there was nothing but champagne to drink.

Today the Welsh Guards have been dressing up the famous mannikin-pis statue in Welsh uniform. It's always dressed up on fete days and he's going to be dressed up in the same uniform every September 3rd. As I've been saving so much money by not being allowed to sleep with anyone I've bought you a little present which I'll send on.

All my love dearest

RB

220)   287225 Capt R Barer RAMC
                                                  94 Light AA Regt RA
                                                  BLA

                                                  Late July/early August

Dearest Gwen
Sorry you wasted your time at Stoke Newington. I suppose you looked up the *London Gazette* – I know they took it there, I haven't seen the citation

252

myself yet so I don't know what it's for . . . was going to send you the ribbon but will wait as the France and Germany star and 39-45 star are coming out and you'll be able to sew on all three together. The MC ribbon is blue and white. Hope you went to Oxford. Max deserves a good telling off and it'll probably do more good coming from you. He's too casual for words, but will go to no end of trouble when one least expects it.

You must try and get Geoff Allsopp [*regimental friend*] up to dinner one night – about the 12th perhaps. He likes <u>plain</u> food – nothing fancy – no mayonnaise – rather like your Pa. Very fond of tinned pineapple if you can get it! Lots of bread and butter. No currants or sultanas. Hope photo of G arrives before he goes on leave. Really think there may be a hope. G mustn't appear too high-class for him [*Geoff desperately wanted a girlfriend*].

Book has come, very useful. Bought several books in Brussels – will tell you about them later. Had rather an embarrassing incident at the Ball. About midnight someone rushed in and asked for a doctor. I was grabbed and told there was a girl who'd been taken ill suddenly. I rushed upstairs and saw a girl who looked rather embarrassed. Eventually she points to a spot of blood on her skirt and it dawned on me. I said I didn't normally carry sanitary towels around with me at that hour of the night but I managed to get her fixed up with an ordinary towel. Anyhow you'll be glad to hear she was the only girl I spoke to during the whole of my time in Brussels. I think you might have a <u>little</u> confidence in me.

All my love dearest

RB

221)

287225 Capt R Barer RAMC
94 Light AA Regt RA
BLA

Tuesday 31st July

Dearest Gwen,

Please forgive me for upsetting you like that. I didn't mean you to take it that way at all. Obviously one can't blame women doctors as a class – I don't suppose they had anything to do with the decision – it was probably made by some stupid old man trying to be chivalrous. What has caused a lot of unfavourable comment however is that people remember what a fuss the women's bodies like the medical women's federation made at the beginning of the war to get women equal status – insisting that they should go into the RAMC and not the ATS and so on. Now these people are conspicuous by their silence. You're wrong about it not affecting our length of service for that reason. In addition there'll be fewer doctors and therefore fewer can be spared for release. Anyhow it's no use worrying about it now. I certainly didn't mean to hurt you – that's the very last thing in the world I'd want to do. Hope you managed to go to Oxford after all. I wouldn't worry about a doctor for my Ma. I know how she feels and it would embarrass her to have a young woman. A good kind middle-aged family doctor is more in her line but I don't think there's any point having a regular one – it would only worry her. She gets on very well really, you'll find.

Sorry dear, another blasted mine has gone off – must go and deal with the bits and pieces.

All my love

RB

[*I must have gone to Oxford to look for a house and probably Max had promised to take me but didn't turn up!*]

222)

287225 Capt R Barer RAMC
94 Light AA Regt RA
BLA

Monday 6th August

Dearest Gwen,

Got your letter with the photos and notes. Photos are marvellous. RG looks a scream – so pensive. My old Gert has her hair all over the place as usual and could also do with a bit of fattening up but otherwise she's the dear old hag I love. They're very good photos. Have you sent my Ma any? She'd love them. Get 2 enlargements of the upright one showing RG in full. We can get enlargements of the others later, when prices are cheaper. Everyone's been saying what a handsome baby he is – he still seems to have your nose. On second thoughts get an enlargement of the one with you smiling as well.

Don't think Allsop will be able to come on the 12th – his leave's been put back a day. Somewhere about the 16th would be better. I'll try and let you know the exact date he expects to land.

The weaning schedule seems quite reasonable. I see the child is virtually weaned by 8 months. I see no reason why the process couldn't be hurried a little in a healthy baby provided such things as vitamins are watched. You must feed yourself up too dear. Try and put on at least a stone.

The notes on myopathies are very interesting. There's obviously an awful lot of work to be done. Will write to Uncle.

All my love dearest – can't stop looking at the photos.

RB

223)

287225 Capt R Barer RAMC
94 Light AA Regt RA
BLA

Wednesday 8th August

Dearest Gwen,

No letter today. The General has just been round to lunch, which was very good – he nearly fell asleep! Afraid I shall probably have to go to Buckingham Palace sometime – probably when I'm on leave.

Your notes on Muscular dystrophies were very interesting. It's all very well saying that muscles with recently acquired functions escape and those developed earliest in the foetus are affected but there must be some more fundamental reason, e.g. some difference in structure, chemical composition or blood supply. In particular the difference between the two heads of the sternomastoid must surely depend on some structural property, even if there is a hormonal influence at work the selective distribution still has to be explained. I notice one or two references to glycogen and hypoglycaemia. Has anyone determined the glycogen content of the affected muscles in these diseases, or is there a normal difference in glycogen content of those muscles liable to be affected? It might be worth staining for Glycogen in various muscles. I think there is a lot of work that can be done on the sympathetic in relation to muscles and a lot of Hunter's work has never been repeated.

Incidentally I can't remember anyone ever suggesting that myosin may be the toxic agent in crush syndrome. If myosin is indeed adenosine triphosphate, the liberation of large quantities of this into the blood stream might be expected to interfere with carbohydrate metabolism throughout the body and in the kidney, where it is so active. It might cause liberation of adenosine or adenylic acid derivatives which are themselves capable of causing many of the symptoms of shock. Green thinks these products are liberated by muscle injury and cause the syndrome. However the liberation of any enzyme might cause far more to be liberated in other parts of the body.

All my love dearest
RB

224)   287225 Capt R Barer RAMC
                                            94 Light AA Regt RA
                                            BLA

                                            Saturday 11th August

Dearest Gwen,
Two letters at long last. Have just heard about the Jap surrender. It really is amazing and most unexpected. Even at the very worst I should be out within a year and you've nothing to worry about now.

Afraid Allsopp's leave has been put back another day! Should leave tomorrow (12th). When does G go back?

Sorry you found my remarks about the long-haired gents obscure. What I meant was that a lot of us, especially they, are going to be sadly disillusioned about certain people [*our gallant Soviet Allies*] we were so keen to emulate and on whose behalf we once signed a certain document at UCH [*as students to our deep regret in later life, we had once sent a telegram to Churchill: 'Open a second front now'*]. Afraid the outlook is most depressing.

All my love dearest

RB

225)   287225 Capt R Barer RAMC
                                            94 Light AA Regt RA
                                            BLA

                                            Sunday 25th August

Dearest Gwen,
Hope you're getting better weather than we are. It's scarcely stopped raining for a week. Went to a farewell party for the CO of 128th FA, who's

being demobbed. There weren't many of the old crowd there – in fact it doesn't look as if the Division will last very long once demobbing gets going. Wish I could hear something definite. I must say the prospect of winter here is not very pleasant. I don't know if you read some of the accounts in the papers of the happenings in eastern Germany and the conditions of the refugees around Berlin. It's quite sickening and I have not the slightest hope for the future of Europe. The trouble is that things are bound to get worse. Conditions in the big towns will be desperate. You've probably heard that the Americans have advised as many people as possible to leave Frankfurt. I'm sorry you didn't understand my remarks about certain people. Perhaps if I say I was referring to the country where my parents came from you will understand. You yourself made a eulogistic remark about them in one of your letters about a week ago. You had better save your eulogies till you know the truth – which is far from pleasant. However I'll tell you when I come on leave.

All my love dearest

RB

226)   287225 Capt R Barer RAMC
                                            94 Light AA Regt RA
                                            BLA

                                            Monday 26th August

Dearest Gwen,
Two of your letters today. You can tell Lewis's quite definitely that I returned M's *War Surgery* at least 2 months ago. It's possible of course that it got lost in the post. I think it was soon after I came back here from leave – probably early June.

We must see about a house at Oxford when I come on leave. Did my Ma give you any idea whereabouts in Oxford this house she saw was? £1950 is a lot of money – was it a specially big house? What did you mean about your Pa buying it? I presume you mean he'd sell Watford and buy one in Oxford with the money. On the whole I'm against your moving this winter as things may be rather difficult in a house by yourself.

I wonder if you could look up the subject of clubbing as I have a most remarkable case. It's by far the best example of clubbed fingers I've ever seen and would make a wonderful picture for a medical book. The finger tips are enormously expanded, with very curved nails and great heaped spongy nail beds. I can find no cause – no history of chest trouble or congenital heart – never been ill – plays football etc. without getting breathless. He says he remembers his fingers being like it at the age of 10, so it's probably congenital. Can you find out about congenital clubbing. I'll try and get a photo taken and probably take him up to a hospital one day.

All my love dearest

RB

ENCLOSURE: GAD FAREWELL PARADE AND NOTE RE MC FROM ST ANDREW'S

227)   287225 Capt R Barer RAMC
                                          94 Light AA Regt RA
                                          BLA

                                          Thursday 29th August from PARIS

Dearest Gwen,

Well here I am in Paris. Sorry about the delay in writing but I've been travelling and I arrived too late for the post yesterday. Paris seems scarcely touched by the war and everything seems to be functioning normally except that cafes shut at 11 p.m. The prices are pretty high but it's possible to get most things. I'm off to the Palais de Decouverture today. It's a big science museum which I first saw at the exhibition here; they've kept it going. It used to be marvellous – with all sorts of experiments and demonstrations – even better than S. Kensington. I haven't been to Janine and I don't know if I'll go as it would be a pity to waste a morning if she's away. However I'll see. I fulfilled a sordid ambition last night and went to see the Folies Bergères. Once you've got used to the sight of titties flapping in the breeze it's extremely good. The stage settings and costumes are magnificent – like one of those lavish Hollywood productions. I was surprised at the number of women there – both French and WACS and ATS – the audience, 50% Americans, were very amusing. Whenever a girl came on wearing anything they yelled 'Take it off!' It's a remarkable institution really. Nearly all the best artists in France – people like Maurice Chevalier and Josephine Baker have acted there. Even the star has to expose her bust – a pretty searching test. We must go there together sometime.

All my love dearest
RB

228)

287225 Capt R Barer RAMC
94 Light AA Regt RA
BLA

Friday 30th August

Dearest Gwen,

Well I went along full of good intentions to see Janine this morning but I'm afraid they're all at Yvetot. The caretaker said Janine was very ill, but I don't know what's the matter.

Paris really is a beautiful place, there's no doubt about it. Brussels is dingy by comparison. I went to the Palace of discoveries yesterday it's still extremely good though damaged by fire. They have some first class optical and electrical demonstrations – polarisation and interference etc. – far better than S. Kensington in that respect.

Saw an amazing vaudeville act today – a man disguised as a monkey and just as agile. He picked things up with his toes and then proceeded to climb over the stalls among the audience! He sat on the backs of stalls and pretended to look for fleas in people's hair. Of course he raised a tremendous laugh when he molested a couple of WACS. He then climbed up to the balcony and waltzed around the rail. I should think he would make a wonderful cat burglar or mountaineer. Afraid I've not bought anything as prices are quite ridiculous. Even a cheap doll costs £2.

All my love dearest, hope to have a pile of mail waiting for me when I get back.

RB

PS Haven't slept with anyone yet but have had plenty of invitations!

[*So there are no letters during September. R came on leave. We went to Oxford and found a little house in Headington, which was to be our first home. We had a wonderful time.*]

[From Eye Club, Brussels, presumably on way back from leave.]

229)
                  287225 Capt R Barer RAMC
                  94 Light AA Regt RA
                  BLA

                  September 1945

Dearest Gwen,
Just a note from the Eye Club. I managed to get a lift here from Calais and am spending the night in Brussels. I went to the Ballet this evening. It was quite good but they didn't do any of the well known pieces.
    Let me know all about the house dearest and thank you for a lovely leave.

    All my love

    RB

230)
                  287225 Capt R Barer RAMC
                  94 Light AA Regt RA
                  BLA

                  Tuesday 8th October

Dearest Gwen,
Two of your letters today. It's a bit of a blow about the curtains etc. – especially the nice carpet in the drawing room. However we'll manage somehow. I shouldn't be surprised if we have some curtains in one of the packing cases at Hibberds. I hope you've been accommodating over the garage. She did say they might rent it if we didn't want it. I should certainly get the sweep to do the chimneys. Also ask about coal etc.
    I'm now installed in my new quarters. I've got a lovely little room in a very nice house. It's got a nice wash basin set in a green tiled wall. The wallpaper is light cream and I've got half a dozen van Gogh's pinned up. There are lots of lights and switches – all controllable from the bed, which makes reading in bed a pleasure. There's only one snag. One of the officers messed about with the plumbing so that now we get nothing but hot water from <u>all</u> taps! To our consternation we also get hot water in the lavatory! It's

Father and son – Highgate, Sept 1945

quite alarming to pull the chain and get a great column of steam rising from the pan! It should be nice in the winter time.

I'm off to a farewell dinner to the General tonight. It's really very sad to see the old Division breaking up like this. He was the last symbol of the good old days.

All my love dearest, am longing for you

RB

231)   287225 Capt R Barer RAMC
                                                                        94 Light AA Regt RA
                                                                        BLA

                                                                        Thursday 11th October

Dearest Gwen

Well I've got some news for you at last, but all very unexpected. I'm being posted for the time being as RMO to the 2nd Welsh Guards – formerly our RECCE tanks, so I now have all the armoured cars and half tracks you used to natter about. I'm going there on Monday. There's going to be an awful lot of work there as I shall have to look after one of the Irish Guards battalions as well, plus our machine gun company and engineers – over 5,000 men in all! However, it'll be quite a nice change and I much prefer it to a hospital. Living in a Guards mess should be quite amusing. Incidentally for God's sake don't send me any more once used envelopes, or I shall get thrown out! We shall be at Bensburg, about 10 miles east of Cologne and not very far from Burscheid [*where our great friends lived*]. Fortunately too there's a general hospital almost on the doorstep so I'll be able to go to clinical meetings.

Regarding your ideas on carcinogens, why don't you look up some of Hinshelwood's stuff and see if you could fit in the effect of carcinogens with his ideas? I should think he'd be quite interested. Carcinogens might affect only one of the two enzyme systems he postulates – in fact they might be of the utmost importance for his theories.

Was most startled about G [*UCH friend*]. Can scarcely believe it. However, from the facts it rather looks as if she was in the wrong – especially if she ran away so soon. Did she get divorced? Anyhow dear, we'll never run away from each other – that's one thing I'm quite certain of. I love you more and more every time I think of you, you old darling.

All my love sweet
RB

PS Start writing to me at 2nd Welsh Guards, BAOR (British Army of the Rhine)

232)   287225 Capt R Barer RAMC
                                              2nd Welsh Guards
                                              BAOR

                                              Post marked 16th October

Dearest Gwen,

Well I've now moved in to my new job. It seems quite pleasant and I have very good accommodation. Oh, dear, I don't know what to do about your latest effort. Whether to be angry, amused or amazed. Darling, let's drop the silly subject once and for all. You know perfectly well that you're the only thing I care about in the slightest. I don't even think about anyone else, let alone speak to them. Please dear, don't say anything like that again. Things have been absolutely perfect, for me at least and you make me very upset when you say they're not. You really must stop this silly habit of seizing on something I say and turning it over and over in your mind until it reaches ridiculous proportions. Please believe me darling I just haven't room in my heart for anyone but you.

All my love sweetest

RB

233)

287225 Capt R Barer RAMC
2nd Battalion Welsh Guards
BAOR

16th October [*R's 29th Birthday*]

Dearest Gwen,

No letters for 2 days now. I expect they're still going to the 94th so am awaiting a whole bunch.

Am gradually settling in here. They seem quite a decent crowd. The CO, Windsor-Lewis, is a most remarkable man. He has the DSO and bar and MC. He was captured in 1940 but escaped though wounded in the leg. He's rather eccentric and eats by himself in his room. He was quite pleasant to me however and tried to ask about my MC. It doesn't cut much ice here however as there are 4 in the regiment. I have 2 sergeants in my RAP – one has the MM. The regiment goes in for an immense amount of spit and polish which must certainly impress the Germans. I have to walk along the road at the salute and every few yards a guard presents arms! We have a bugler sounding calls about 6 times a day.

All my love sweetheart, am dying for a letter

RB

PS Have written to Uncle Spencer

234)

287225 Capt R Barer RAMC
2nd Battalion Welsh Guards
BAOR

20th October

Dearest Gwen,

Two of your letters have caught up with me today, including the photos. They're really surprisingly good aren't they? I think the two with you holding him are the best of RB (minus cap). He's got a most roguish expression in the one in which he's about to suck his fingers. Will send them back direct to my Ma.

Glad you've got things fixed about the house. Mrs S seems to be very thoughtful and helpful. It would certainly help you enormously if she got the shopping for you. I don't suppose it makes much difference where you register nowadays – the rations are much the same and she is probably the type of person who is a good shopper.

You women are a dreadful lot. An Irish Guards sergeant came to see me this morning and showed me a letter to his wife. His 5 year old son has developed an urticarial rash and he has bad acne himself. His wife thinks he has VD and refuses to sleep with him! I've just had to write her a letter saying he's not got VD, but the man is so upset I've had to send him to a specialist and get a blood test. It's funny but it's always the wrong men who get blamed.

All my love dearest

RB

235)

287225 Capt R Barer RAMC
2nd Battalion Welsh Guards
BAOR

Monday 29th October

Dearest Gwen,
Got your letter of last Friday. Hope your interview with Miles goes OK.

Had a most remarkable day today. The Irish have just recaptured a Guardsman who escaped from their Guard house a few days ago. He was marched in for me to examine this morning and I saw he had a good growth of beard. He said that during his absence he had associated with an Indian and had decided to change his religion from RC to Mohammedan! I gather the RC padre nearly had a fit. Anyhow the CO ordered that his beard had to come off forcibly. In the course of this he managed to get hold of the razor and slashed his arm, cutting the brachial vein and losing a lot of blood. At the moment he's locked in the sick bay with two guards by his side.

I see the papers are making a lot of fuss of what goes on inside detention barracks. I agree that we don't want any inhumanity or cruelty, but from reading the papers one would think that the victims are all sweet little angels. Actually most of such men are hardened criminals and often very desperate. This particular man was one of a group who had escaped from the guard room by picking a hole through a 15 inch brick wall!

I found the enclosed while looking through some old papers. It's reprinted from some of the daily papers of the time. It's rather 'journalese' but it gives a fairly true picture of what was happening at a time when B would probably have said the Guards were getting themselves killed just for fun.

All my love dearest

RB

236)   287225 Capt R Barer RAMC
                                             2nd Battalion Welsh Guards
                                             BAOR

                                             6th November

Dearest Gwen,
Got your letter of 3rd today. Am glad you met Peter [*UCH friend*]. He seems to have had a very good time – I rather envy him! Glad Jules and Dawson are well [*a surgeon and a young doctor from UCH who had both been imprisoned by the Japanese*]. I heard an Australian talking about the Burma railway on the wireless the other day (by the way what about our wireless from Jones Bros.?). This Jap business is very queer. He said many of the officers were quite decent and some even went out of their way to be kind. On the other hand others were extremely brutal. Have managed to buy a handbag – rather like yours but of soft leather. Will probably send it to Janet but I may be able to get a better one. Had an interesting case yesterday. Acute melancholia with suicidal tendencies – was found sobbing bitterly with a loaded rifle by his side, rather interesting as he has full insight but is afraid of insanity.

Enclose an old order of the day of the advance on the Rhine, in which some people seem to think we played no part!

All my love dearest

RB

237)

287225 Capt R Barer RAMC
2nd Battalion Welsh Guards
BAOR

Friday 9th November

Dearest Gwen,

Got a couple of your letters and photos today. The snaps are not so nice as the last lot. Will send them on to my Ma.

Sorry you got held up by the bus strike. I have absolutely no sympathy for such people. They do their cause and the Labour government a great disservice. All the Tories go around saying how incompetent the government is – they can't even control their own people. The men who died in this war didn't go on strike, neither did they complain that they were working too hard on too little pay. There are several dockers in this Battalion and their remarks about their colleagues are unprintable. What a pity it is that the government never seems to have the guts to take some really decisive action, like calling up all unofficial strikers – there are plenty of men in the forces only too willing to take their place.

Went to dinner with the local Mil government people yesterday. They certainly do themselves well!

All my love dearest

RB

238)

287225 Capt R Barer RAMC
2nd Battalion Welsh Guards
BAOR

12th November

Dearest Gwen,

Two letters today. I wouldn't worry about the rent for the garage if Mrs S really does do the shopping for you. It would be worth far more than 5/- a week for that, as it's an enormous saving in time and health. Occasional lifts and errands would also be extremely useful, so I should say nothing about it unless she offers to pay. Darling you needn't worry about my doing too much coaching. I should like to do a little for the fun of it – quite apart from any financial considerations, but as you say we must have as much time as possible together. I'm not in the least interested in money, as long as we can manage on our income. The only snag is any sudden large expenditure e.g. buying a house, but I'm sure we'll manage.

Please do buy the coat for Linda [*daughter of a Barer family friend*] and as quickly as possible. I ought to have bought something myself long ago.

All my love dearest

RB

239)   287225 Capt R Barer RAMC
                                                   2nd Battalion Welsh Guards
                                                   BAOR

                                                   15th November

Dearest Gwen,

Got 2 of your letters today. I'm quite sure my Ma would like to look after RG a few afternoons a week. She doesn't go out much and would probably be delighted . . .

You ask me to describe some of the officers here. They seem quite a decent lot, though it's a bit shaking to talk to someone and then discover he's Sir . . . or Lord . . . or Lord . . .! For the most part they're very young – mere boys straight from school. Some are going back to Oxford as students so I shall probably see them again. It was quite amusing the other day as I found myself the senior Officer at dinner. I had to be served first and no-one could start before I did, nor could another course be served before I finished the previous one. However, the mess is quite pleasant and informal really.

All my love dearest – think of you always.

RB

240)

287225 Capt R Barer RAMC
2nd Battalion Welsh Guards
BAOR

18th November

Dearest Gwen,

Two letters at last. I set off for Burscheid this afternoon but unfortunately I ran into 2 blown bridges and a minefield, so I had to turn back. However, I hope to go next week.

I agree that Palestine decisions are reasonable in the circumstances. What a pity that it has taken all this time and the greatest massacre in history to realise that it's time the problem was solved! The extremist acts of violence, though reprehensible, spring from a feeling of utter desperation. No attempt was made to solve the problem during the past 30 years and I'm quite sure that if matters had not been brought to a head by these acts of violence the matter would have drifted on for another 30 years. Even now, 6 months after the end of the war Jews are dying in thousands all over Europe, many of them under conditions approaching the concentration camps. That is difficult to believe but I've seen it myself, and if you remember the official American commission said the same thing a couple of months ago. Despite that no attempt was made to find a solution to a matter of desperate urgency, until now. Can you wonder that a few hotheads tried to take the matter into their own hands? It's easy to condemn but you mustn't forget that by smuggling in illegal immigrants, hundreds of lives have been saved.

As regards Palestine itself, agreed it's not the ideal solution, but even so it's quite capable of holding another million people. Do you believe for one moment that if the country were rich in natural resources we should allow the Arabs to stand in our way if we wanted to colonise it? I think the natives of Java and French Indo-china have just as much 'right' to their country as the Arabs, but it's strange that no-one ever dreams of criticising the Dutch or French for wanting to return – or, if you please, ourselves, for helping them!

Assuming there are ethical grounds for colonisation, namely the moral right of a more highly developed people to use the land to its best advantage, I think those conditions are well fulfilled in Palestine. There would certainly be no question of exploitation of the Arabs. Their standard of living has risen enormously and thousands have migrated to Palestine – in fact the Arab population has doubled in the last 30 years. It is the ruling class of Arab land-owners who have opposed Zionism because it has shown them in such a bad light. Just take a look at a map of the Arab countries and you will see how tiny Palestine is as compared with Arabia and Egypt. It's ridiculous to say that the Arabs have no 'lebensraum'. If the Jews left Palestine, it would become a desert again within 5 years. Only last night we were discussing the problem at dinner. An officer of the 1st Battalion, which has been in Palestine for the last couple of months, has just sent us a letter describing conditions. He said that he had gone violently pro-Arab and anti-Jew, but he had now completely changed his opinions. The letter caused a great deal of discussion and the CO has had it passed round the battalion. The trouble is that most Englishmen think of Arabs as fine honourable sheiks dashing around on beautiful white horses while their conception of the average Jew is someone like Shylock. Be that as it may I'm afraid the problem has been so mishandled by now that Palestine offers no real solution owing to the antagonism of the Moslem world. Lets hope some other solution will be found. What a terrible pity it was that Hitler didn't solve the problem completely!

All my love dearest

RB

[*Enclosed terrible cartoon of European Jew.*]

World Copyright Reserved.

"Hurry—this door's open already!"

241)
287225 Capt R Barer RAMC
2nd Battalion Welsh Guards
BAOR

29th November

Dearest Gwen,
Letter of 24th came today.

Regarding your query re Haberdashers school. I knew it quite well. We used to play them at games. It had a very good reputation as a good sound grammar school – rather like my own. I don't know what it's like now but I should say it's pretty good.

For goodness sake <u>don't</u> write to the papers or MPs about Palestine. It won't do any good. People do realise the urgency of the problem – most of the newspapers have stressed it. Despite that however it was announced yesterday that the Anglo-American committee would take 4 months to reach a decision. As regards present conditions there are many things better left unsaid. As you said, Harriman's report received very little publicity – about as much as reports of the concentration camps before 1939. It did have one effect however – the dismissal of General Patten. I quite agree that Palestine could not take several million people within a month. I think you greatly overestimate the numbers involved. It's very doubtful if there are more than a million Jews left in Europe outside Russia and of these not all would want to go. The use of British troops to hound down the few unfortunate illegal immigrants who thought they'd got away to safety is disgusting and inhumane. It's very reminiscent of the attitude towards people who escaped from Germany in 1939.

All my love dearest
RB

242)
287225 Capt R Barer RAMC
2nd Battalion Welsh Guards
BAOR

1st December

Dearest Gwen,
Glad to get your first letter from our new home (OXFORD!). Am dying for

a bit of news but I quite understand that you must have been very busy. Am keeping the picture of RG being held by Mrs Jones. It's a bad picture but magnificent pose. Will send the other back soon.

Dined in state with the CO last night. It was like living in the pages of the *Tatler*. There was an English Countess there. The world appears to be composed of Eton, Mayfair, St Moritz, Biarritz, Juan-les-Pins and Cannes. However it was all quite amusing and pleasant and I can keep my end up.

Am hoping to go to Burscheid tomorrow as I have some films.

All my love dearest

RB

PS Will probably be coming on leave <u>early</u> in January!

243)
                    287225 Capt R Barer RAMC
                    2nd Battalion Welsh Guards
                    BAOR

                    7th December

Dearest Gwen,

Sorry I raised false hopes about my leave. Afraid I won't be coming on leave in January after all. However you may be interested to know that I shall be coming home to stay – yes, the impossible has happened at last and I have just signed my acceptance of Class B release! I'm not sure exactly when I shall come. It'll take a couple of weeks to find someone to replace me and for me to hand over and sort out my kit so on the whole I think it would be best if I came after X-mas – say the beginning of January. I know you'll probably try and persuade me to speed it up but honestly dear there are very good reasons for my not coming before so you'll have to be patient. Anyhow it'll only be 3 weeks. Am going to write to Le Gros [*Professor Le Gros Clark, future boss at Oxford*] – I don't suppose he knows, and will try and apply for one of those grants. In the meantime it might be a good idea if you made tentative enquiries at a reasonable clothiers shop and perhaps they could reserve me a sports jacket and pair of flannels – even though they don't know my size. It must save some time. You might also enquire how long it takes to make a suit nowadays.

I shouldn't worry at all about Florey [*I had applied for a part-time job with him and failed*]. There are plenty of other possibilities. After all he probably has everyone working on antibiotics and hasn't any room for some completely new branch. Hinshelwood might be more interested. [*Professor of Physical Chemistry and Nobel Laureate with whom I did get a job.*]

Anyhow dear I'll start sending my kit home in small parcels. Can you send me a couple of cheques from our new bank as I want to pay my bills?

All my love dearest – only 3 weeks before we're together <u>for ever</u>.

RB

244)   287225 Capt R Barer RAMC
                                                    2nd Battalion Welsh Guards
                                                    BAOR

                                                    17th December

Dearest Gwen,

Got your letter of 14th today. Sorry I was cross about the letters but just at the time I wanted news your letters were particularly rushed. For example you told me practically nothing about your interviews with Miles and Florey. However only another couple of weeks before we can dispense with letters. Hope you're settling in better now. It certainly must make a difference having most of your shopping delivered. I should think life will become gradually easier as more restrictions go.

Have heard from Otto's parents [*Otto was German Medical orderly who went into Sandbostel with R*]. He's alive and well and is at present in Munich. They didn't say if he'd had Typhus.

All my love dearest

RB

[Next letter in awful writing – R was ill with influenza.]

245)   287225 Capt R Barer RAMC
                                                2nd Battalion Welsh Guards
                                                BAOR

Dearest Gwen,

Sorry I've not been able to write much in the last couple of days. Am just recovering from the effects of 'flu' – the real thing I think, fortunately without any complications. The main unpleasant feature was the extreme weakness and loss of appetite (!). However I'm much better now and hope to resume normal work tomorrow.

Got your letter enclosing Le Gros's letter, <u>don't</u> try and change his mind dear. There must be some very good reason behind it. £512 is a very satisfactory sum anyhow. As far as I'm concerned it's much better to get a proper University Department job than a grant. There's something much more permanent about it and a grant might have some irritating conditions attached to it. Le Gros knows perfectly well what our financial position is and I'm sure he must have a good reason – after all it's his department's money he's paying out.

I wonder if the allowances are tax free? In any case we shall have an income of over £400 tax free, which should be adequate, even if we don't supplement it.

Glad the maid's OK. You <u>must</u> keep her.

All my love dearest

RB

246)   287225 Capt R Barer RAMC
                                                2nd Battalion Welsh Guards
                                                BAOR

                                                24th December

Dearest Gwen,

One letter today. Am on my feet again but alas my appetite is well below normal, let alone Xmas! Will probably make up for it when I get home. I felt sure there was some reason like the one Weddell gave you. I'm glad they visualise the prospect of my staying on, as I'd certainly like to stay there for a few years at least. Oxford ought to be an ideal place in which to work, and it's an ideal stepping stone. I thought you'd start asking questions sooner or later despite your good intentions. However I can't explain all the reasons for my not coming sooner. Anyhow it's only 10 days!

All my love dearest

RB

[*On 1 January 1946, a bitter night, I had just put RG to bed and was looking out of the window. A familiar figure in uniform was just opening the garden gate! He had come! So our life together began at last. It was very good and lasted forty-five years. Sorrows and domestic difficulties came our way at times as to everyone, but it was a great love and it lasted. Indeed it got better.*]

CHAPTER X

Report on Sandbostel Concentration Camp, 1945
Diary of German girl at Sandbostel

[*This report was handed in to the British Embassy in the Hague in 1997 by Herr Ing J. Boonenberg, when he, belatedly, received a campaign medal! He had known RB when he served as an interpreter to the 94th LAA Regiment. He had been in the Dutch Resistance! I have since met him and we have become good friends. His service with the BLA was clearly the high spot of his life and he has kept in touch with old colleagues.*]

SANDBOSTEL – APRIL 1945
by CAPTAIN R BARER, MC, RAMC, RMO, 94 LAA REGT
RA

The attack went in at 1430 hrs. It was a fine sight – the waves of Grenadier Guards walking steadily toward the camp – no fuss, no hurry, they might have been on the parade ground. A few yards away a tank was giving supporting fire from its machine guns, and every few minutes a cloud of smoke would rise from a bursting shell.

Yes, it was something to remember, this final attack on Sandbostel; but as we waited in the rain we felt no elation, for inside the camp we knew we should find an enemy far more deadly than any weapon devised by Man – TYPHUS.

We first heard definite reports about Sandbostel two weeks before its capture. A patrol of the Household Cavalry had got quite near the camp and had caused some confusion among the camp guards who thought our main body was coming. A number of British Secret Service men had escaped a few days later and they gave us very useful and accurate information about conditions in the camp. Sandbostel was really Stalag XB and originally contained only prisoners of war of all nationalities; about 25,000 in all. Recently, however, the SS had brought in about 8,000 political prisoners from other concentration camps, and despite the horrified protests of the German Commandant, had dumped them in a corner of the camp. The SS allowed no one to enter the political prisoners' compound. They even refused the German

276

CSM Winter . 108938.
S.O2

Rpt on Prisn Camp.

The foll inf has been recd from CSM Winter 108938 who escaped fm the camp on 22. Apl 45.

Camp capable of holding abt 60,000.

At Present Constitute

British off.

Admin - Fresh Col.

Conditions British not bad. clen.

PSl prs v. bad. Many French

? c 7 cases Typhus.

dying 30 / day mostent

Food shrt Drunken 5 Dys.

Water poor.

Fixed documents.

1 Brit Dr. Capt Sapford.

bignest abt 1 km. prs 1000 Br 100

Camp Doctor permission to enter. It was obvious that conditions in the compound were very bad – every day great piles of corpses appeared outside the huts and more than 500 were buried in a communal grave.

Then had come the great day when a few armoured cars bearing the 'Eye' sign had appeared on the horizon. With characteristic courage the SS packed up and went. The German Camp Commandant and his staff remained, but handed over the administration of the camp to Colonel Albert, a French prisoner of war. A French Naval Medical Officer, and the German camp doctor were able to enter the political compound and at great risk had removed a number of Typhus cases to a separate hospital hut. This was an important piece of news. It confirmed the presence of Typhus, though we had no idea of its extent. It meant that extreme care would have to be taken in capturing the camp to ensure that none of our troops contracted the disease. Plans were made accordingly. Orders were issued that no troops were to enter the camp itself until a Medical Officer had reported on the typhus situation. All troops were to be dusted with anti-louse powder and if possible inoculated. No prisoners were to be allowed to leave the camp as there was a grave danger that the disease might get spread about the countryside and among our troops. What we feared most was the possibility that thousands of prisoners, crazy with joy at their release, might surge forth to thank their liberators, infecting them in the process.

One morning the great news came. The Guards Armoured Division was going to liberate Sandbostel.

I had just come from Westertimke Naval Camp to make my report when the ADMS told me that the Irish Guards were being ordered to take Sandbostel. I contacted them only to find that the plan had been changed and the Grenadiers were to do the job. We found the Motor Grenadiers eventually, and also a long column of cars bearing a PWX contact team composed of officers of every nationality.

These were to enter the camp as soon as I had reported on the Typhus situation. We waited at the Battalion Headquarters for a while, listening for wireless news from King's Company, who were doing the attack. While we waited two very ill-looking Russians who had escaped from the Camp came along. They looked as if they had Typhus so we put them in a barn, intending to take them back to the camp. That may sound cruel but it was impossible to allow them to wander about spreading Typhus. This incident gave us some foretaste of the sort of thing we should be up against.

At last King's Company announced they were within sight of the camp. We got into the jeep and drove off. It seemed a dreadfully long and depressingly empty road and not even our Red Crosses, revolvers, and Winter's cocked Sten, which I clutched nervously – I was terrified lest the darned thing should go off – could contrive to make the journey a pleasant one. However we got to Company Headquarters at last, after dealing with a badly wounded German woman on the way, and were met with the familiar phrase 'The bridge is down'. We decided to go on and have a look at the bridge, about half a mile down the road.

After a few hundred yards we got a thrill. The road ran along a ridge and there below us, about 800 yards away we could see Sandbostel Camp and the hospital. Everything looked so quiet and peaceful, even through the binoculars, that we were almost tempted to stroll across the fields into the camp. However a few bangs from an enemy SP made us decide not to tarry, particularly as the GP vehicle (Jeep) was in full view of the enemy, so after taking a peep at the bridge and the Sappers we turned round gingerly and laboriously in the middle of the road and went back to Company Headquarters. A few minutes later some wounded came by. The SP had started firing down the stream at the Sappers, wounding their officer and a tank crew. The building of the bridge had to be abandoned.

It soon became clear that Sandbostel would not be taken that night. A patrol got across the stream but ran into trouble, and the place was too strongly held to be captured by one company. We discussed other means of entry. It was known that the camp guards were only too anxious to hand over the camp. Indeed, an envoy had come out offering us a safe conduct. Unfortunately it was one thing to get a safe conduct from the camp guards, but quite another to persuade the German troops defending the area to allow us to enter. I decided that it was not worth risking being sniped merely to enter the camp at night. In my case we could not have done any useful work under the circumstances and it was practically certain that the camp would fall the next day.

Thus it was at 1430 hours on the next day we stood in the rain by the stream watching the final attack. This time the attack was on a battalion level, with artillery support. The Germans were dug in all round the edge of the camp and hospital so that our gunners had to be very careful where their shells dropped. It speaks volumes for their accuracy that practically no damage was done to the camp itself. After half an hour enemy resistance began to weaken and the Grenadiers began to clear the nearest edge of the camp perimeter. The Jeep was performing valiant service evacuating casualties to the Grenadiers RAP. I had cursed when I had to have it converted to carry stretchers but the inconvenience was more than worth it. I was making arrangements with the Grenadiers to go across the stream in an assault boat when I caught sight of a familiar figure. It was Capt. Harry Wilcox, a former Adjutant of this regiment, now a press representative. We decided to go in together. As we prepared to go we saw two figures walking across the field towards us from the camp. They were quite nonchalant about it, as if going for a Sunday walk. They turned out to be a Polish General and his Adjutant. The General wished to see the Divisional Commander in order to 'congratulate him on his very nice attack'. I tactfully suggested that it would be better if no one left the camp until the Typhus situation was settled, so he contented himself with handing over numerous messages for Polish Generals and cabinet ministers.

At last we got into the boat and crossed the stream. In addition to the Polish General and his Adjutant, Winter and Otto, my English-speaking German medical orderly, had begged to be allowed to come. We set off across the field. It was raining and quite noisy so we walked fast in order to gain the cover of the trees outside the camp. The General decided that it was not in keeping with his military dignity to walk so fast, so he lagged behind. He appeared to be discoursing on the beauties of nature to his Adjutant, but the latter looked as if he would rather have caught a train. For my part I had no wish to cut a dashing figure – it would have been difficult, anyhow, in my sodden Jeep coat. At last after picking our way past a few dead Germans we got to the camp hospital. Here we got a tremendous reception. There were 2,000 patients and 40 doctors of all nationalities. I was introduced to all the doctors and had to salute and shake hands with each one individually. At last I managed to take a pencil in my aching hand and made a few notes. The hospital appeared to be well equipped and very well run. I made a note of certain medical requirements and after a final salute all round I made my escape, still flushed with embarrassment.

By this time the further end of the camp had been cleared of the enemy and there were only a few airbursts dropping, so we made our way into the camp itself. If I had felt embarrassed before, I soon felt a thousand times worse. As we approached the wire there was a tremendous burst of cheering from thousands of prisoners of war. I noticed that behind one stretch of wire there was a number of people in black and white striped suits. Many of them looked terribly thin and ill. Some of them cheered but some just stared, as if unable to understand what was happening. These were the political prisoners.

We made our way down the main path through the camp, towards the main gate. The whole road, about 800 yards long was lined by dense masses of cheering prisoners. Everyone saluted us and we tried to return the salutes. At last we arrived at the main gates and were greeted by the French Commandant. He was very helpful, and so also was Dr Baziel, the French Naval Medical Officer in charge of the Typhus ward. He confirmed the presence of Typhus, of which there were 122 cases in the ward and an unknown number in the political compound. To my great relief there did not appear to be any contact between the prisoners of war and the political prisoners, and the Typhus was entirely confined to the latter. This made things infinitely easier, as there was no reason why the prisoners of war should not be evacuated as soon as conditions allowed. Putting 25,000 people in quarantine would have been no joke. It was clear that there were two very distinct communities in Sandbostel. The ordinary prisoner of war camp was quite well run, as I saw for myself later. True, food was scarce but there was a good stock of Red Cross parcels. Opinion was unanimous that life would have been almost impossible without these parcels. The camp guards were elderly men and had behaved quite well. Medical attention was first class. Most of the prisoners, even the Russians who got less to eat than the others, looked quite well and showed no signs of gross starvation. Indeed, it was my impression that so long as a man kept himself occupied and exercised he remained healthy. The type of man who fell ill was often the one who got thoroughly browned-off, took no exercise, but lay in bed. Boredom seemed more dangerous than starvation.

We made our way towards the political compound, but first we called in at the British and American compounds. All seemed to be well here and there were several recent arrivals from the Division. Of course everyone was busy brewing pots of 'char' and one lucky gang was frying spam and chips – I could have done with some myself. The prisoners were housed in wooden huts and slept mostly on wooden double bunks with blankets. Ablutions and latrines were poor but passable. I mention these things in order to contrast conditions in the prisoner of war compound with those in the political compound. I have heard many apologists, both German and British, try to explain away conditions in concentration camps as being due to a breakdown of the supply system caused by bombing of transport and the approach of our troops. Sandbostel gives the lie to this excuse. There we had in one camp, on the one hand prisoners of war humanely treated, with no evidence of serious supply difficulties, and side by side with them political prisoners kept under conditions which beggar description. No words of mine can ever convey the full horror of what I saw there. A combination of Charles Dickens and Edgar Allen Poe might have done so, but I doubt it.

We approached the political prisoners compound and I saw the gate was marked with the skull and crossbones, with the word 'Typhus' underneath. Suddenly I was panic stricken as I had left the tin of anti-louse powder in the Jeep. However, it was too late to do anything so I kept quiet. The first thing I noticed in the compound was the smell, which got stronger as we approached the huts. I cannot attempt to describe it, but I never got rid of that smell from my nostrils for several days. Outside the huts odd groups of men were standing or lying. Some of them tried to raise a cheer, but it was a poor hollow affair.

One creature who looked like a skeleton wrapped in parchment gave us a smile of welcome and a wave. At least that is what I think he tried to do, but the smile was like a death grin and the wave was like a slow motion film. We entered a hut and the smell grew stronger. I steeled myself and threw open a door. I made a mental vow that if anyone rushed forward and tried to embrace me I should kill him. No one rushed forward. We looked into a room about 30 feet long and 15 feet broad. It contained about 30 men and four bunks. About six of the men were dead. Twenty were lying on the floor or on the bunks, too ill to move; the rest sat or stood around the room. Little groups of dead, the living and dying were huddled together for warmth. About one man in four had a blanket. Two men squatted in the middle of the floor emptying their bowels. Another was vomiting over his neighbour. The floor was covered in filth.

We closed the door and walked along the dark passage. The floor boards were rotted through and slimy with filth. I stumbled over something in the dark. It was a corpse. The next room was smaller than the first. In one corner two creatures were huddled close together with their arms round each other. Their great black eyes stared at us, but they gave no sign of recognition or emotion. One whimpered and bared his teeth in a snarl, I was reminded suddenly of chimpanzees at the zoo. We went on from room to room and hut to hut. In one place a man who said he was English rushed forward and shook my hand. I did not have the heart to withdraw it. An American did the same in another hut. Ruefully I thought about the anti-louse powder. Each room, each hut, had some new horror. In some huts the inmates were all French, in others Russian, others Dutch, and so on. Every country was represented, including Germany itself.

There were no sanitary arrangements at all. If a man wanted to relieve himself he went outside if he was so inclined, otherwise he just did it where he lay. His neighbours were beyond caring. Nearly everyone had diarrhoea, the type of diarrhoea caused by long starvation. The whole place was crawling with lice, but it was impossible to tell who had Typhus and who had not. Outside the huts the ground was fouled by excreta, and corpses were lying all over the place. No attempt was being made to have them removed. It was a fantastic sight, completely unreal and beyond ordinary human understanding. I toyed with the idea of pouring petrol round the place and setting the whole lot on fire. In my state of mind at that time the idea did not seem ridiculous; indeed it seemed to be the only possible solution. I just could not see how we were going to save more than a few of these people, who were dying at the rate of several hundreds per day. We left the political compound at last and I hurriedly rinsed my hands in a puddle of rain water. There was a bite at the base of the middle finger of my right hand, which the Englishman and the American had shaken. I consoled myself with the thought that young and healthy people didn't often die of Typhus and anyhow there was not much sense worrying with Jerry airbursts only a couple of hundred yards away. Besides, life did not seem very desirable at that moment. Otto's eyes were filled with tears. He was bitterly ashamed of being a German. I was ashamed of being human. No animal could possibly have sunk to such depths of cruelty.

We made our way back towards the stream passing little groups of Grenadiers digging in for the night. The shells were nearer now and I shuddered to think what might happen if Jerry shelled the camp systematically. As we walked through the trees I realised something for the first time. 'Did you feel any pity?' I asked Capt. Wilcox. 'No,' he replied. 'It's a strange thing isn't it?' It was true. The things we had seen were so terrible that all feelings of sympathy or pity had been driven out. All I felt was horror, disgust, and I am ashamed to admit it, hate.

Hate against the prisoners for looking as they did, for living as they did, for existing at all. It was quite unreasonable but there it was, and it gave us one possible explanation of why the SS had done those things. Once having reduced their prisoners to such a state the only emotions the guards could feel were loathing, disgust and hate. Do not think I am apologising for the SS, I am not. I shall have more to say about those criminals later, but I am merely trying to find some reason for their extraordinary behaviour. Capt. Wilcox busied himself with his pencil and notebook, taking down a statement from Otto.

He also asked Winter for a statement as the first Gunner, indeed the first British soldier, to enter the camp. Winter preened himself and decided that Hull wasn't so bad after all. We got back to the Jeep at last and smothered ourselves in anti-louse powder.

That night the Sappers completed the bridge. That night too several hundred frenzied political prisoners rushed the barbed wire fence and broke out of that camp. Orders were issued to round them up and send them back. Anyone failing to stop when called upon was to be shot. These were hard decisions, but very necessary. The next morning when the bridge was finished I got my Field Ambulance section and Hygiene section up to the camp and set about delousing. People began to arrive in large numbers. The PWX contact team began to sort out 25,000 prisoner of war. The ADMS and DDMS arrived and a medical conference was held. Our old friend the Polish General, who had insisted on being present at all discussions though he understood not a word of English, sat down at the head of the table and waited for us to start. I was on the verge of screaming by now and managed to control myself sufficiently to suggest that the general was not really interested in such mundane subjects as latrines and lousiness. Fortunately he agreed. In addition to the medical problem there was the supply problem, and we were fortunate in having the full co-operation of the Q staff of 30 Corps. The Corps Commander himself arrived and said we were to go to him personally if any difficulty arose.

That evening a Field Ambulance arrived and I attached my sections to them. We settled down for the night in some huts a little way outside the camp. Intermittent fighting was still going on in the area and just as it was getting dark we were suddenly told that we had located ourselves way out in no-man's-land! However, we decided it wasn't worth doing anything about it. Anyway there was nowhere else to go. Fortunately we spent a very quiet night. The Commanding Officer of the Field Ambulance joined us later that evening. He had just come from a visit to Belsen and was obviously badly shaken by what he had seen there. Belsen was far larger than Sandbostel and contained about 60,000 political prisoners. The conditions were much the same but the presence of women and the vast number of prisoners made the problem far more difficult.

The next morning I handed over my commitments to the Field Ambulance and we left Sandbostel after lunch. As we were leaving a convoy of trucks containing women arrived. These were German women who had been impressed to work at the camp. I think this was an excellent scheme as it is of the utmost importance that as many Germans as possible should see for themselves what conditions were like. The work those women did was highly dangerous but they and the many German nurses who came later were so horrified by what they saw that they worked willingly. The personnel of the Field Ambulance put in some very good work too, and several contracted Typhus. The main task was the removal of several thousand prisoners from their filthy huts to special hospital huts. Most of the prisoners were too ill to walk or even stand. They had to be taken on stretchers, washed, disinfected, their old clothes burned and new pyjamas issued. Those who had obvious Typhus were put in separate huts. Many were too weak to eat and had to be given fluids intravenously until they were able to be spoon-fed.

About ten days after leaving Sandbostel I found myself in charge of the German Naval and Military Hospitals in the Cuxhaven area. I spoke about what I had seen to many of the German doctors. Some believed me but others thought it was just propaganda. One or two laughed outright. I got permission to take a mixed party of Naval, Military and Civilian Doctors, and a well known lawyer, to Sandbostel. An immense change had been brought about in that short time. An entire CGS had been brought in. The place was swarming with German women and nurses. The hospital huts contained about 2,000 cases. Several thousand had been evacuated. Even then the political compound had not been entirely cleared. There were still over 1,000 prisoners living under much the same conditions as before. We went round the hospital wards and the German doctors were obviously impressed.

Even in their new surroundings, in clean pyjamas, and having been washed, the prisoners were a terrible sight. One could still feel very little but horror. They didn't look human and few of them behaved humanly. Many of them would pull their bedclothes off and wave their spindly limbs in the air. One poor wretch was wandering about stark naked making whining noises, with a bed pan in one hand and a roll of lavatory paper in the other. He didn't seem to have any idea what to do. Several patients in each ward were receiving a continuous intravenous drip of plasma – the only way they could be fed. Others were being spoon-fed by German nurses. The German doctors went round asking the patients questions. Many of the latter had no idea why they were there, some had been anti-Nazis or had committed some trivial offence. Others simply said 'Because I am a Jew'. There were several children among the patients, boys of ten to fourteen years of age. One of the huts had been full of them. Many of them had been in concentration camps for several years. It is difficult to conceive what crime they could have committed. Their presence came as a profound shock to the German doctors. I got some of the German doctors and nurses who had been working in the place to talk to the party. It was the same story each time. They all told the truth, interspersed with exclamations of horror and indignation and in many cases extreme shame.

Finally I took the civilian doctors and the lawyer round what was left of the political compound – it was considered inadvisable to take anyone in German uniform. We were most fortunate in being met inside the compound by a Dutch Doctor of Philosophy, who spoke good German. He had written a book against Hitler, and had been removed to a concentration camp when the Germans overran Holland. He was an exceptionally fine type and greeted the Germans without any resentment or bitterness. He merely let the facts speak for themselves and added nothing. We went into the huts. Things had improved considerably as there was now no overcrowding and each man had a blanket – taken from someone who had died. The dead were no longer left lying about the huts, but were arranged in neat rows outside, and covered with sheets. Neat graves had been dug and flowers planted. Crude latrines had been created, but those too weak to stand still fouled the floors where they lay. Men were still dying in every hut. Conditions were still atrocious, but nothing like so bad as when I had left. The daily death rate had fallen from hundreds to about 50, but the number of Typhus cases was increasing. In all there were 800 cases. I have seldom seen such a change as occurred in those German doctors. I remember one in particular, who had laughed at my stories. He was not laughing now. He was almost crying with shame and horror. It was a very silent and depressed party, that left Sandbostel that day.

These are the facts about Sandbostel, as I saw them. It is not a pleasant story, but the story is a good deal pleasanter than the actual conditions. There are many horrifying stories I could tell – authenticated cases of cannibalism, men's livers being cut out and gnawed raw before they were even dead; men's eyes being plucked out in struggles for bits of potato peel. But I have tried to restrict my story to what I saw with my own eyes. In conclusion there are a few comments I should like to make. I hold no brief for the German people but it is only fair to say that my considered opinion is that the vast majority of them knew nothing of the conditions inside concentration camps. These places were closely guarded by SS and no ordinary German was allowed anywhere near them. Those few people who were allowed out after serving a term were far too terrified of returning to relate their experiences. The terror of the Gestapo and SS is something which I hope we in England shall never know. It is most important that the entire German people should be told of these things. Films and articles are not enough, they leave one with a sense of unreality. I remember reading about and seeing pictures of Belsen and Buchenwald and feeling quite unmoved. The ideal thing would have been to take the entire population around these camps but that, of course, was impracticable. The next best thing I feel, would be to take some of the German Doctors and nurses who worked at these camps on lecture tours round Germany.

There are many Germans who have been imprisoned in these camps who would be only too glad to relate their stories. I cannot help feeling that unless every single German gets a true picture of what has happened in Nazi Germany this war will have been fought in vain. Finally, there is the problem of the SS and the Gestapo. I think there is only one solution – complete extermination. I am quite aware that many non-Nazis were forced to join the SS in recent times, but I feel it would be better to let the innocent suffer rather than let a single guilty man escape. Any one who can stand by and watch human beings treated as they were at Sandbostel and other places has forfeited the right to live. After a war which has cost us so many fine and useful lives it would be wrong to be unduly squeamish about worthless lives. There is only one satisfactory treatment for a foul cancer – cut it out!

PRELIMINARY REPORT ON P.O.W.CAMP
SANDBOSTEL(9235).

The camp was entered at 1600 hours 29.Apr.

General description:
    There are 4 main areas:
1) P.O.W.Camp
2) P.O.W.hospital
3) New hospital for typhus cases
4) Guards quarters,which will be used as a hospital for political prisoners.

Prisoners:
Total	nearly 23000 composed as follows:	
Political prisoners	7500	
Military prisoners:		
British and U.S.	390	
Belgian	290	
French	2280	
Polish	2500	
Italian	230	
Roumanian	11	
Russian	5300	
Czech	480	
Jugoslaves	1700	
Patients in hospital	2000	

Conditions: General conditions in P.O.W. Camp hard but reasonable.Conditions in pol.pris.compound apalling.Most of these pol.pris. are suffering from severe starvation,about 700 can not get up and have to be helped to eat.The barracks are extremly filthy;no sanitary arrangements are provided and the dead the dying and the living are all mixed up together.Until the 20th of April these prisoners had no medical attention many hundreds have died and have been buried in a large communal grave.

Typhus: Dr.Basiel who is in charge of the ~~civilian~~ pol.pris.medical service states that there are 107 cases of typhus.It is very difficult to be certain of the diagnosis as it is hard to distinguish between typhus and the terminal stages of starvation.However,there are 5 certain cases of typhus and 3 death have occured since the patients have been isolated.The incidenc of lousiness is very high.Energetic measures have been taken to deal with the situation and the risk of spread beyond the pol.pris.compound is small.

Immediate requirements for political prisoners:

1) Typhus vaccine 8ooo doses
2) cardiac stimulants,coramine,digitalis,strychnine,
3) unsweetened condensed milk,8ooo tins
4) intravenous fluids-plasma,glucose saline.
5) surgical dressings for 4oo patients
6) hypodermic syringes and needles.
7) charcoal,kaolin,and sulphaguanidine tablets for dealing with the large number of cases of diarrhoea.
8) soap,1oooo bars.
9) anti-louse powder,1 ton
1o) suites of clothes and under-clothes,8ooo,
11) blankets,at least 8ooo.
12) ambulances and lorries.

General camp requirements:

There is enough food for 7 days but no bread.Bread for at least 13ooo is needed. Cooking facilities are very poor and one or more field-kitchens would be useful.Water is normaly pumped by electricity but there is no current.There are some pumps runned on diesel-oil there is sufficient oil in(6oo liters) to last 4 days.

Hospital:

One kilometer from main camp.2ooo patients 2oo stretcher cases.4o doctors under command of colonel Kuzenkoyytch.Well equipped. No urgent requirements except bread.Can work at least one week without help.There are 2o polish woman workers in the hospital.

German personnel:

23o guards,4 officiers,2 doctors,15 woman civilian workers.

Remarks:

Disciplin appears good.All necessary steps are beeing taken to deal with the typhus epidemic.It is essential that only really nece= ssary personel be allowed to enter the camp until the exact extent of the typhus outbreak is known.A dusting station is beeing set up at the entrance to the camp.The situtaion,though bad,is not quite so serious as earlier reports may have suggested.This is mainly due to the energetic action of the camp medical staff.

Capt.R.A.M.C.
R.A.C. 94 L.A.A.Regt.R.A.

ELFIE WALTHER: DIARY

28 April 1945, evening

I have just received my conscription papers. An English officer and a German came and brought me the letter. I am to be in front of the Town Hall tomorrow morning at seven, with things for several days. They want to send us away. Mother thinks that we might be deployed as foreign workers. I don't believe it. We are much too young.

1 May

We have been told that we are to clear up a camp near Hamburg. I got a dreadful shock and had to think of the pictures at home. A concentration camp! I had heard enough about them over the last few days. I hope we don't have to go into the camp with all the dead people, I thought . . .

In Wildeshausen we saw traces of the battle. Houses burnt down everywhere, burned-out cars and tanks. Between Bassum and Harpstedt we went past a huge camp of tents. There seem to be Russians and Poles there. They were setting about burning all sorts of things. Some of them stood by the side of the road and shook their fists at us. They called abuse after us. We were afraid, and hoped that the car would drive past quickly. But to our horror, it stopped, and we had to get out amidst the taunts and shouts of the foreigners. It was driven home to me how it is to be afraid of violence. My heart was in my mouth.

Suddenly we saw a large POW camp. Once again Russian soldiers were standing behind the fences and staring at us. That was Sandbostel, south of Bremervörde. We turned off and drove to another corner of the camp. There were huge barracks there. We were told to clean out these barracks and prepare them for political prisoners from a concentration camp who were camping nearby. First we had to clean out a barrack for ourselves . . .

After we had made the barracks reasonably clean, we moved in. There are two sacks of straw between three of us. Now we are sitting here and waiting for further instructions. And for something hot to eat! For days we have not had a square meal. All we have had is the bread that we brought with us, and chocolate which the English gave us.

1 May 1945, late in the evening

I have just head the most terrible news. I must write it down today. We have one candle, so it's possible . . .

In the hospital barrack there were three old medical orderlies from the time when the camp had housed POWs. We stayed there for a while and asked them questions. Then they started to tell us things that gave us shivers down the spine. I can hardly repeat them, it is so incredible! But I will try in a few words. When the guards from the POW camp had disappeared SS soldiers brought prisoners from a concentration camp. Where it was, the orderlies didn't know. The prisoners were in incredibly bad condition, half dead, half starved.

They were driven out of the railway wagons or tipper trucks – I didn't quite understand this – with bayonets. They were beaten and stabbed with the bayonets. According to the orderlies, the SS treated them dreadfully. Most of the prisoners remained lying where they were unloaded. They could hardly walk, staggered, fell. Then suddenly the SS disappeared because the British were advancing. They just left the poor people lying there in the rain and dirt.

And that is how the British found them. They had to have help and people to look after them as quickly as possible. That is why they had the idea of getting schoolgirls in – and that is why we are here. Tomorrow we will have to wash and clean up the prisoners! Then they are to move into the barracks that we have cleaned. The orderlies didn't know any more than this . . .

I am dreadfully mixed up. Can this be true? If it is as the orderlies have told us, then the pictures of Bergen-Belsen are certainly true too. And what else might there be that we have no idea of? Is this what our soldiers were fighting for? Is this what the German people have been suffering for? Those pigs were lying to us, and now we have to bear the consequences! I am terrified of tomorrow. What will happen tomorrow? No one will be able to sleep here tonight. Everyone is speechless and listens to our report with unbelief.

2 May 1945

. . . Nobody at home would believe us if we told them about it. I couldn't stop thinking about how we had loved and honoured the Führer. Everything that he told us was a lie! What is this thing that was called National Socialism? We always thought that it was something beautiful and noble.

Why is everything so cruel? Why do they kill innocent, helpless people? One can't treat one's enemies like that! It is incomprehensible. Last night I finished with everything that I used to believe was good. People are vile pigs – all of them, including me. And there is meant to be a God? And he allows all this to happen? . . . I haven't seen a prisoner yet, and I notice that I am glad. I am frightened of seeing them. How can we apologize? . . .

4 May

Today we cleaned out another two barracks. So much dirt! We can't wash at all, and look like pigs. When we asked an English officer if we could wash somewhere he snapped at us not to put on such airs and graces. The prisoners had not been able to wash for years. I believe we already have lice . . .

4 May, evening

I was happy too soon. It is cruel in the typhus barracks. I lack the right words to describe all the misery. They are hardly people. Skeletons lie there in their filthy beds, smeared with excrement from head to foot, and stare at us with huge eyes . . . How ashamed I am in these minutes to be German! We caused this! And my mother does not believe that Germans could do something like this!

5 May 1945

When can we go home? There are so many rumours. We have heard that Hitler is dead. And all the others. Himmler is said to have been captured. I wonder if the war is over everywhere . . . Today two men died. We had to carry them out. Some never open their eyes. They just lie there and moan. Sometimes there is no sound any more. Then the others say he is dead. When we dragged the dead men out, the others immediately pounced on their few personal belongings. Their feelings have been dulled . . .

I had never seen a dead person before. Today I had to carry two. When the first one died I could not control myself and broke down in tears. He was a Greek. At the end his breath rattled and he kept beating the wall with his fists. When the other patients who could stand saw me crying, they smirked. They have seen so much, death does not mean much to them anymore. And the British had their satisfaction when they saw that we didn't know what to do. One has the feeling that they want to punish us because we are Germans. Understandable . . .

6 May 1945

More and more sick people are being brought in. There are 6 barracks in our complex, and all are overcrowded. Another 600 new patients are to be brought today. But yesterday and today more than 100 people died.

In total, an English soldier told me, there are more than 3,000 people in the camp . . .

Our mental state is much worse than our physical condition. We will never lose these impressions. What we experience here cannot be described in words . . .

Evening

This afternoon I was close to despair. Inge has dropped out too, and I have to do all the work in our barracks alone. As everything takes longer, some of the patients become quite aggressive, and I was really scared. Thank goodness there is also a room with nice, educated people in it. They come from Holland and Belgium. Some of them are doctors, and then there is a lawyer, he always consoles and encourages us.

Just imagine: someone who has suffered so much at the hands of our people encourages us! He says that what we are doing here is wonderful. But, he says, it is shameful that people who are still half children have to put in order the mess that adults have created. All this man did was to make a comment against the German occupation in Holland. For this, he was taken to a concentration camp . . .

7 May 1945

. . . The suffering here is so dreadful. Sometimes I think I can no longer bear it. So many people die. Wrapped in blankets, these skeletons walk – or rather, stagger – between the barracks. There really are children – gypsy children – among them. I can't understand it! They even put children in concentration camps!

Many of us are seriously sick. The British seem to be worried. Up to now they have taken little notice of how the German schoolgirls are. We have lice and are dirty. Many of us have no changes of clothes. Our coats and jackets are wet through because it is always raining, and our shoes are soaked and completely filthy . . .

8 May 1945

. . . Some women from the village helped peel the potatoes. They could give us some news from outside. The war is said to be over. Foreigners – I mean foreign workers – are living under dreadful conditions in the villages. I wonder if my parents are still alive? I am terribly worried. Men and women from the village have to bury the dead. We just put them outside the door. They are buried in a mass grave. An old woman who was crying all the time sat next to me.

When another woman cursed the SS and said that they would all be shot now, the woman next to me started to scream dreadfully and suddenly cut her artery with her potato knife. We were all frozen with terror. Someone called for help. The Frenchmen came from the kitchen, bandaged her arms, and took her away.

Later we were told that this woman had a son who had been in the SS. And when she heard that all SS people were to be shot, she did not want to live any longer. Her husband had died in the war. What fates people have! . . .

293

10 May 1945
We are leaving tomorrow! Quite suddenly! I can hardly believe it. After lunch our replacements arrived, 100 girls from Bremen. They didn't even have any luggage with them – they thought they were just going to look at a camp. Well, they'll have a good look round!

11 May 1945
I am home again, after a two-hour journey. In spite of the curfew in Delmenhorst, we ran home from the market place. My parents could not speak for joy. While we were away, nobody knew where we were.

. . . It is nice to be at home, but it is different from how it was before. I have experienced too many dreadful things. One needs time to cope with it.

I haven't told anybody anything, although everybody asks all the time. I simply can't yet. Perhaps I am afraid that they won't believe me?

Postscript
Soon after, at least twenty-five of my school friends went down with typhus, including my friend Rosi. We were injected afterwards. But for many it was too late. Three days after my return, everyone in my house had lice.

My parents were speechless when, one evening, I told them about the horrors. A world collapsed for them too, and at that time we didn't even know that everything I had seen was nothing compared with what had happened in other camps, and especially the extermination camps.

CHAPTER XI

30–40 years on, unbearable memories

NIJMEGEN REVISITED FORTY YEARS ON

In 1982 R was president of the Anatomical Society of Great Britain and Northern Ireland. A joint meeting with the Dutch Anatomical Society was held in Nijmegen. We went together. I was anxious because I knew R would have to make a speech and feared the memories would be too much for him. We flew to Amsterdam and went to Nijmegen by train. As we approached I saw R go to the window as we crossed the railway bridge and look across to the famous road bridge. The time for his speech came. 'This morning,' he said, 'I escaped from the meeting and wandered round the town. I found the place by the bridge where I, together with an American MO, set up my aid post. We saw the Guards tanks rush the bridge and the Americans cross in assault boats. We tended British, American, Dutch and German casualties. I went and looked at the road on the far side and saw why we could not get further . . . After the battle we were withdrawn to rest in a Dutch village and realised that the people were starving. If any of you are about 40 years old, you may owe your lives to our Quartermaster who distributed tins of bully beef to pregnant Mothers . . .' This speech was very much appreciated by our Dutch Hosts, also by a 42 year-old Welshman whose father had been killed in that battle and whom he had never seen.

SANDBOSTEL RECALLED 1971

In 1971 we were attending a scientific congress in Munich. We had dinner one night with two American friends. One of us commented on the Congress brochure, which began 'from the rolling hills of Dachau . . .' We thought this very insensitive. The American husband said, 'Do you think we should take our daughter to Dachau?' I asked her age. 'Ten,' he replied. 'No,' I said, 'she is too young.' I turned to R and said 'What do you think?' He simply burst into tears. I remembered that for a long time after the War he had nightmares about Sandbostel. It had not been mentioned for many years but clearly the memory was still unbearable.

295

OBITUARY 1989

Professor Robert Barer

The microscope has its place in the media language of our time. Hardly a month goes by without its being reported that some matter or some institution is to be put 'under the microscope'. The image of the microscope too has become a symbol, for promoting the idea of research, often in connection with the development of household products. But, while the microscope of metaphor and symbol undoubtedly lives, so does the real microscope. Invented in the seventeenth century, this device continues to evolve and offer new information. Robert Barer was deeply involved in the world of real microscopes.

As a student at London University he had awesome abilities. While taking Honours in Physiology by day he obtained a First in Physics by evening study, then took top Honours in the MB BS examinations. These were his paper qualifications and with them, in January 1946, after his war experience as Captain in the RAMC, he was appointed Demonstrator in Anatomy at Oxford. Inspired by A.V. Hill, he became a biophysicist exploiting contemporary physics for exploring cells. He invented important microscope methods for weighing and chemically characterising cells. In the university he taught anatomy. Ideas for instruments flowed from him: micromanipulators, calorimeters, infra-red and phosphorescence microscopes, the early TV-based image analysers.

Some of a bewildered anatomical establishment saw him as 'just a gadgeteer'. Others with greater insight realised that he sought truth in structural biology by extending the variety of the available experimental repertoire. His knowledge of optics was almost unrivalled, and as a scientist he gained the regard of many, including the Nobel Prize Winners Zernike, Florey and H.A. Krebs, and it was the last of these who, in 1962, recommended Sheffield University to him and him to Sheffield.

Sheffield anatomy was of the most traditional kind, but from within this Barer grew a large department pre-eminent in the research and teaching of microscopical science. The preclinical curriculum too was to be modernised. In 1963 even changes in the tempo of anatomical teaching aroused fierce comment and the introduction of microphones into the dissecting room was

Professor Robert Barer

viewed by some as portending a kind of Orwellian doom. The effort required for this cost a curtailment of research time, although even so several machines for single cell study marketed by British companies were based on his expertise. But as a professorial contemporary put it, he 'spent his substance pushing against the dead hand'.

His department made its mark, however, and its offspring have continued to do so, a success due in no small part to his ability to choose staff and to school them. A fine writer himself, numerous articles from his juniors went to press with the benefit of his literary coaching, yet without his name appended. Distressed if you received injustice, he was very sharp if he felt you were less than just. He could be a formidable judge. Colleagues have said they could quarrel with him as if with their own family.

Like my genetic father, he set standards, gave and expected things; omitted to tell things. Just as my genetic father said nothing of Passchendaele, so Robert Barer said nothing of his time in the Guards Armoured Division. Of his staff only his technician, himself a D-Day veteran, heard of Barer's exploits in burning tanks and of the casualty clearing station he organised beneath Nijmegen bridge. As the first allied officer to enter the typhus-infested Sandbostel concentration camp, he witnessed scenes of horror. We were conscious of the profound effects of these experiences, yet did not know of the experiences.

It is sometimes said that the success of a professor is estimated by how many new professors spring from his guidance. In Barer's case it is more than 10. He, with others, brought anatomy in Britain into the fold of modern quantitative biology. It is an irony that the most obvious present sign of their success is the competition not with the dead hand, but in a monetary climate, with the prevailing fashion, molecular biology.

Mike Williams

Robert Barer, anatomist, born London 16 October 1916, MC 1945, Arthur Jackson Professor Human Biology and Anatomy Sheffield University 1963-82, married Gwendoline Briggs (three sons), died Sheffield 10 June 1989.